A GAME OF TWO HALVES?

The Business of Football
A GAME OF TWO HALVES ?

Edited by

Sean Hamil, Jonathan Michie and Christine Oughton

FOREWORD BY ALEX FERGUSON

MAINSTREAM
PUBLISHING

EDINBURGH AND LONDON

First published in Great Britain in 1999 by
MAINSTREAM PUBLISHING COMPANY (EDINBURGH) LTD
7 Albany Street
Edinburgh EH1 3UG

ISBN 1 84019 225 3

A catalogue record for this book is available from the British Library

Typeset in Berkeley Book
Printed and bound in Great Britain by Butler & Tanner Ltd

Contents

List of Authors

Dr Anne Bourke
Department of Business Administration, University College Dublin

Rob Branston
Department of Commerce, Birmingham Business School, University of Birmingham

Dr Adam Brown
Department of Popular Culture, Manchester Metropolitan University, and a member of the Football Task Force Working Group

Nestor Duch Brown
Departament d'econometrica, Estadística i Economia Espanyola, Universititat de Barcelona

Armand Carabén
L'Elefant Blau Independent Barcelona Supporters Group and currently a financial consultant to several Spanish and international companies. From 1970–75 he was the general manager of Barcelona Football Club, when he famously signed Johann Cruyff

David Conn
Freelance journalist for national newspapers, magazines and documentary television and author of *The Football Business* (Mainstream Publishing, 1997)

Professor Keith Cowling
Department of Economics, University of Warwick

Jeanette Findlay
Department of Economics, University of Glasgow

Alfons Godall
L'Elefant Blau Independent Barcelona Supporters Group

Sean Hamil
Department of Management, Birkbeck College, University of London

Professor William L. Holahan
Department of Economics, University of Wisconsin

Juan Laporta
President of L'Elefant Blau Independent Barcelona Supporters Group

Simon Lee
Department of Politics, University of Hull

Brian Lomax
Chairman of Northampton Town Football Club Supporters Trust and elected director of Northampton Town FC

Professor Jonathan Michie
Department of Management, Birkbeck College, University of London

Jordi Moix
L'Elefant Blau Independent Barcelona Supporters Group and regional director of Metrovacesa, Spain's second largest real estate company

Dr Christine Oughton
Reader in Management, Birkbeck College, University of London

Shay Ramalingam
Management Consultant, Arthur Andersen

Professor Roger Sugden
Department of Commerce, Birmingham Business School, University of Birmingham

Shraddha Verma
Department of Management, Birkbeck College, University of London

Andy Walsh
Chairman, Independent Manchester United Supporters Association

Acknowledgements

The following chapters were commissioned specifically for this book. We are therefore grateful to the authors for having undertaken this work. The chapters were written during the course of 1998 and were then presented and discussed at a meeting of all the authors in February 1999, following which they were revised for the book. Several other experts attended that meeting to comment and make suggestions for redrafting, and we are therefore grateful to the following colleagues for this: Ernie Battey, Lloyds Bank Project Finance; Lucy Burns, Government and Parliamentary Relations Manager; Michael Crick, Shareholders United; Dr Chris Forde, Leeds University; Professor Andrew Gamble, University of Sheffield; Simon Grover, University College, Northampton; Diana Jackson; Gavin Kelly, The Fabian Society; Michael Kitson, St Catharine's College, Cambridge; Soo Hee Lee, Birkbeck College; Emily Lomax, Lancaster University; Simon McNeil-Ritchie, Hamilton Laird Consulting; Roland Muri, Birkbeck College; Steve Parrott, Birkbeck College; Dr Jenny Piesse, Birkbeck College; Huw Richards, freelance journalist; Nick Toms, Independent Manchester United Supporters Association (IMUSA); and Dr Peter Trim, Birkbeck College.

We are particularly grateful to the members of the Barcelona supporters campaign group L'Elefant Blau, for travelling from Barcelona. Hearing of their campaign to maintain their club as precisely that – a club, owned and run by its members – in face of the new commercialism, was inspiring to all who heard them talk during the day as well as over the previous evening. Their delegation included Armand Carabén, the general manager at the time Johan Cruyff was brought to the club, as well as Alfons Godall, Joan Laporta, Jordi Moix, Joan Sola and Albert Vincens.

Thanks also to Steve Warby who organised the February meeting, helped with the production of this book and at the time of writing is preparing for a conference in July 1999 at Birkbeck College on the governance and regulation of professional football.

Others who were unable to attend the February meeting but who nevertheless provided valuable advice include Dr Simon Deakin, Reader in Law, Cambridge University; Gordon Farquhar, Radio 5 Live;

Mark Longden, Coalition of Football Supporters; Stan Metcalfe, Professor of Economics, Manchester University; and Malcolm Sawyer, Professor of Economics, Leeds University.

We are grateful to Bill Campbell, Sarah Edwards, Andrea Fraile and Elaine Scott of Mainstream Publishing for the speedy turnround of the manuscript.

Jonathan Michie would like to express his special gratitude for various advice and assistance from Carolyn Downs, Director of Leisure, Calderdale Borough Council; Alex Michie, a football manager (fantasy league) always almost on the edge of a dramatic breakthrough to success; and three-year-old Duncan Michie whose personal friendship with Paul Scholes is – quite literally – fantastic.

Finally we are grateful to Alex Ferguson for taking the time to contribute the Foreword to this book. It is particularly appropriate for a book edited from a Department of Management that we should have this contribution from someone who must be one of the country's outstanding managers not just in football but across the board.

Sean Hamil, Jonathan Michie, Christine Oughton
Department of Management, Birkbeck College
May 1999

Foreword

There is no doubt that football is now big business. New opportunities are opening up. But if these are to be taken rather than squandered, intelligent action is required.

The government should therefore be congratulated on launching the Football Task Force to report on what can be done to ensure the best possible development of the game for the largest number of people. But the issues involved are far too important to be left to the Task Force alone, or even government. More input is needed from people in the game itself. We all need to be involved in these discussions and decisions – the game's administrators, the clubs and the fans.

Firstly, there is a danger of over-commercialisation, in particular with the inflation of players' salaries. This will have to be addressed, sooner rather than later. We are already seeing clubs in financial trouble. The influx of TV revenues has gone largely in increased salaries. There has also been the fantastic development of football stadia across the country and through the divisions. But as any football fan will tell you, the hugely increased revenues certainly haven't gone to keep ticket prices down.

One of the reasons the money has gone disproportionately to top players' salaries is the Bosman ruling. Clubs have had to sign their players on longer contracts. And this has involved increasing salaries.

So far the pressure has fallen most heavily on the smaller clubs. But unless something is done, the big clubs will start to suffer too. And fans will get priced out of grounds.

Of course, fans are tremendously loyal. And they want their players to be well rewarded. But there is a limit to how far they will be prepared to pay for multi-million-pound salaries. Sooner or later this issue will need to be tackled. It would be best if the initiative came from the players' representatives themselves. The Professional Footballers Association in this country needs to take a responsible view of their members' interests as a whole, right through the leagues, and also of the game as a whole. But it's also an international problem – the players' representatives internationally should be talking about this, in the interests of the game as a whole and ultimately in the interests of their own members.

The second main point I would make is that while the new broadcasting developments – especially pay-per-view – promise large revenues to the bigger clubs in particular, it is in everyone's interests to maintain some degree of league balance. The Premiership is a fantastic league because there's fierce competition. On their day, anyone can beat anyone else. And that's how it should be. But if the authorities are to ask the large clubs to share these increased revenues through the league, for the good of the national game, something should be given in return.

For clubs playing in European competitions, a mid-season break would allow them to compete on equal terms. There should also be flexibility when it comes to arranging domestic fixtures, as there is on the continent. Helping our own clubs in Europe would benefit the whole game. It would increase the number of places English clubs get allocated. It would give more European experience to English clubs, which can only help the players, particularly by learning more of the tactics and how the game is played on the continent. It could only be good for the national team.

These are exciting times. I welcome the national debate that is emerging on these issues. If we can make the right decisions now, there are fantastic opportunities right through the game – from increased international success, through to improving facilities for the millions of people who play football week in, week out.

Certainly, football is big business. But it also plays an important role in the country's social and cultural life. Some may see it as just about money. I see it as much more important than that.

Alex Ferguson
May 1999

Introduction

Sean Hamil, Jonathan Michie and Christine Oughton

Over the last ten years, British football has been transformed. Up until the early 1980s it was largely a loss-making social institution with clubs privately owned by local benefactors. As we approach the millennium it is increasingly being incorporated into the commercial 'leisure' sector. (Football clubs are listed on the Stock Exchange under 'Leisure, Entertainment and Hotels'). Ownership by institutional and multi-national investors is becoming the norm as private owners sell out. The large clubs have been transformed into highly profitable purveyors of the full gamut of leisure-related product lines. Critical to this transformation, televised football has become *the* key weapon in the battle for viewers by satellite, cable and digital TV (including pay-per-view).

Amidst all this change the role of football as a social and cultural institution in Britain, and indeed the world, has remained largely intact. But tensions between the new commercialism and football's social purpose have become intense. The institutions of corporate governance which served football adequately when it was a loss-making passion catering to 'fans' whose core interest in the team was in its expression as a vehicle for social solidarity, a passion we term 'fan equity' (see chapter 1), are no longer adequate to effectively manage the extraordinary commercial pressures unleashed in the industry.

Football has been extensively analysed from a sociological perspective, most notably with regard to the football hooligan phenomenon. As the industry has become more profitable it has been subject to a growing body of analysis from a conventional economic and financial perspective. While important, none of this work to date has really succeeded in explaining the current dynamics of the industry. The existing literature generally lacks the necessary breadth to encompass an understanding of either the influence of 'fan equity', or an appreciation of the importance of maintaining and enhancing what we term 'positive league balance' (see chapter 6). None of the existing work, therefore, really gets to the heart of why it is so

13

necessary that the game be protected and developed through regulatory intervention (although the Football Task Force has done useful work, on which see chapter 3). Neither the UK football industry nor the sports markets generally, have been analysed to any extensive degree with regard to corporate governance issues and their relationship with 'fan equity'. This book sets out to fill that gap.

Birkbeck College's Department of Management has established a research programme on how regulation of the football and broadcasting industries might best be reformed to meet these new challenges. A successful conference in February 1999 brought together leading academics, policy-makers and analysts to discuss future possibilities for the governance of professional football. This book brings together the results of these discussions.

Critically, the key theme of all the contributions is that there are alternative governance structures to those currently being employed in the headlong drive toward greater commercialisation of the game. Plcs are certainly not the only option, and may not even be the most appropriate. The various alternative structures discussed in the following chapters (especially 8–13) are more in tune with the historical roots of the game in local communities, and more appropriate in terms of securing both the game's financial future and its critical role as a cultural and social asset.

The opening chapter by Sean Hamil ('A Whole New Ball Game? Why football needs a regulator') sets the scene by outlining the central importance of structures of corporate governance in determining the success, or otherwise, of the industry. This is because of the 'social' character of the good which football provides. He argues that the value of this 'social' element (described as 'fan equity') to the financial success of clubs is not fully appreciated by the current owners or regulators (the Football Association) of the sector.

He begins by explaining the critical role of regulatory intervention through the recommendations of the 1990 *Taylor Report* and significant public subsidy for ground rebuilding via the Football Trust, in reforming the industry in the early 1990s, and how this laid the ground for increased TV monies. He describes the chronic problems of financial and operational mismanagement that characterised the game's administration up until the early 1990s and which still persist at many clubs.

He then examines the subsequent movement by club owners to capitalise on the increased value of clubs, firstly by floating them on the Stock Exchange and, in what looks like the second wave in the development of a market in corporate control, the attempted sale of clubs to media conglomerates. Chapter 1 therefore argues, in a theme developed in many of the subsequent chapters in the book, that without effective regulatory intervention, current developments threaten to destroy the central character of the game by leading to a fragmentation of the traditional league structures. Instead, an élite of major clubs, retaining no real link with the communities from which they sprung, may break away. He argues that the failure of the Football Association (FA) to meet its responsibilities as an effective regulator has been an important facilitating factor in this negative development.

Hamil concludes by arguing that regulatory intervention has dealt with the ground safety issue. Significant further regulatory intervention is required to address the wider corporate governance issues thrown up in recent years by the headlong commercialisation of the game.

David Conn's 1997 best-selling book *The Football Business* (Mainstream) was the first publication to present a sustained critique of how increasing commercialisation was in danger of destroying the distinctive qualities of football as a key national cultural asset. In chapter 2 ('The New Commercialism') he brings the story up to date. Conn begins by setting out the history of the game from its earliest inception to the present day. He outlines how, while initially football clubs in the late Victorian and Edwardian era were set up primarily as sporting and community institutions, the explosion in the popularity of the game attracted a breed of businessmen bent on profit, in not dissimilar fashion to today. The same processes of consolidation were set in train. However, on that occasion, the Football Association and Football League intervened decisively to protect the sporting character of the game. The introduction of the FA's Rule 34 explicitly barred business people from making money out of the game via dividends or salaries, thus dramatically reducing the value of clubs as speculative business ventures. An extremely equitable form of financial redistribution of gate receipts, later extended to TV revenues, was introduced which served to maintain a high level of competitive uncertainty in the game.

Chapter 2 then outlines how a culture of amateurishness combined with parsimony with regard to ground improvements developed among clubs as a breed of director intent on securing local prestige at little cost was attracted. This culminated in the stadium disasters of Bradford, Heysel and Hillsborough. Conn notes that a supreme irony of the *Taylor Report* is that while it is most remembered for its recommendations on improving ground safety – the implementation of which has revolutionised the quality of British stadia – it also made a number of other recommendations aimed at preserving the unique cultural status of the game via the reform of its governance and administrative structures, which were never acted upon.

Conn argues that the failure to follow the wider remit of Lord Justice Taylor's recommendations has allowed a situation to arise whereby, with the influx of TV monies, football has been made increasingly attractive to a new generation of acquisitive businessmen, but on this occasion there has been no decisive regulatory intervention to prevent rampant commercialisation. He argues that fans have been increasingly exploited in a rapacious fashion. And that the erosion of redistributive rulings, when combined with this commercialisation, has set in train a powerful process of consolidation which is likely to lead ultimately to the breakaway of leading clubs from existing structures. He explains the manner in which the FA's Rule 34 was effectively side stepped, and the poverty of vision of the FA itself in the face of these developments.

Chapter 2 concludes by arguing that there must be a restoration of effective mechanisms for financial redistribution among clubs and a return to some form of social ownership structure. Conn argues that football needs a single executive body to regulate the game.

In chapter 3 ('Thinking the Unthinkable or Playing the Game? The Football Task Force, New Labour and the reform of English football') Adam Brown outlines the background to the formation of the government's Football Task Force. He sets out its aims and objectives with regard to the governance of football, and assesses both its progress to date and the prospects for meaningful change in the governance of football in England. Although writing in a personal capacity, he brings to bear his unique insight as a member of the Task Force Working Group. While at the time of writing (May 1999) the Task Force's work is not yet complete, he nevertheless offers an intriguing analysis as to the possible direction its findings, if taken up by government, might lead.

Brown explains the origins of the Task Force's remit in the Labour Party's pre-1997 election policy document, *Charter for Football*. While on the face of it the influx of TV money meant that financially football had never had it so good, the *Charter* tapped into a popular perception of a game mired in sleaze (the bung scandal), rocketing ticket prices, merchandising policies which appeared to exploit fan loyalty, a continued lack of representation for fans at all levels of the game and governing bodies seemingly incapable of providing leadership in the face of this hydra-headed challenge. He explains how, with the setting up of the Task Force in July 1997, the original broad sweep of the *Charter's* recommendations were incorporated, but in heavily diluted form. Critical omissions were the lack of any investigation of new formulas for administering the game and the associated reform of the FA, and any investigation of TV's role in football.

He documents how the Labour government's concern that the Task Force proceed on the basis of consensus served to critically complicate its work, as inevitable tensions erupted, most notably in the resignation of the Professional Footballers Association (PFA) representative Gordon Taylor after Task Force chairman David Mellor criticised players' attitudes to community work in a newspaper article.

Chapter 3 concludes by arguing that, while it is not possible to predict what the outcome of the Task Force's deliberations will be prior to the completion of its work, it nevertheless seems clear that some form of government-appointed regulator would be the logical outcome from the substance of the Task Force deliberations.

In chapter 4 ('The BSkyB Bid for Manchester United Plc') Simon Lee analyses the background to BSkyB's 1998 bid for Manchester United against the backdrop of developments in the political economy of football since the Hillsborough disaster. Lee argues that Manchester United in many ways represents a high-water mark of a financial model of corporate governance that has pervaded English football during the 1990s. For the future, the pursuit of short-term shareholder interest which this has involved needs to be replaced with an alternative stakeholding model of corporate governance which would recognise the status of supporters as major stakeholders in the English game.

Reaction to the BSkyB bid from within English football and without is assessed in the context of the impact of increasing TV revenues and the widening gap between the richest and poorest clubs in English football. Chapter 4 argues that neither the competition authorities nor BSkyB would have needed to have been involved in the future governance of English football, had the FA and the Football League launched the fundamental reassessment of English football which the *Taylor Report* called for in 1990.

Chapter 5 ('Football and Broadcasting and the MMC Case') by Jonathan Michie and Christine Oughton examines the reasons why BSkyB's attempted acquisition of Manchester United was blocked by the Monopolies and Mergers Commission and the Secretary of State for Trade and Industry. The chapter starts by considering the 'peculiar' nature of the football industry – the 'brand' loyalty of the fans, the links between clubs and their local communities and the collective nature of the league system which combine to make the industry particularly vulnerable to anti-competitive behaviour and raise a number of public interest concerns. The analysis then turns to the anti-competitive effects of the attempted acquisition on the broadcasting and media markets. BSkyB's attempted take-over raised three separate areas of concern regarding anti-competitive threats and restrictions on competition. Firstly, it would have led to the market for watching Manchester United at the ground and the market for watching Manchester United live on pay TV being controlled by a single company. This opens up the possibility that the company could raise prices at the ground with the intention of shifting the demand from those fans priced out of the stadium on to its other market, Sky Sports. Secondly, if the bid had been successful it would have distorted the bargaining process for rights to screen Premier League matches, creating restrictions on competition. Finally, the attempted acquisition would have weakened the competitive position of BSkyB's rivals and strengthened BSkyB's already dominant position in pay TV. The attempted take-over also raised the possibility of BSkyB subsidising Manchester United in order to 'buy' success on the field. If the BSkyB bid had been successful and was followed by other broadcasters acquiring Premier League clubs, cross-subsidisation would have exacerbated growing inequality and competitive imbalance. The MMC broadly accepted these points and recommended that the merger be blocked on the grounds that it would have reduced competition in broadcasting and adversely affected the quality of English Football. Michie and Oughton argue that this decision needs to be built upon, firstly to prevent any other media company–football club mergers, and also to prevent greater inequality of wealth between clubs by the uneven distribution of broadcasting revenues and the over-commercialisation of the game generally.

Chapter 6 ('Revenue-sharing from Broadcasting Football: the need for league balance') by Jeanette Findlay, Bill Holahan and Christine Oughton, focuses on the impact of income from live TV broadcasting on league balance under different systems of league organisation and regulation. The chapter looks at three interrelated aspects of live television broadcasting: firstly, the motives for revenue-sharing and the impact of the current rules for revenue-sharing on league balance; secondly, the effects of a move away from the current system of collective league bargaining to a system where each club sells the right to broadcast its matches individually; and finally, the incentives for revenue-sharing in a system of vertical integration, where all aspects of a club's activities – from the pitch to the television screen – are owned and controlled by a broadcasting company.

The impact of broadcasting revenues takes on particular significance at this time as debates about the future organisation of football are taking place against the backdrop of the case brought by the Office of Fair Trading (OFT) against the Premier League in the restrictive practices court, and also the government's April 1999 blocking, on the recommendations of the Monopolies and Mergers Commission (MMC) inquiry report, of the take-over by BSkyB of Manchester United.

The authors argue that all of these aspects of football organisation and regulation are inextricably linked and therefore any attempt to reform the current system of regulation needs to deal simultaneously with rules regarding the sale of broadcasting rights, revenue sharing and ownership structures. They conclude that there is an urgent need to examine the impact of broadcasting revenues on league balance (and league fragmentation) under different distribution rules, and systems of corporate governance in football more generally.

The question of the valuation of players' contracts in club financial balance sheets and annual accounts is addressed by Jonathan Michie and Shraddha Verma in chapter 7 ('Is Paul Ince an Asset or a Liability? Accounting and governance issues in football'). Following new regulations requiring football clubs to include players as assets in the balance sheet, the authors discuss the issues involved. Under the new rules, players are to be classified as intangible assets for accounting purposes and the chapter suggests that there are indeed strong arguments for so doing. In particular there is a danger that clubs may be undervalued if players' contracts are not included, thus leaving them vulnerable to asset-stripping take-overs.

Chapter 7 also considers other governance issues, arguing for greater representation for small shareholders. This is particularly crucial in the event of a take-over attempt. Most small shareholders are fans who have usually bought shares for reasons of emotional commitment rather than just a crude calculation of financial gain. This reflects the particular status of football clubs as social and cultural assets. The authors argue that prospective buyers should have to demonstrate that any take-over is in the public interest. Likewise shareholders should not be forced to sell against their will, as currently happens when 90 per cent of the shares in a company are acquired.

In chapter 8 ('Whose Game is it Anyway? Stakeholders, mutuals and trusts'), Jonathan Michie and Shay Ramalingam argue that mutual organisations are effective in removing stakeholder conflict. This has been demonstrated in particular in the financial services industry in the form of mutual assurance firms and building societies. Michie and Ramalingam argue that this form of organisation would suit the culture, ethos and objectives of football clubs and should be encouraged. Short of mutualisation, clubs such as Barnsley Football Club in Britain and the Green Bay Packers in the US are at least examples of widespread local and fan ownership. The chapter discusses how fan involvement might be institutionalised through the progressive transfer of shares to Trust status.

The subsequent chapter by Anne Bourke ('The Evolution of Irish Plc Co-operatives: lessons for English football clubs') considers possible alternative ownership structures for football clubs in the light of the experience of dairy co-operatives in Ireland. While on the face of it there are major differences between the dairy and football industries, they do share two key characteristics. Like football clubs they play a major role in providing social cohesion, in this case in rural areas in the Republic of Ireland, by guaranteeing a market for their farmer-owners' produce. And in the early 1980s this industry, like football, was regarded as under-capitalised. Chapter 9 explains how the dairy co-operatives squared the circle of maintaining co-operative ownership by their farmer-suppliers with raising capital to fund modernisation and expansion in a competitive marketplace by adopting a hybrid structure of co-operative plc status. Stock-market-quoted subsidiaries were created with full plc status but remained under majority control of the dairy co-operatives and their farmer-owners. This co-operative/plc status thus served to protect community ownership rather than serving as a vehicle for destroying it, as has happened in the case of football in the UK. Bourke argues that it is not too late for football clubs to learn from this example.

In chapter 10 ('Modern Corporations and the Public Interest'), Rob Branston, Keith Cowling, Nestor Duch Brown, Jonathan Michie and Roger Sugden consider the controversial issues of corporate governance from the broader perspective of the democratic deficit that characterises most large corporations. An analysis of large corporations across a range of business activities shows that there is a widespread problem of hierarchical decision-making that tends to serve the narrow interests of an élite few. The issue of who takes the key decisions, and in whose interests, takes on particular significance with the attempted take-over of Manchester United by BSkyB and the emergence of other media groups showing an interest in English soccer clubs. The authors argue that if corporations are to be governed in the 'public interest', the governance process needs to be characterised by more participation and greater democracy. They suggest that this might be achieved by a regulator for football with responsibilities that would include monitoring the activity of clubs and their controllers to ensure effective representation of the public interest in strategic decision-making.

Chapter 11 ('Supporter Representation on the Board: The Case of Northampton Town FC') by Brian Lomax, chairman of Northampton Town Supporters Trust and elected director of Northampton Town Football Club, discusses how and why the Trust was formed in 1992. Following the launch of the Trust and its involvement in running the club, average gates have risen from around 2,000 to over 6,000 per match. There was also a marked improvement in the club's performance, with two Wembley play-offs and promotion to the Second Division of the Nationwide League. Off the field, the Trust has fundraised and paid over £90,000 into Northampton Town FC. The Trust owns over 7 per cent of the total shares issued. It was also instrumental in cementing a three-way partnership between the club, the Trust and the local authority to build a new stadium with award-winning facilities for disabled access. The experience at Northampton Town has been endorsed by the Football Task Force and paves the way for supporter involvement to become the norm rather than the exception in football.

In chapter 12 ('The Struggle for Democracy at Barcelona FC'), four members of L'Elefant Blau (The Blue Elephant) – Armand Carabén, Alfons Godall, Joan Laporta and Jordi Moix – outline the struggle by supporters to maintain the democratic traditions of Barcelona Football Club. In recent years, Spanish football has undergone a deep transformation as the vast majority of clubs has been transformed from non-profit associations to private corporations. Today, only four professional football clubs out of the 42 playing in the national Spanish leagues are not corporations. Barcelona Football Club (or 'Barça' to its friends) is one of them. The Blue Elephant is an association of Barça fans that was established in 1997 with the aim of democratising the club and preserving its original status as a non-profit sports association. Chapter 12 documents the erosion of the traditional democratic rights of club members that has occurred in recent years. The Blue Elephant aims to reinstate and enhance the club's democratic tradition and strengthen its ties with the local community to ensure that Barça is not run along narrow commercial lines but rather serves the broader interests of supporters.

The book concludes with a discussion by Jonathan Michie and Andy Walsh of a range of ownership and governance options for football clubs ('What Future for Football?'). Chapter 13 begins by explaining the catalytic effect of the 1998 announcement of BSkyB's attempt to take over Manchester United in crystallising fears among concerned fans about the effectiveness of existing structures. Michie and Walsh outline how a strategy by individual businessmen in controlling positions at several clubs, notably Martin Edwards at Manchester United, has seen the legal status of clubs move from that of quasi-public bodies (as statutorily embodied in the FA's Rule 34), to decisively privately owned businesses (through the creation of holding companies), enriching these same businessmen in the process.

Chapter 13 demonstrates that the current regime of regulatory oversight, as administered by the FA, has been inadequate in the face of these developments. Indeed, to some extent the FA could be said to have collaborated in creating many of these problems. The authors then outline a range of alternative ownership structures for clubs, most notably trust status, and discuss how these might be achieved. This final chapter concludes by calling for government intervention to facilitate the creation of such structures. Michie and Walsh argue that this agenda is not only necessary to meet the remit that the government itself gave to the Football Task Force, but is also necessary for achieving other key objectives of government, most noticeably the tackling of social exclusion – a process dramatically illustrated at many football grounds by the pruning out of low income supporters by high ticket prices.

There is clearly a problem. Tony Blair was quite right in 1995 to express concern:

> I worry that a game in which one individual is deemed to be worth £7 million and whose club must raise the money with ever more lucrative and exclusive television deals, merchandising and expensive seats, is a game which may lose touch with its roots. I worry that fans are taken for granted. I worry that the television deals are ignoring the smaller clubs which desperately need support, and creating a class of bigger clubs that becomes ever more voracious in its quest for success. I worry, too, that the dividing line between marketing and exploitation may have been crossed amid the plethora of ever-changing strips.

The subsequent chapters demonstrate that such fears are indeed well founded. In what follows, the various authors outline the necessary solutions. It is to be hoped that these ideas will now be acted on by the government, by the game's regulators and by the clubs.

1. A Whole New Ball Game?

Why Football Needs a Regulator

Sean Hamil

Until the early 1980s football clubs were mainly loss-making. They were primarily social – as opposed to commercial – institutions. Clubs were privately owned, usually by locally based, wealthy and indulgent benefactors motivated by a desire for prestige in the local community, some sense of *noblesse oblige*, or just pursuing a hobby. As real incomes increased, spectators were turning to other leisure pursuits. Attendances were declining.

By contrast, in 1999 the industry is increasingly being incorporated into the conventional commercial 'leisure' sector (with stock-market-quoted firms listed under 'Leisure, Entertainment and Hotels'). Ownership by institutional or multi-national corporate investors is on the way to becoming the norm as private owners sell out. The large clubs have been transformed into highly profitable purveyors of the full gamut of leisure-related product lines, attracting an increasing number of spectators from across the full range of income groups.

Two key factors have driven this transformation: the opening up of this previously closed sector to market forces and effective governmental regulatory intervention.

The influence of market forces has critically been felt through the ascension of televised football (and professional sport generally) to the role of the key software in the battle for viewers in the burgeoning multi-channel TV and related-media industry. This has dramatically increased the financial value of football clubs. However, even the most forthright proponents of market-based frameworks for developing the industry in the future acknowledge the central catalysing effect of governmental regulatory intervention in the industry's recent transformation.

Regulatory intervention: the catalyst for change

The problems of football in the 1980s have been well documented. Indeed the industry could be said to have been in an almost perpetual state of crisis since the early 1970s. Jennet and Sloane (1985), in their critique of Sir Norman Chester's Football League-commissioned report (*Football League*, 1983), succinctly summarise the parlous state of the game in 1983. Attendances had declined from a peak of 41.3 million in 1948–49 to 18.4 million in 1983–84. In only 18 clubs were current assets in excess of liabilities. The Chester Enquiry was in part a response to an earlier Football League document starkly entitled *Fight for Survival*. The chronic lack of investment in grounds coupled with inadequate management of clubs was to culminate only a few years later in the Heysel (1985), Bradford (1985) and Hillsborough (1989) stadium disasters. The *Taylor Report* (1989 and 1990) lays bare the catalogue of incompetence and negligence in stark detail. Something had to be done if the game's future was to be secured. It is one of the paradoxes of football as an industry that while it had long played a central role in the cultural life of the nation, in terms of business entrepreneurship its waters were stagnant. The *Chester Report* highlighted most clubs' lack of commercial awareness and a general absence of responsiveness to consumer demands.

The business management techniques employed by most clubs had remained virtually unchanged for nearly seventy years. A study of clubs' accounting practices by Arthur Andersen & Co. in 1982 found these to be 'chaotic'. Until very recently football's reputation for mismanagement made the investment community highly sceptical of the sport as an industry:

> Traditionally their [football club] marketing strategies were unsophisticated, their internal cost controls have been slack and their accountancy practices have been archaic, village hall stuff [according to the *Financial Times*] (Cheffins, 1997a, p. 75).

Indeed there remains some scepticism as to whether the majority of football clubs will ever make good investments in the conventional sense. An article specifically examining the prospects for UK football clubs on the Stock Exchange observes:

> . . . it may be that recent economic changes in football do not provide a solid foundation for continued growth and strong share performance . . . present patterns suggest only a small handful of clubs will benefit. Those buying shares in teams that

are not in the financial élite thus may well not earn a favourable return from their investment. (Cheffins, 1997b, p. 108.)

If football was a conventional industry, firms which fail would exit the marketplace leaving the remaining clubs to grow stronger by attracting 'customers' from defunct clubs. Or underperforming clubs would be acquired by more effective management teams. In football, as a rule, neither of these phenomena occur. One reason has been that businessmen didn't generally acquire clubs to make money, and so subordinated profitability to the objective of winning enhanced league position, by means of subsidy if necessary. As clubs were habitually unprofitable there was no incentive for them to be acquired by new owners for profit-maximisation reasons:

> It is quite apparent that directors and shareholders invest money in football clubs not because of pecuniary income but for such psychological reasons as the urge for power, the desire for prestige, the propensity to group identification and the related feeling of group loyalty . . . Football clubs are essentially based on tradition, which derives from their position in the social structure of their particular localities. The gathering together of partisan supporters breeds a club (or brand) loyalty, which *per se* yields utility, so that supporters as well as directors are prepared to donate money without regard to financial gain (Sloane, 1971, p. 134).

More fundamentally, football clubs were never intended to be conventional profit-maximising firms. They were intended to act as sporting clubs. The FA's Rule 34 specifically restricted the size of dividend payments (Conn, 1997, pp. 35, 134–35). This had the effect of making clubs of little value to conventional investors, as was the intention. How Rule 34 was subverted and the implications thereof is dealt with in detail in subsequent chapters.

Conventional economic analysis fails to apply because clubs are effectively local monopolies with allegiances based on emotional and not economic relationships. Were a club to go out of business it is far from certain that its fans would transfer to another team. Changing allegiance is rare: 83 per cent of Premier League supporters have always supported their present club, a figure that might be expected to be even higher for Football League clubs (Smith and LeJeune, 1998, para. 1.20). So club owners have had no incentive to see their local rival go to the wall; if anything they had an incentive to see them survive so they could bank the gate money from the local derby.

Football occupied a backwater of ineffectual self-regulation. The result was the catalogue of ground safety disasters culminating at Hillsborough. The resulting regulatory intervention forced the industry to modernise its facilities, and hence itself. Not only that, but this regulatory intervention was augmented by a significant subsidy from the public purse (rather unusually so in the context of the general thrust towards deregulation of economic activity experienced during the 18 years of Conservative government from 1979 to 1997), via grants from the Football Trust. The Trust had been charged by government in 1990 with responsibility for helping professional clubs meet the costs of the *Taylor Report*. In addition to its traditional income from the pools companies' Spotting-the-Ball (later Littlewoods' Spot the Ball) the Trust received the proceeds of a reduction in pool-betting duty to fund its work. In total, the Trust distributed £150 million to clubs in the FA Premier League, the Football League and the Scottish Football League between 1990 and 1997, enabling Taylor-related stadium rebuilding projects costing over £500 million (The Football Trust, 1997, p.1).

The revenue from Spot the Ball has now been discontinued and from 1998 the Trust's work is to be funded by the FA Premier League, the English Sports Council and the Football Association. The Trust's activities have expanded beyond the Taylor-inspired stadia improvements to embrace investment in grass-roots activities via the Football in the Community Programme.

The capital investment facilitated by the Football Trust's activities paved the way for increased attendances at games, rising 15 per cent between 1990–91 and 1994–95 (Salomon Brothers, 1997, p. 26). Maintenance of safety and comfort standards at Premier and Football League grounds is exercised through the issuance of ground safety licences by the Football Licensing Authority (FLA), a remit devised for it by the *Taylor Report*. The FLA's best known function has been to enforce the government's policy that every club in the Premiership and First Division of the Football League had to make its ground all seated by August 1994 or by three years after its promotion into the First Division. It now undertakes a wider safety regulatory brief. It is a tribute to the influence of the FLA and its perceived success in contributing to the raising of standards in British grounds that its advice was sought by the organisers of the 1998 World Cup in France, and the 2000 European Championships in Belgium and Holland (FLA, 1997). Like the Football Trust, it offers a successful model of regulatory intervention in an industry which had shown no signs of being able to reform itself.

These regulatory interventions enabled football as an industry to reconstruct itself as a reformed and 'clean' activity in the eyes of the wider non-traditional football-supporting public. It is one of the two central arguments of this chapter that this reconstruction from impoverished ugly duckling to golden goose would not have occurred without regulatory intervention. There would have been no television-money revolution without regulatory reform.

The role of television

The emergence of satellite TV has had a major impact on football. The satellite companies, chiefly BSkyB, needed an attractive software to draw viewers who were also prepared to pay the extra cost, away from terrestrial channels. It is now widely acknowledged that the key 'software' was the rights to televise live football. It is also the case that the advent of satellite TV, and in particular BSkyB's aggressive and innovative marketing techniques, enabled football to make the crossover into mainstream popular culture via fashion/lifestyle/entertainment products.

The sums of money TV companies were prepared to pay for television rights meant that it became possible for a minority of clubs to pay extraordinary sums of money to players, and still make handsome profits.

The current BSkyB deal for exclusive rights to the English Premier League amounted to £670 million for the 1997–2001 seasons – nearly 3.5 times the price paid for the previous contract in 1992. The BBC agreed to pay £73 million to show highlights on *Match of the Day* from 1997 to 2001, versus £4 million for the previous contract in 1992 . . . gate receipts as a percentage of total (UK football club) revenues are forecast to decline to 32 per cent in 2000 from 39 per cent in 1996. Television has become the most important factor, given that it supports football's other future value drivers, sponsorship and merchandising (Salomon Brothers, 1997, pp. 27, 32).

This influx of money into football encouraged many club owners to float on the Stock Exchange while retaining controlling interests. It became obvious that the nature of the relationship between club and fan had changed dramatically. The flotation of most football clubs brought significant windfall profits to controlling directors. This process has raised significant corporate governance problems. The money raised has often initially come from small shareholders, who buy out of a sense of fandom, and therefore are likely to pay more than conventional institutional investors. An implication, as Conn (1997, pp. 164–76) explains, is that owners are simply cashing in some of their capital at inflated prices while retaining control. The financial experience of the fan-shareholder has so far not been good. The starkest example is the case of Newcastle United where, in November

1998, the directors agreed to sell their controlling interest in the club to the cable TV company NTL at a price, 111.7p, significantly below the original flotation price of 135p. While this may have represented good business for Newcastle's major shareholders, the Hall family and Freddie Shepherd, who had originally bought the club at a fraction of this price, it was decidedly bad business for the fans who bought shares in the club at the original flotation price. The *Financial Times* reported the following exchange at the company annual general meeting:

> Newcastle United football club has been sold down the river by Cameron (Hall) Developments (the Hall family's holding company) to suit themselves . . . Freddie Fletcher, chairman and chief executive responded by pointing to the fall in value of other listed football clubs (whose value had fallen much further). 'There's not a shadow of doubt the football sector isn't as frothy as 18 months ago.' (*Tighe*, 1998, 22 November).

The paper's influential *Lex* column observed:

> A public auction would have been better for minority shareholders, but when did their voices ever count? (*Lex*, 1998, 22 November).

NTL withdrew their bid in April 1999 following the MMC's ruling against BSkyB's bid for Manchester United.

So while on the surface talk was of a renaissance in the industry, underneath the surface discontent bubbled:

> This should have been a golden age . . . to be a football supporter. Heysel and Hillsborough were in the past. We had seen off the hooligans and nearly all the fences. Where we were once the enemy within, we were now the height of fashion . . . TV programmes, plays and even opera took an interest . . . Football shirts were everywhere. There was a boom . . . This should have been everything we ever wanted. Instead, just when it was, at last, all right to be a football fan, everything went sour (Horton, 1997, pp. 13–14).

> For all the talk of the glories of the Premiership and the new fans coming into the sport and the economic benefits of the game to its localities, there is a pervasive air of discontent among fans (Dempsey and Reilly, 1998, p. 241).

Fan equity

What is 'fan equity' (Salomon Brothers, 1997; Gorman and Calhoun, 1994) and why is it important? Fans buy merchandise as a means of associating themselves with their sporting heroes, but also as a means of expressing solidarity with their fellow fans. Organised sport, and football in particular, draws on an emotional investment by the fan in the competitive proceedings which is highly unusual in the context of the typical consumer/producer interaction. It is this ability to attract paying viewers at the grounds and through television, and sell related merchandise, which makes sports clubs/franchises valuable as businesses. And as the experience of UK football clubs demonstrates, this value has been rising. According to the *Deloitte & Touche Annual Review of Football Finance*, the average English club's turnover has grown at 20 per cent compounded annually over the last five years (Boon, 1998, p. 5).

This raises the question of what it is that fans are consuming. The answer is what Salomon Brothers term 'fan equity', or an 'irrationally loyal customer base':

> Fans are the customers in the sports business. And the relationship between a team and its supporters is exceptional in the sense that the customers do not need success. The target is desirable for them, but not a condition for their support in the short term . . . Fans can therefore constitute for some teams a real asset of truly intangible nature, as an essential part of the team's revenue is generated from the support it receives (Salomon Brothers, 1997, p. 9).

For Salomon Brothers the fans' relationship with their team is 'irrational'. In fact the fan-club relationship is easily explainable – but not in the terminology of free market economics. Firstly, 'fan equity' is antipathetic to commodification, which is the driving force behind recent commercial trends in the industry. The organisation of consumption in a capitalist economy is fundamentally about the packaging of goods/services for purchase by individual consumers, about transforming products/services (however intangible, for example, a desire for status symbols through personalised number plates) into a commodified form so that they can be sold on as products. However, 'fan equity' is difficult to commodify on a sustained basis. For, critically, the core component of the 'fan equity' phenomenon is the opportunity it offers to supporters to engage in solidaristic behaviour with other fans with whom they share a common identity. Not only is it about a shared solidarity with those who support your team, crucially it also incorporates a competitive relationship with those who don't. The football club is the vehicle for this 'shared' experience, for this 'community' of interest. Its essence is the collective and not the individual. It is not even like other cultural activities such as going to the theatre or cinema. As Smith and LeJeune (1998, para. 1.11) observe, while football is a form of entertainment, the competitive element is paramount and essential to its appeal. The claim sometimes made that football is merely a branch of show business is misleading and trivialises the game.

It is instructive that the report of the Football Task Force, *Investing in the Community*, the most recent investigation into the health of the industry, offers substantial evidence in support of this contention that football is different from other industries because it is fundamentally about the community and not the individual, about a sense of shared emotional ownership (Football Task Force, 1999, pp. 37–46).

Even a club like Manchester United, which draws many fans from outside of Manchester, taps into a deep emotional well. To a large extent this reflects the mystique that the club acquired following the Munich air disaster in 1958, and subsequently in the 1960s when its identity became caught up with a wider affiliation with the romance, music and social liberation of that decade perhaps best typified by the career of George Best, the first footballer of the modern era to cross over into popular culture. However, it remains true to say that the core support remains in the local Manchester area.

Football without fans with a shared emotional investment in their team's performance, and an emotional investment in the failure of their competitors, doesn't work – neither as a human experience nor as a commercial venture. This is what makes it different from conventional marketplaces:

> As a Newcastle United fan said after the club's managing director had drawn parallels between shopping at Safeways and following Newcastle United: 'I don't go around wearing Safeways replica shirts. I don't wait for hours to get on a coach to go and see Safeways in other parts of the country. I don't pay £340 for a season ticket to go to Safeways.' (Cheffins, 1997b, p. 109).

Commercial forces threaten to corrode 'fan equity', and also 'competitive uncertainty', which refers to the requirement that there be 'real competition' between clubs, with the possibility left open that even the smallest may achieve glory if they organise successfully. A thriving football fanbase depends on the existence of real competitive uncertainty. Free-market forces such as those currently shaping the direction of football are antipathetic to both the 'fan equity' and 'competitive uncertainty' concepts. As with the historical case of ground safety, the football industry appears unable to recognise this fact, or to produce a regulatory framework which will work to protect its key assets. The goose that lays the golden eggs is in danger of suffocation. This is because both the new owners of football clubs and the current dominant regulator (the FA) appear to misunderstand the importance and nature of 'fan equity' and 'competitive uncertainty'.

Institutional ownership of clubs will erode links with local geographic identities, which is at the root of the 'fan equity' concept. It will set in train oligopolistic tendencies which will reduce the overall level of competitive uncertainty in the process. This might even involve consolidation among clubs, along the lines of when the late Robert Maxwell attempted to merge Oxford United and Reading into the contrived 'Thames Valley Royals'. *The Guardian* reported discussions about a possible triple merger between Oldham, Bury and Rochdale, to create a club possibly called Manchester North End (Chaudhary, 1999, 9 January). Regardless of whether or not such mergers take place there is a growing divide between the powerful élite clubs and the rest. The end result of this trend could well be a small number of financially successful clubs engaged in gladiatorial combat, like the International Wrestling Federation, but with a fanbase that is no longer emotionally involved in the traditional sense, but are instead attracted by the concept of the 'big event'. Those clubs left on the outside, robbed of the opportunity or even possibility of one day scaling the divisions like a latter-day Wimbledon, are likely to wither on the vine condemned to a twilight existence. Football as a national cultural asset will have died.

The fundamental danger of the current commercialisation is that the fan will no longer feel any 'equity' in the game. The more insightful commercial analysts recognise this risk. For example, Salomon Brothers acknowledge that 'fan equity' can be eroded by lack of sensitivity which would be 'value-destroying' for football, with insensitive scheduling of broadcasts in terms of timing, or 'abusive pricing' cited (1997, p. 10). But there is no appreciation in that document of the scale of the potential crisis set in train by unchecked commercialisation:

> Many loyal supporters . . . could stop attending matches because of blatant commercialism. Other fans, bombarded by media 'hype' might abandon small clubs in the lower divisions to support a coterie of widely publicised élite teams. The destruction of the sport's working-class roots and community

traditions could then easily follow. If this occurs and football at the same time falls out of fashion with affluent sectors of the population, the sport's economic future would be bleak indeed (Cheffins, 1997b, p. 107).

The new affluent supporters are more fickle than their traditional lower-income counterparts. According to Premier League fan surveys:

> Season ticket holders earning over £30,000 per year were the least committed attenders of home matches of their clubs (54.2 per cent attended all home games, compared to 75 per cent of those earning £15,000 or less), and ascribed a much less significant place to football in their lives as a whole than poorer supporters (Smith and LeJeune, 1998, para. 2.8).

The cords of community, be they local, emotional or both, which have tied clubs to their supporters and which are at the heart of its success are close to being severed:

> Football clubs owe their support to the . . . belief, that they are driven by a common purpose, that they form a community in which the players, supporters and directors work together and pull in the same direction. Never has this been less true than it is today, and nowhere is it more false than at the new élite. These clubs have nothing in common with the people who support them . . . Between us and them (the multi-millionaire owners and exorbitantly paid players) there is no community. And football is embittered by the conflict that results (Horton,1997, p. 18).

Tellingly, television host Johnny Vaughan (most recently of Channel 4's *Big Breakfast Show*) remarked in an interview in *Esquire* magazine entirely unrelated to football:

> I went to England–Poland at Wembley a while ago, and I just couldn't shout any more. All I could see were 11 millionaires running around. And, I dunno, something's gone . . . (cited in Bastable, 1998, p. 22).

As any reading of the *Taylor Report* would quickly confirm, football needs to be managed in a businesslike fashion. But as an industry it is inappropriate to use conventional governance techniques and structures. It is not just a business, but also a social and cultural activity.

Competition or consolidation?

The move towards consolidation goes against one of the longest-established and central guiding principles of successful organised sport:

> ... it is a unique feature of professional sporting activity that in order to produce a saleable output, clubs must combine together to produce a game. Therefore competition is characterised by mutual interdependence, such that a club can only survive provided other clubs remain viable entities ... The paradox of competition in football is that whilst a club's objective is to finish the season in a higher league position than any of its rivals, it also has a vested interest in the continuing success of its rivals in the league, for the more successful the rival in terms of league position and popularity, the larger will be the total attendance resulting from the common product ... Uncertainty, as well as the quality of the football, creates interest (Sloane, 1971, pp. 123–24).

All serious analyses of the economics of sports as a business recognise this central point:

> Sports leagues are in the business of selling competition on the playing field, leading to what Walter Neale (1964) termed 'The Peculiar Economics of Professional Sports'. The special problem for sports leagues is the need to establish a degree of competitive balance on the field that is acceptable to fans (Fort and Quirk, 1995, p. 1265).

In the United States this involves extensive financial cross-subsidisation between sports clubs within their respective leagues. Consolidation, in whatever form, be it the actual breakaway of some clubs to form a 'Super League', or the *de facto* breakaway of an élite group on the basis of financial power which effectively buys guaranteed high league position on an ongoing basis, threatens this competitive balance.

The new commercialism is creating a handful of 'super clubs', who by dint of their financial power, can more or less guarantee that they will be able to finish in the top ten of the Premier League each year. Below them are a group who, while they are too weak to join this group, are too strong to be relegated. Next come a group who are constantly yo-yoing between the Premier League and Nationwide Football League First Division.

As the recent discussions regarding a European Super League

independent of the current UEFA structures indicates, this group of 'super clubs' may eventually detach themselves from the structures that have sustained and nurtured their development over the last 100 years, the English and Scottish leagues and their systems of promotion and relegation, with negative consequences for football as an industry and as a cultural asset. Essentially, the economics of the industry have degenerated into a free-for-all, with the big clubs benefiting at the expense of the small:

> The future of football will follow the course of every 'industry' which has been subjected to the divisive acid of 'market forces', guided by no more human force. The result is 'consolidation'. Every decision will be taken on the basis of whether it will make more money for the already rich (Conn, 1997, p. 287).

The race is on to see which clubs will be included in the 'select' and oligopolistic band of top clubs, and which will be excluded.

The move towards consolidation threatens the financial interests of those, often fans who have invested for emotional as well as financial reasons, who have invested in lower division clubs in the expectation that their value will rise if and when they achieve promotion. As fan loyalty is to some extent dictated by the existence of the possibility, if not the probability, that one day their team will scale the heights of the game's competitive structures, the elimination of this possibility, through the establishment of 'Super Leagues' of various kinds which preclude relegation or promotion, will seriously depress the financial value of such clubs, as well as undermining fans' emotional 'equity' investment in their team.

Even those with only a financial interest in the industry recognise that consolidation, taken too far, could have negative consequences for the long-term financial health of the game:

> The economics of sport is tied to a guaranteed competitive balance within a league, as uncertainty over the outcome feeds the fans' support and interest. However, the increasing polarisation among Premier League teams, both in terms of results and revenue base, endangers this principle (Salomon Brothers, 1997, p. 3).

Even the FA Premier League, which has done so much to accelerate this process of consolidation and fragmentation, has belatedly woken up to the threat it poses, although its concern was the financial threat posed by the setting up of a European Super League, rather than by any great concern to protect fan interests. A consultancy report commissioned by the Premier League to examine the 'Implications for football and TV in Europe' of the setting up of a Super League observes:

> Together the threat of relegation from premier divisions and the possibility of qualification for European competitions have created all-season excitement for most club supporters in spite of there only being a handful of clubs with realistic expectations of winning the league title within domestic markets . . . [but the setting up of a European Super League with certain 'super clubs' gaining automatic entry each year would mean] . . . Domestic tournaments would lose relevance as they become less competitive due to automatic European qualification for the top clubs (Oliver and Ohlbaum Associates Ltd, 1998, pp. 5–6).

The need for rules

The *Taylor Report* (1989; 1990) and the *Chester Report* (1983) chronicle the shortcomings of the game's management and regulation. The attempts by the first clubs to raise money on the stock-market, such as Tottenham Hotspur, were dogged by scepticism regarding the quality of their management and governance. Even in the post-Taylor era they continue to inspire little faith. Dempsey and Reilly (1998) detail the culture of cash payments, and often downright illegality, which has characterised the recent history of many clubs. They observe:

> Senior executives at many publicly limited (football) clubs concede in private that the share-price slump of the football sector on the stock-market is in part due to worries about the business standards of the game (Dempsey and Reilly, 1998, p. 206).

In the most extraordinary recent example of poor business management, the former owner of Doncaster Rovers football club, Ken Richardson, was jailed in March 1999 for four years for plotting to burn down the club's main stand. The plot came to light when the hired arsonist left his mobile phone at the scene and was quickly traced and arrested.

The *Financial Times* (Gapper, 1999) reported that the Independent Television Commission (ITC), which is responsible for the regulation of all commercial broadcasting, was opposed to the take-over of football clubs by media companies as it would impede the sale of broadcasting rights. It rejected the alternative of imposing conditions on such take-overs on the grounds that they might not be enforceable as the low standards of corporate governance in the management of football clubs meant some could not be trusted to stick to conditions on how they should behave. Even the Football Association recognises that there is a governance problem. Following the FA enquiry into transfer irregularities triggered by the acceptance of cash gifts by then Arsenal manager George Graham (the so-called 'bung' scandal), its chair Sir John Smith, a former deputy commissioner of the Metropolitan Police, was asked to extend his enquiry to:

> . . . inquire into the manner in which football regulates its financial affairs and to make recommendations to the Football Association as to how to ensure and maintain the integrity of football and to promote accountability in the way it operates . . . (Smith and LeJeune, 1998, Summary).

His findings make interesting reading:

> Since it is so successful, why should football bother about its occasional scandals? Why meddle with a success story? Does it matter if the world of football is tarnished by rumours of financial misbehaviour? There is a tendency for people within the game to dismiss this subject with a cursory statement: 'that's football', as if it were the natural order of things for financial misconduct to be part of the game (Smith and LeJeune, 1998, para. 2.1).

This is an extraordinary admission. Yet Sir John's recommendation (Smith and LeJeune, 1998, Summary: Recommendation 3) that an independent compliance and monitoring unit be set up by the Football Association to monitor finances, deal with appropriate complaints and investigate serious financial irregularities has not been acted upon.

The role of the FA as regulator has been particularly deficient leaving the industry effectively rudderless in terms of regulatory strategy. As David Conn presciently observed in conversation with a perplexed Graham Kelly, then chief executive of the FA:

> . . . but all markets, even in this country (the UK), have regulators. Even the privatised industries have . . . Oftel, Ofgas, Ofwat . . . And their jobs are to make sure that prices stay affordable, that excessive profits aren't made and that money is ploughed back in investment. And that seems to be precisely what has happened in football: increased prices and excess

profits, not enough investment in the long term. And in this industry, you, the FA, the governing body, are the regulator (Conn, 1997, p. 284).

Conclusion

Football is entering a potentially self-defeating spiral. The irony is that the requirement that there be even minimal standards of regulatory intervention is not in itself terribly radical. Michael Porter, doyen of business strategy at Harvard Business School, has famously made the point in the context of environmental regulation, that regulatory intervention can actually enhance the financial quality of industry performance. Nowhere is this clearer than the football industry, where its very salvation from the social, cultural and economic nadir of the late 1980s would not have been possible without the regulatory changes set in train by the *Taylor Report*.

Regulatory intervention has resolved the problem of ground safety. But what gives the requirement for more effective regulatory intervention particular urgency is the need to move beyond ground safety issues in order to protect the football industry's value as a social and cultural asset, as well as an economic activity; and to preserve the pyramid structure of leagues which provide the appropriate level of 'competitive uncertainty' on which the English and Scottish games have thrived. This intervention needs to be underpinned by the recognition that there are other stakeholders in football than just the shareholders and employees. A more inclusive form of structure is required, more radical in its design and thinking. There is nothing 'natural' about the increased commercialisation of football, just as there was nothing 'natural' about the appalling standard of ground safety prior to the *Taylor Report*, or the extraordinary poor quality of financial probity observed by many clubs. As other chapters in this book argue, there are alternatives. But they must be underpinned by the creation of a strong regulator.

References

Bastable, M. (1998). 'The Esquire Interview: Johnny Vaughan'. *Esquire,* December, pp. 21–27.

Boon, G. (ed.) (1998). *Deloitte & Touche Annual Review of Football Finance.* Manchester: Deloitte & Touche.

Chaudhary, V. (1999). 'Oldham push for triple merger of league clubs'. *The Guardian,* 9 January.

Cheffins, B. (1997a) 'UK football clubs and the stock-market: past developments and future prospects: Part 1'. *The Company Lawyer,* Vol. 18, No. 3.

Cheffins, B. (1997b). 'UK football clubs and the stock-market: past developments and future prospects: Part 2'. *The Company Lawyer,* Vol. 18, No. 4.

Conn, D. (1997). *The Football Business: Fair Game in the '90s?* Edinburgh: Mainstream Publishing.

Dempsey, P. and Reilly, K. (1998). *Big Money: Beautiful Game.* London: Nicholas Brealey Publishing.

Football League (1983). *Report of the Committee on Football* (Chairman Sir N. Chester), Lytham St Annes: The Football League.

Football Licensing Authority (1997). *Annual Report and Accounts.* London: Football Licensing Authority.

The Football Task Force (1999). *Investing In The Community.* A Report submitted to the Minister of Sport on 11 January. London: Football Task Force.

The Football Trust (1997). *Annual Report.* London: The Football Trust.

Fort, R. and Quirk, J. (1995). 'Cross-subsidization, Incentives, and Outcomes in Professional Team Sports Leagues'. *Journal of Economic Literature,* Vol. XXXIII, pp. 1265–99.

Gapper, J. (1999). 'ITC calls for halt to Man Utd bid'. *Financial Times,* 12 February.

Gorman, J. and Calhoun, K. (1994). *The Name of the Game: the business of sports.* New York: John Wiley and Sons.

Horton, E. (1997). *Moving the Goalposts: Football's Exploitation.* Edinburgh: Mainstream Publishing.

Jennett, N. and Sloane, P. J. (1985). 'The future of league football: a critique of the Chester Committee of Enquiry'. *Leisure Studies,* 4, pp. 39–45.

Lex (1998). 'Newcastle United'. *Financial Times,* 18 December.

Neale, W. (1964). 'The Peculiar Economics of Professional Sports'. *Quarterly Journal of Economics,* 78, February, pp. 1–14.

Oliver and Ohlbaum Associates Ltd (1998). *Super Leagues and Super Clubs: The Implications for Football and TV in Europe*. Oliver and Ohlbaum Associates Ltd.

Salomon Brothers (1997). 'UK Football Clubs: valuable assets?'. *Global Equity Research: Leisure*, November. London: Salomon Brothers.

Sloane, P. (1971). 'The Economics of Professional Football: The Football Club As A Utility Maximiser'. *Scottish Journal of Political Economy*, 17 June, pp. 121–46.

Smith, Sir J. and LeJeune, M. (1998). *Football: Its Values, Finances and Reputation*. The Football Association.

Inquiry by the Rt Hon Lord Justice Taylor (1989). *The Hillsborough Stadium Disaster: Interim Report*. Cm765. London HMSO.

Inquiry by the Rt Hon Lord Justice Taylor (1990). *The Hillsborough Stadium Disaster: Final Report*. Cm962. London HMSO.

Tighe, C. (1998). 'Newcastle Utd shareholders pack a punch'. *Financial Times*, 22 December.

2. The New Commercialism

David Conn

In order to see how English football has changed and produced such extreme inequalities since 1992, it is necessary to consider the system which was in place previously. Football started in this country, and its development has generally been a process of evolution, with little overall planning. But from the beginning football always considered itself to have a sporting ethos and to aim to play a beneficial role in society. Even as it became professionalised, the game's governing bodies saw it as their duty to maintain the underlying sporting ethic. The league structure was ordered to maintain some equality between big and small clubs, and the clubs themselves were subject to FA regulations to protect their sporting character and prevent them being treated purely as businesses to make profits for shareholders.

In 1992 the First Division was allowed to break away from the rest of the Football League, with the backing of the Football Association. This constituted a betrayal of a century of the traditional structure, and it was done on the threshold of an unprecedentedly huge TV deal for football. The Premier League did that deal and shared very little of the £305 million which flowed from it. The FA allowed its own rules to be broken to allow flotation, and so the major shareholders, chairmen and a few others, made a fortune on shares bought cheaply under the previous structure.

No other regulation was put in place, except the *Taylor Report* injunction to build all-seater stadia, for which the clubs were given a subsidy of public money. The top clubs have raised their prices more than 300 per cent since then and indulged in many more money-making activities. In 1997 a four-year TV deal was done worth £670 million, still with only 20 Premiership clubs. The Football League clubs have done their own deals, and there is some redistribution from the Premier League, ring-fenced for ground improvements and for the setting up of academies. But it is utterly insufficient. Generally the game suffers from huge inequality and, despite the full houses which attend Premier League matches, many supporters who came to football in the previous era have been disenfranchised by the rising prices and exploitative culture at their clubs.

It is instructive to understand that this is not mere opinion, but that the current 'free market' age constitutes a departure from football's sense of itself throughout its previous history, in which FA and League strove to balance the needs of commercialism with the central spirit of the game.

Early football

Football originated in England. Its rules were developed in the public schools of the nineteenth century. It was played for pleasure, and encouraged by the 'games ethic' generation of headmasters who saw in it the social and moral benefits of 'sportsmanship', alongside its obvious provision of organised physical exercise. The Football Association was formed in 1863, its original purpose to unify the games being played in the various schools and universities under a single set of rules.

Football was taken out of the upper-class environment around the 1860s and 1870s, spread largely by university graduates. It was substantially promoted by churches and schools, who saw the game's potential for encouraging physical health and some moral values in still rawly industrialised cities. The game rapidly became phenomenally popular. Clubs sprouted all over the country, in particular the North and Midlands, formed by people who wanted to play the game, or teachers, vicars, or businessmen who wanted to encourage it. Most relevantly in terms of the development of the professional game, the more prominent clubs began to attract huge crowds, which from the beginning appear to have been fiercely partisan.

The FA insisted from the beginning on the amateur ethos, believing that payment of players would corrupt the purity of the game. But competition between clubs, particularly in the North, led around the mid-1880s to regular illicit paying of players. In 1884 the big clubs threatened to break away from FA control if professionalism were not legalised. The following year the FA finally legitimised professionalism. It did so reluctantly, persuaded by the argument that it was now inevitable and if the FA persisted in the ban, professionalism would continue underground and become impossible to regulate or control. From the beginning, therefore, the governing body aimed to regulate commercialism to protect what it believed to be inherent sporting values.

Early professional football

Problems sustaining regular fixtures for football clubs, which now had wage bills to maintain, led to a proposal from William McGregor, chairman of Aston Villa, to form a league. The Football League, the first professional football league in the world, came into existence in 1888, with 12 clubs competing.

The FA remained the 'governing body' of football. It remained amateur in its ethos, responsible for every club and league in England and for upholding football's rules. The Football League was registered with the FA, which set the regulatory framework.

Early regulation of football

League equality

From the beginning it was considered important to maintain equality in the Football League. The League's policy was that it would be bad for the game if the big city clubs were to dominate purely because they could make more money through the gate. For almost a century, the rule was maintained that clubs shared gate receipts equally. Later there was also an overall levy: every club paid 4 per cent of its season's gate money into a central pot and this was distributed equally to all clubs.

The maximum wage

The other measure aimed at maintaining equality between member clubs was the FA's imposition of a maximum wage on players. In retrospect this is generally accepted to have been an unjust and unwelcome product of England's class system – a restriction by the upper-class FA on the rights of the working-class players – and it lasted until 1961.

Governance of member clubs

Following the onset of professionalism, and particularly when, soon after, the first enclosed football grounds began to be built, football clubs began to form themselves into limited companies. Before this, they were all membership clubs, usually run by committee.

Mostly the clubs formed limited companies as a defensive measure, to protect the members from becoming personally responsible for the expenses of the wage bill and the cost of building the grounds. Most football companies remained clubs in spirit, run by local burghers and businessmen, and were concerned purely with playing the game as successfully as possible. However, it is utterly mistaken to assume the culture was purely philanthropic. The popularity of the professional game attracted entrepreneurs who were interested in football as a commercial endeavour. Three examples illustrate this: Liverpool FC, Chelsea FC and Portsmouth FC were all set up as professional football companies, having had no previous tradition as sporting clubs, purely as commercial ventures for their owners.

It is crucial to understand this early era of football in order to throw light on our current era. Now, 'market forces' are causing gross inequality, with many lower division clubs threatened with extinction while Premiership plcs are coveted by some of the biggest corporations in the world. In the City, analysts talk approvingly of the inevitable 'consolidation' of the football 'industry'. But had it not been for the FA and League's sense that its game was to be different from normal commercial industries, this consolidation, effectively the dominance of only a few large professional clubs, would have happened a century ago.

As noted above, the League was concerned to redistribute money between the large and small clubs, and early this century the FA moved to protect the sporting character of the professional football clubs. The FA imposed rules which were inserted into professional club-company articles of association. The rules are still nominally in force today:

The FA Rule 34

Briefly, the FA's regulations were as follows:

1. Nobody could draw a salary for acting as a director of a football club. (This has been changed twice: in 1981 a single full-time director could be paid. Now there is no restriction on the number of directors who can be paid, but they must work at the club full-time.)
2. Nobody could derive major income from owning football company shares; the dividends were restricted to 5 per cent of the shares' nominal face value.
3. A football club company was protected against asset stripping. If a club were wound up, any surplus assets had to be distributed to sporting benevolent funds or other local sporting institutions.

These rules – effectively a framework of corporate governance – were aimed at maintaining a spirit of public service, not profiteering, in the people who came to own shares and run the clubs. Rule 34 prevented a businessman from making money out of a football club either via salary or dividend. And he could not wind up a successful club because all surplus assets had to be distributed. These rules set the culture for the running of the clubs by local businessmen who, whatever personal benefits they derived from their involvement with the football club, could not treat it purely as a business endeavour.

The development of professional football

Professional football thrived, exploded in popularity, and by 1921 there were four divisions. The amateur FA and professional League had some practical administrative conflicts, but in general there was harmony between the two bodies for the decades until after the Second World War. Players unionised and had periodic conflicts with their stubborn governors.

With regard to the running of the clubs, broadly speaking, most were taken over by businessmen who presented their activity as a form of public service. Directors generally came to describe themselves as 'custodians', 'putting something back into the town', their job to hand the club in good health to the generations to come after them. This is still a common self-description at many lower division and non-league clubs.

In these days of football plcs run as investments for shareholders, such a culture might seem ideal. However, the 'custodianship' was often merely the public rationale for a self-serving group of businessmen, varying greatly in competence and concern for the game and its supporters. As clubs became communal focal points, directors enjoyed public profile, made contacts, received perks or even made money illegitimately out of them. It is arguable that the amateurishness, combined with the class system, created poorly run companies in which complacent owner-directors regarded supporters as a rabble and failed to provide for their safety, let alone comfort.

Yet it is worth making some general observations about the beneficial aspects of the 'custodians' culture. It has become commonplace, largely because of the Hillsborough disaster, to dismiss the whole way in which football was run pre-1990s, as shambolic. Of course, the failures which led to the disaster were shameful and inexcusable. However, it is false to place the current arrangements in direct comparison with those in place at the time of the disaster, and to draw the conclusion that current arrangements must be better because a disaster on such a scale is mercifully unlikely in the modern rebuilt grounds. There were several benefits of the old regulated system which have to be acknowledged.

It is no accident that football clubs survived and became magnets of loyalty to generations of supporters. Football clubs' very survival springs from the fact that they were protected against being mere companies competing in a branch of the entertainment industry. The restrictions against profit-making helped keep the cost of watching football affordable to most working-class pockets. Entry was informally free for children even at the great grounds. This accessibility and popularity meant that football became a great binding force in popular culture very quickly. Support came to be passed down the generations and became a family (or father and son) experience.

The redistributive nature of the League (and the maximum wage) ensured the survival of 92 clubs – very few professional football clubs have gone out of business in over a century, despite variable quality of management for most of their histories. The lack of professionalism and often petty provincialism of the clubs would not be acceptable today, but nevertheless there was a public service ethos and culture in the running of the clubs, League and FA, which contributed to the game's success and popularity and the survival of so huge a population of clubs.

The arrival of television and sponsorship revenue

Sponsorship and television made their first inroads into football in the '60s. The big clubs were more attractive to the sponsors and TV companies, but the League's structure and system of governance ensured that all income was treated as the League's, and distributed equally throughout the 92 clubs. In 1965, the BBC paid £5,000 for the first regular highlights package on British television – *Match of the Day*. The money was redistributed equally, every club receiving little more than £50 each.

The money grew with the success of football on television, and with it came resentment from the big clubs at having to share it with the small. By the early '80s, a new younger breed of chairmen began to drive to keep more of the money, particularly after 1981 when for the first time clubs were allowed to pay full-time directors. By 1983 threats were being made by the big clubs to form a breakaway league. Concessions were given by the small clubs, ceding more money and voting rights to the big clubs. First, the overall gate levy was reduced to 3 per cent, then the home clubs were allowed to keep the gate receipts.

In 1985 the so-called 'Big Five', Manchester United, Liverpool, Tottenham, Everton and Arsenal made a serious threat to break away, which produced further concessions on the distribution of TV money. In 1988 the big clubs did what amounted to a private deal with ITV to see themselves shown almost exclusively on ITV. Nevertheless, the League held on to its four-division, 92-club structure and a proportion of the TV money was distributed to all clubs. The clubs, companies in structure, still did not charge high prices to watch football, which remained widely accessible as a live experience. People continued to invest their emotions and loyalties in these institutions, which were clubs in a more general cultural sense. Even now most people refer to them as clubs, very rarely as companies, or plcs, which most of them are.

'The new commercialism': a chronology

The development of English football into its current state of inequality, money-making at the top and poverty below, was beginning with the breakaway talk of the early and mid-'80s. The chronology of how the breakaway finally came about begins at a terrible and sobering point: the Hillsborough disaster.

The Hillsborough disaster

At Hillsborough in 1989, 96 Liverpool supporters were killed, crushed to death, at the FA Cup semi-final against Nottingham Forest.

The *Taylor Report*

Lord Justice Taylor was appointed to conduct an official inquiry into the disaster. He produced two reports. The first, the *Interim Report*, identified the particular causes of the disaster, which he found, in summary, to be: an appalling record of safety management by Sheffield Wednesday Football Club; a failure by the local council in its safety regulatory duties and mismanagement of the crowd on the day by the South Yorkshire Police.

It is worth reflecting briefly on the disaster within the terms of this book. Football's corporate governance is seen at its wretched worst in the failures which led to the disaster itself. The football industry now is seen in a barely improved light by the bereaved families. They perceive it to continue to be run out of similar self-interest, mostly by the same people who were in charge of football then. Sheffield Wednesday, for example, has had no concerted change of staff, and the safety officer in 1989 is still the club secretary. There has been little or no spirit of recompense or even responsibility from the football industry to the families. The families, who have had to bear the enormous cost of protracted legal procedures themselves, have been given almost no financial assistance from football, despite clubs having been given around £200 million of public money as a direct result of the disaster. Only this year, a decade after its failures led to the disaster, has Sheffield Wednesday agreed to place a memorial to the disaster at Hillsborough itself, done grudgingly following a threatened boycott by Liverpool supporters of this year's match between the two teams.

Lord Taylor's final report was concerned with the more general issue of safety at sports grounds. His report recommended legislation to make England's football grounds all-seater. Taylor commented more widely, however, on football's general institutional failures. In summary his analysis was as follows:

– the League and the FA had both failed to regulate member clubs effectively in terms of fulfilling their safety duties

– the ethos of public service in the boardroom was being widely betrayed:

> As for the clubs, in some instances it is legitimate to wonder whether the directors are genuinely interested in the welfare of their grass-roots supporters. Boardroom struggles for power, wheeler-dealing in the buying and selling of shares, and indeed of whole clubs, sometimes suggest that those involved are more interested in the personal financial benefits or social status of being a director than of directing the club in the interests of its supporter customers (Taylor's Final Report, para. 53).

Taylor concluded his indictment of football with an observation that the game remained phenomenally popular and he called for fundamental reform in order for it to serve its public in the future.

> The lesson is surely that now is the moment for the fullest reassessment of policy for the game (Final Report, para. 58).

No such full reassessment ever took place. The government only enacted the all-seater requirement. They did not insist on further reforms, either of the clubs or the increasingly troubled administrative structure. So the government agreed to give public money, in the form of grants to fund the rebuilding, to the very directors who had been so criticised in the report.

The post-*Taylor Report* rebuilding of the grounds

Taylor recommended that the government reduce the levy on pools betting duty, and give the difference to the Football Trust who would award grants to the clubs to fund the rebuilding. The Football Trust awarded grants close to £200 million to the football companies, in £2 million maximum awards for each stand. Some examples are as follows: Manchester United received £3.4 million public money, Chelsea £4 million, Sheffield Wednesday themselves £3.6 million.

Taylor noted the 'communal culture' of football club support and the fact that much of the support was working class. He said that the rebuilding should not be an excuse for increased ticket prices: 'It should be possible to plan a price structure which suits the cheapest seats to the pockets of those presently paying to stand. At Ibrox, for example, seating is £6, standing £4.' (Final Report, para. 72).

The League's 1990 proposal to the FA to unify

In 1990 the Football League produced a document *One Game, One Team, One Voice*. It was prompted by the horror of the Hillsborough disaster and also the forthcoming expiry, in 1992, of the 1988 TV deal. The League foresaw a yet bigger TV deal being done, and could see the potential for dissent and possible breakaway attempts by the big clubs.

The League's proposal was simple: unity. The FA and League would bury their differences. A new 12-man board would be formed, six from each organisation, to run the whole of football, professional and amateur, from top to bottom, for the good of all. Commercial and TV deals would be done for the whole of football and money distributed according to the needs of running a healthy game.

The big clubs' move to break away

Only one month after the publication of the document for unity, the League's Big Five clubs met in secret with Greg Dyke of LWT to see whether he would be prepared to buy the TV rights if they were to form a breakaway Premier League. He said he would. The purpose of the breakaway was simple: so that the top clubs would no longer have to share TV revenue with the other Football League clubs – or the rest of football.

The FA's response: the 1991 blueprint

The big clubs needed the backing of the FA if their breakaway was to be legitimate. David Dein and Noel White of Arsenal were deputed to go to the FA to ask for backing.

The FA was working on its own document, which it had begun as a response to the League's *One Game, One Team, One Voice*. They saw the proposal for unity merely as a threat to their own administrative pre-eminence, and so they saw the big clubs' desire to break away as an

48

opportunity to deal a fatal blow to the Football League. The FA agreed to back the breakaway Premier League in the subsequent document: *The Blueprint for the Future of Football*.

Thus the traditionally amateur governing body of the game, which had always seen its role as regulating the commercialism of the professional game for the common good, betrayed its own history by backing a breakaway of the top clubs on the threshold of a huge influx of TV money. The *Blueprint* also contained the fateful advice that football should move upmarket to chase 'more affluent middle-class consumers'. The *Blueprint* contained no provision that any of the new wealth should be shared with the rest of football. In an interview with me for *The Football Business*, Graham Kelly, then chief executive of the FA, said it was not even considered. Redistribution, part of football throughout its history, ended in 1992, with the blessing of the FA.

No coherent or convincing explanation has ever been produced by the FA for having so betrayed their governance traditions by backing the breakaway. *The Blueprint* envisages an 18-member Premier League tied into a system which promotes excellence, leading to success for the England team. But this was never structurally implemented, and indeed the top clubs refused to reduce in number from 22 to 18. In my interview with him, Graham Kelly admitted that the primary motivation of the FA was self-preservation, that they saw the League's proposals as a threat, and the *Blueprint* itself makes a call for the FA to be pre-eminent in football administration.

In my view this action by the FA effectively constituted an abdication of their right to govern football for the common good. Reform of football's corporate governance has to involve major reform of the FA, and a clarification of its role, aims and responsibilities. It always regulated football for the end of maintaining its public service, sporting character, and a reformed governing body – or regulator – needs to be constituted to do that in the context of the new pressures of a fiercely commercial age.

The Premier League breakaway in 1992 and the first Sky TV deal

The 22 First Division clubs broke away from the rest of the Football League clubs to form the FA Carling Premiership in 1992. Litigation from the Football League produced an agreement to give the League around £3 million per year as compensation.

In the event, Greg Dyke did not win the TV rights for ITV. Sky TV won the rights in a deal with the BBC whose headline figure was £305 million. This was shared almost completely by only 22, later 20 clubs.

The 'new commercialism' in the Premier League

The purpose of the Premier League breakaway was simply to make more money for the big clubs and their owners. No internal regulations governed the relationship between the club and its supporters, and the clubs began to look to maximise income from all possible sources.

Contrary to the spirit and letter of the *Taylor Report*, the rebuilding programme itself, funded with public money, became a springboard for commercialism. The stands were almost all built to accommodate corporate entertainment, banqueting and conference facilities which would be put to work on non-matchdays as well as matchdays. But neither this nor the TV money went to subsidise ticket prices. On the contrary, clubs were allowed to raise their ticket prices, which they have done dramatically and massively above the rate of inflation. Rises of over 300 per cent since 1989 would be a reasonably accurate average.

The price rises have led to a significant number of people being excluded from being able to watch football. Recent work has been carried out by Leicester University to assess this. Anecdotally, there is no question that many people who supported their clubs all their lives have found themselves priced out of going. It is increasingly difficult for people to afford to take their children to matches, and the prices are prohibitive to most teenagers. Football has barely begun to address the question of whether, in cashing in so heavily on the supporters built up in a previous, more communal culture, the next generation of football followers is being priced out.

In addition, clubs entered a new era of merchandising, including the mass manufacture of replica kits, whose colours change with increased regularity. The quality and sophistication of the clubs' merchandising has been quite rudimentary, yet supporters have been ready consumers. The loyalty and culture of football support meant that demand for tickets was 'inelastic' – people would continue to pay the increased prices, and they were 'brand loyal' to the merchandise. A report in March 1997 by City analysts UBS described football supporters as a 'captive market'.

Flotation of football clubs

Tottenham Hotspur were the first football club to float, and did so in 1983. In order to do this, they simply bypassed Rule 34. They formed a holding company, Tottenham Hotspur plc, making the football club, Tottenham Hotspur FC, merely a subsidiary of it. All the assets including the ground were transferred to the holding company. The holding company was expressly stated not to be subject to the FA's own rules.

I have not found a satisfactory answer from the FA about the process by which this was allowed to happen, and why the FA allowed it. It seems to be part of the general loss of any sense of direction or clear idea of the FA's purpose in the modern era. In an interview with the FA's current lawyer, he suggested simply that Rule 34 was outdated and that the market should be allowed to do its work – an extraordinary view from the governing body.

Tottenham's float was not a success, but with the promise of the breakaway and Sky deal, other clubs were nevertheless still encouraged to float themselves in the '90s. Manchester United followed suit, an initially lukewarm float which has become the most profitable of all the new football plcs, and in 1998 was the subject of a £623-million bid from BSkyB itself.

All the football companies, in order to float, followed Tottenham's example, forming holding companies to bypass Rule 34. They all expressly admitted this in their prospectuses. (See chapter 10 for the relevant wording from the Manchester United prospectus).

Most of the football companies floated in a busy period between mid-1996 and 1997. Some 20 football companies are now listed on the full stock-market or Alternative Investment Market. They are subject to no specific regulation by reason of being football companies, and have indulged in the relentless commercial exploitation of the 'captive market' described above. It has been one of the lesser acknowledged aspects of the current transformation of football that one of the driving forces of this has been the prospect for major shareholder/chairmen making vast personal fortunes out of their football club shares.

Flotation as a means of personal money-making

Flotation was presented to the public, and to the football club, as an unarguably beneficial process for a football club. It was also presented as a means for ordinary supporters to have a stake in their club. In any analysis of flotation, and amongst proposals for a different form of football club ownership, its benefits have to be acknowledged along with its disadvantages.

One clear potential benefit is that flotation presents a relatively easy way to raise new capital. New issues of shares are bought up by institutions and their investments can be put to use by the football clubs. However, the record of football club flotations in this area is poor. Most of the flotations occurred after the major capital expenditure of the grounds being rebuilt. Much of the money raised by the flotations was spent on transfers of players, which led to further inflation of the transfer market and players' wages. Nevertheless, in any proposals to outlaw further flotations or to mutualise the clubs, thought has to be given to alternative ways to raise capital.

A close examination of the reasons for football club flotation leads to the inescapable conclusion that a central motivation was simply for the major shareholders to cash in on their shares. In *The Football Business* I documented how much shares in various football clubs were bought for, and compared them with their values inflated by the 'new commercialism' and flotation. Shares bought cheaply in the years when football was governed by a different culture, by rules of redistribution and Rule 34, are now worth huge sums in the age when football has become a stock-market activity.

Football was never intended to be a purely commercial endeavour and the clubs were built up over a century in which they were preserved from being mere investment vehicles. The current major shareholders, Martin Edwards, Sir John Hall, Doug Ellis, Ken Bates etc., have broken away from the rest of football and its rules for their own commercial ends, exploiting a century of support and tradition to make very quick, enormous fortunes for themselves. Several football club shareholders, including now Peter Johnson of Everton, are resident offshore in order to be exiles from capital gains tax.

The opportunistic zeal with which such personal fortunes were made could hardly represent a more shameless flouting of the spirit and analysis of the *Taylor Report*. Ticket prices rose, scant attention was paid to the 'communal culture' and little if any concerted thought was paid to 'the welfare of grass-roots supporters'. The very directors so criticised by Taylor embarked on a drive to maximise revenue and their own fortunes, using as a springboard Taylor's own report and the grants which followed. It is a bitter irony that following the *Taylor Report*, and partly as a result of it, the same directors who had been so criticised were allowed to indulge in more 'boardroom struggles for power, wheeler-dealing in the buying and selling of shares, and indeed of whole clubs,' than ever before, for huge, unprecedented 'personal financial benefits'.

Wider inequality in football

The Premier League breakaway and the consequent huge fortunes made by a few individuals at the top has produced huge inequality in the game. Redistribution ended just as the money became big enough to restore the fortunes of the whole of football. In the lower divisions, many football clubs are struggling. Wage inflation has come down from the Premier League, but the revenue has not come down to keep pace with it. Many semi-professional clubs are in trouble, suffering from having to compete with Premier League hype and games being televised in mid-week very much more often. At the grass-roots of the game, the municipal playing fields where Premier League clubs find their talent and on which the vast majority of the football population play the game, local authority cuts have led to facilities deteriorating into a state of squalor and disrepair.

The future: the need for reform

It is not difficult to see what needs to be done to reform football in this country. It is not simply a matter of opinion that the game should be run in a more civilised, socially responsible way – for all its history until 1992 structures were in place which aimed to preserve its sporting heart. The primary needs are for unity in the administration of the game, some equality and redistribution of the game's vast income, and for reform in the ownership and running of the clubs themselves. In effect, the twin forms of regulation – redistribution of money and Rule 34 – have to be restored in a form adapted to modern needs.

In *The Football Business* and in a submission to the Football Task Force I have proposed, broadly speaking, the following:

Unity in football administration

The game's governing bodies should unify, and a single executive board should rule the game from top to bottom according to the needs of all. Given the lamentable recent record of football's governance, some form of public accountability needs to be built into this.

A 'pyramid' of football

As with most other countries, an end to the historic division between League and FA would produce a coherent football pyramid. The top league of 20 clubs would be the apex of a system which would stretch from the professional game, through semi-professional and right down to the grass-roots.

Redistribution of money

A united game of football would ensure that money from TV and commercial deals would be redistributed fairly to ensure the overall health of football for the people who play and watch it. The top clubs would no doubt get a higher proportion of the money than the rest of football, but the current levels of inequality would not be tolerated.

Reform of the clubs

The flotations and developments such as the BSkyB bid for Manchester United have concentrated minds on the need to reform the football clubs. It is a historical accident that football clubs became companies – this was mostly a defensive measure against the cost of professionalism and building grounds. Rule 34 was in place to prevent the clubs becoming investment vehicles and to preserve an ethic of public service. The club-companies now have no such regulations to encourage or preserve a sense of community or even responsibility to their supporters.

I believe a key aim now of those concerned about what has happened to football should be to consider other models for the ownership and running of the clubs. The other chapters in this book represent in my view a very useful starting point for this. Most supporters recognise that football clubs have a particular character as a focus for sport, community and loyalty, and are different from commercial companies making products for consumption. It is only since 1992 that football itself has failed to preserve a sense of this in its structures.

Historically, the period following the *Taylor Report* can now be seen as a missed opportunity. The clubs ought to have been reformed then, along with the rest of football. With public and major television money coming in, the finance was there to effect reform. Despite this, the issue should be addressed to reform the clubs as much as possible now.

Some form of mutualisation, of democratic ownership and control by the supporters, is clearly the desirable model to follow. We have excellent domestic examples at Bournemouth and Northampton Town, and there are European supporter-ownership models to learn from as well. The fact of clubs having floated in this country and the high valuations they enjoy on the stock-market present their own problems. But it is clear how the clubs should be constituted; practical ways need to be developed for reform to be effected. I believe at least that a substantial proportion of football club shares should be owned in a collective way by supporters, who would then elect a representative on to the board. This is broadly the position at Northampton Town, which has set excellent examples in areas such as anti-racism and disability access, and has been successful on the field.

Other regulation

A game with a conscience, unified and run according to the needs of those who love it would no doubt avoid exploiting its public. For the moment, at the very least, some regulation needs to be built in to keep prices affordable to people for whom football is an important part of their lives and part of social inclusion. There also needs to be regulation of merchandising, of television coverage, and further work done to make football clubs responsive to their public responsibilities.

The prospects for reform

The Football Task Force report, *Investing in the Community*, was an encouraging step towards reform of football. Although there are limitations to it, it did, at least, put the need for redistribution and the parlous state of the grass-roots, on to the mainstream agenda, alongside other constructive proposals relating to supporter ownership and players working more in the community. There appears to be a willingness from the government to do something about what it recognises to be problems in the way football has been exploited and is now being run. What remains to be seen is how much it is prepared to do, how far it is prepared to go.

Books such as this one are important in formulating practical proposals, and these have to be translated into real reforms. It is vital that measures be brought to bear as soon as possible, given the prospect of further commercialisation and the threat of a European Super League being formed without a redistributive system to preserve football's wider population. Given the appalling record of football's own self-governance in recent years, I am in no doubt that change has to be insisted upon and enforced by government legislation. Advice, encouragement and reliance on football's own goodwill will founder on the twin curses, there since the beginning of the game, of self-interest and greed.

References

Conn, D. (1997). *The Football Business: Fair Game in the '90s?* Edinburgh: Mainstream Publishing.

Inquiry by the Rt. Hon. Lord Justice Taylor (1990). *The Hillsborough Stadium Disaster:Final Report.* Cm962. London HMSO.

Football Association (1991). *The Blueprint for the Future of Football.* London: The Football Association.

Football League (1990). *One Game, One Voice.* Lytham St Annes: Football League.

3. Thinking the Unthinkable or Playing the Game?

The Football Task Force, New Labour and the Reform of English Football

Adam Brown

The Football Task Force was established within three months of the Labour government's election in May 1997. Whereas previous administrations have legislated on football almost exclusively on a law and order or safety agenda, the Task Force, with a remit to make recommendations to government on areas such as ticket prices and the role of public limited companies, represents a governmental concern with the national game of a kind which is entirely new. As such its progress and prospects raise important questions about the prospects for the reform of the governance of football in England and the adequacy of the government's approach.

This chapter will outline Labour's increasing interest in football as an area for policy intervention; the formation of the Football Task Force, its membership, remit and activities so far; highlight some concerns with its formulation; outline some issues about Labour's Third Way and the government's approach to football; and it will end with a brief outline of a possible regulatory structure and the prospects for it.

I must, however, start by declaring an interest.[1] I have been a member of the Football Task Force Working Group since its inception and more recently have become a member of the Full Task Force. For some of this time I was also a representative on the National Committee of the Football Supporters Association. Furthermore, at the time of writing, the Task Force is yet to report on its final, and arguably most important area of its remit, those issues concerning the commercial activities in the game and its regulatory structure.

This notwithstanding, I will argue that the way in which the Task Force was conceived and organised, its concern with achieving consensus and its departure in terms of remit from Labour's original *Charter for Football* produced when the party was still in opposition, have all negatively affected the prospects for radical change in English football's governance. Despite this, the calls for a new regulatory structure for football have, I will conclude, survived, although the form and extent to which they will be implemented are yet to be determined.

Going up: charting football's rise on the political agenda

The origins of the Football Task Force lie in the Labour Party's *Charter for Football*, produced by the then Shadow Sports Minister Tom Pendry. This document is important for it set out the basis for the formation of the Football Task Force. It was, in many ways, a response to a perceived crisis in English football at a time (1995–96) when the game seemed plagued by bungs, bribery, misbehaviour and bad leadership. For example, Brian Clough was under investigation by the FA for taking a financial 'bung' as part of the sale of Teddy Sheringham to Tottenham; John Fashanu, Hans Segers and Bruce Grobbelaar were charged with match fixing; Eric Cantona had attacked a fan at Crystal Palace.

It was also a response by New Labour to a pace of change in English football, including the emergence of a rampant commercialism following the *Taylor Report,* which had raised fears about the future of the 'people's game'. Thus, although the brave new world of the Premier League was being hailed by some as a roaring success (gates were up, foreign stars began signing for English clubs), concerns were growing about the rise in the cost of tickets, merchandising policies which appeared to exploit fans' loyalty, a continued lack of representation for fans at all levels in the game and a rapidly widening gulf in terms of financial strength between the Premiership and the three divisions of the Football League.

A game which appeared to be mired in sleaze and bad behaviour, to which its ruling bodies appeared incapable of responding, yet where the rich were reaping untold riches and the poor flirting with oblivion, seemed a neat metaphor for a nation still in the grip of a dying Conservative Party leadership also fatally tainted with sleaze.

Furthermore, football had become a very fashionable commodity: its players adorned glossy magazines; Sky television marketed the game to a new audience in a gladiatorial, showbiz manner; literary writers were publishing hugely successful accounts of their lives as fans; and a host of celebrities clamoured to be associated with the game. Even within political circles it became *de rigueur* for MPs to be seen at football matches and to declare their lifelong attachments to the game. The full range of political opinion was reflected, from Old Labourites like Roy Hattersley, to the rising stars, Kate Hoey and Tony Banks, and even ex-Conservative Minister David Mellor, now host of Radio Five Live's *6.06* football phone-in programme.[2] For a political party as keenly media-sensitive as New Labour, football became an obvious choice for populist policy intervention. Tony Blair made the first foray into football in a speech in early 1995, following the purchase by Manchester United of Andy Cole for the (then) record fee of £7 million. Coming alongside a new kit release by the Champions and Double winners, Blair warned of the damaging effects of an overly commercialised game.[3]

Labour's *Charter for Football* began in a series of meetings between Tom Pendry and representatives from a variety of organisations in football, including its leading bodies and supporters groups. The desire to involve all established bodies in the game in the development of the *Charter* was to have a major influence on the membership and structure of the Football Task Force.

When published in 1996, the *Charter* was divided into two main sections, 'A New Task Force for Football' and 'Legislative Measures'. Under the former, the commitment was to create a Task Force 'drawn primarily from bodies responsible for the national game' and whose remit would be: restructuring the Football Association; investigating links with television; the treatment of fans (prompted by growing concern with the treatment of English fans abroad); football's finances; and the rather vague 'looking to the future'. It was, said the *Charter*, 'widely recognised that there was a need for change' and, most significantly, that the Task Force would be *'focusing specifically on the need for improved administration'*. Proposed legislative measures included those to deal with football violence, finance, ground safety, 'rights of fans', 'football for all', the grass-roots and policing.[4] Signed by Tom Pendry and Jack Cunningham, it represented the biggest commitment ever for an incoming government to restructure football.

Whereas the *Charter* was a major commitment by a party in opposition toward its future policy, other noises were also being made: Pendry raised the prospect of a possible reintroduction of terracing, arguing that given technological advances[5] there was no justifiable reason against limited safe standing areas, something backed wholeheartedly by supporters organisations. Labour promised to review the Hillsborough Inquiry and there were commitments to support the FA's bid for the 2006 World Cup following the success of Euro '96. Such a concern with the running of the national sport contrasted sharply with the hostile attitude and law and order agenda of previous administrations.[6]

One other key factor came into play before the Task Force was launched, and that was the shock announcement that the outspoken Tony Banks was to be Sports Minister instead of Tom Pendry. Some put this down to issues of 'Old' and 'New' Labour, as Pendry was unpopular with the twin pillars of the New Labour firmament, Peter Mandelson (then Minister without Portfolio) and Alistair Campbell (the Prime Minister's chief press officer). Given Banks's political history this can hardly have been the whole story, but it was thought, nevertheless, that he would be dynamic, outspoken, and have a media profile suitable for such a fast-paced game. In fact, a number of 'gaffes' early on in his tenure weakened his position and meant that for most of it he has stuck to the agenda dictated by the Prime Minister's office, with radical proposals significantly absent.

Some commentators have argued that Labour and football in the 1990s made perfect partners:

> That it was 'the people's party' which came to the (belated) realisation [that football is more than a game] is surely no coincidence, for there are some uncanny parallels between professional football and the Labour Party. Both born at the end of the nineteenth century, promising some kind of escape from working-class drudgery, they each relied on mass support for their existence and success; and despite their ups and downs, both have remained intimately associated with the whims and wishes of 'the people'. More significantly, both hit hard times in the 1980s, but emerged to bask in the floodlights of 1990s glamour and success.
>
> Football, like New Labour, is now 'cool', cosmopolitan and utterly modern. But both the game and the party have achieved this new-found pre-eminence by moving away from their roots in local communities, by depending heavily on a media image to broaden their appeal, and by striking up unprecedented friendships with the movers and shakers of corporate business and high finance. The Football Task Force simply brings these parallel paths together.[7]

For a new Labour Government entering office, football became hard to ignore given both its own commitments and the increased profile of the game. Furthermore, whereas the administrations of Margaret Thatcher had viewed football, and especially its fans, with considerable hostility, and subsequent Tory administrations had failed to develop a new agenda on the game, it was easy for Labour to pick up the populist concerns about the development of football. For this fitted neatly with its desire to be a modern party and to develop a new kind of politics.

Football was perhaps the one area of sporting and cultural life in which Labour's leaders could be confident of attracting media attention, and the game's new constituency – the 'Middle Englanders' who dominate some radio phone-ins – was exactly that which Labour was interested in. Finally, football was also an area in which the incoming government believed it could intervene in a meaningful way without significant cost.

The Football Task Force: membership, remit and development

Membership

It was on the last day of July 1997, three months into office, that Labour created the Football Task Force. The biggest surprise of its formation was the appointment of ex-Conservative minister, David Mellor QC as its Chair. Although he had already made his mark on the football world as a presenter of Radio Five Live's *6.06* phone-in programme, as well as being a sports columnist for the *London Evening Standard*, and as such had some grasp of some of the issues confronting football fans, it was none the less surprising that Labour entrusted such an obviously high-profile policy initiative to such an outspoken, controversial 'outsider'. In other ways, though, Mellor's appointment represented Labour's commitment to its Third Way, the ill-defined but nevertheless undeniably centrist political philosophy publicly espoused by the party leadership which emphasised involving a broad political spectrum of opinion in decision-making.

The membership of the Task Force closely represented the attitudes expressed in the *Charter for Football*, attempting to bring together all interested parties and seeking consensus on the issues. The desire to involve all interested parties within the 'football community' and to involve all as contributors to the Task Force's recommendations was aimed at both avoiding controversial and public disagreements. It was also in line with the Third Way philosophy, premised as it was on a belief that voluntary agreement would be more effective than prescription. It should be noted that such an approach had as a precedent the broad alliance of football organisations which had been involved in the Kick Racism out of Football initiative. This had managed to get all football organisations bar the Football League, as well as 91 out of 92 league clubs, to sign up to a campaign initially launched by the Commission for Racial Equality but backed by David Davies, the (then) new head of Public Relations at the Football Association (FA). The efficacy of this approach, especially in such a notoriously divided sector as football, will be questioned later.

The Task Force included: Keith Wiseman – soon replaced by Graham Kelly; Peter Leaver (Premier League); David Sheepshanks (Football League); Gordon Taylor (Professional Footballers Association); Sir Rodney Walker (Sports Council); John Barnwell (League Managers Association); David Phillips (Association of Premier and Football League Referees and Linesmen); Graham Bean (Football Supporters Association); Tony Kershaw (National Federation of Football Supporters Clubs); Steve Hennigan (Disabled Supporters Association). Added to this list were Chris Heinitz of the Local Government Association; Sir Herman Ouseley of the Commission for Racial Equality; and Rogan Taylor from Liverpool University's Football Research Unit. Over time the personnel have changed – Kershaw was replaced by Ian Todd, Bean by the new Football Supporters Association (FSA) Chair Alison Pilling, and Eleanor Oldroyd from Radio Five was added as a representative of the media. The Football Trust, the body responsible for administering public investment in the game, was charged with acting as the Secretariat for the Task Force, with Peter Lee as Secretary, and later Andy Burnham as Administrator. Later Sir John Smith, the author of the FA's enquiry into the financial 'bung' scandal (see chapter 1) and the author were added from the Working Group (see below).

Remit

The Task Force was also given a specific remit for its investigations. Seven areas were identified as in need of investigation and recommendations were to be made in separate reports, submitted to the Minister for Sport at the Department for Culture, Media and Sport, under whose auspices the Task Force was established. It is worth noting the exact phrasing of the remit:

> to eliminate racism in sport and encourage wider participation by ethnic minorities in both playing and spectating;
>
> to improve disabled access to spectating facilities;
>
> encourage greater supporter involvement in the running of clubs;
>
> encourage ticketing and pricing policies that are geared to reflect the needs of all, on an equitable basis, including for cup and international matches;
>
> encourage merchandising policies that reflect the needs of supporters as well as commercial considerations;
>
> develop the opportunities for players to act as good role models in terms of behaviour and sportsmanship, and to become actively involved in community schemes;

reconcile the potential conflict between the legitimate needs of
shareholders, players and supporters where clubs have been
floated on the Stock Exchange.

What is significant here is that these areas of remit bore only the
most cursory resemblance to the declared aims of the *Charter*, Labour's
pre-election promise. Gone was a commitment to restructure the FA
and the game's administration – the primary aim of the *Charter*; gone
was the investigation into football's relationship with TV (recently
revived in a back-bench Early Day Motion and the subject of two
Department of Trade and Industry inquiries[8]); gone were
considerations of supporters' rights; and although commercial aspects
of the game were included, it was much less wide ranging than the
commitment to investigate football's finances in the *Charter*. Some of
these issues, such as the role of fans in running the game, had been
highlighted in the *Charter*, although others were quite new, reflecting
the (largely media-driven) public image of the game, such as players
acting as positive role models for young people, and merchandising
policies. However, add to this the Home Secretary's rejection of a
reopening of the Hillsborough Inquiry and the rejection of any rethink
on reintroducing terracing, and it seemed that Labour's commitment to
grasp the football nettle had certainly diminished since coming into
office.

The Task Force was launched at Charlton Athletic, with Sports
Minister Tony Banks declaring that:

> the government has decided to establish a Football Task Force
> to ensure that those in a position of power have an opportunity
> to hear the views and suggestions from all quarters of the game
> . . . There are questions, not just of access for minority groups
> such as the disabled, but how clubs can avoid alienating the less
> well-off from the sport that they love.

Again it is notable here that the emphasis was not on a wholesale re-
evaluation of how the game is run, as promised in the *Charter*, but on
rather vague notions of allowing those in power to hear fans'
complaints! The choice of Charlton for the launch was significant said
Banks, because:

> they have a very strong anti-racist policy. They have a member
> of the supporters organisation on the board, they have close
> links with the community and have maintained reasonable
> ticket pricing following their flotation on the stock-market . . .
> showing that financial success and stability can be achieved

> alongside a close working relationship with the supporters that make the game what it is.[9]

Thus Charlton was also important for attempting to highlight the kind of partnership between club, local authority and community which the government found very attractive and sought from the Task Force. The fact that by 1998 Charlton were charging one of the highest Premiership prices for away fans showed the weakness and temporary nature of this approach.

Reaction to the establishment of the Task Force was mixed and far from welcoming. Some sports journalists criticised the appointment of Mellor, arguing that as a 'Johnny-come-lately' to the football party he was inappropriate. Others suggested that given his role as a 'shock jock' of radio football he would produce 'more heat than light'.[10] Some sections either criticised the government for being involved in football at all, or questioned whether it could have any meaningful impact.[11] The City of London financial establishment declared itself 'neutral' and the Task Force 'an emotional appointment about an emotional issue'[12] reflecting their strictly commercial concerns, and arguably their lack of understanding of the football business. There were cautious welcomes from fans' organisations, who at least felt that they would have an input into government thinking – a sharp contrast to the wilderness years of a series of unsympathetic Conservative sports ministers – although they were quick to highlight the growing support for a reintroduction of terracing, omitted in the remit.[13] What was certain was that the Task Force was going to face an uphill struggle for credibility both within football and in the wider public.

Working Group

There were a number of issues which immediately became apparent to those involved and represented, to some, a lack of clear vision as to how the Task Force should be established and a rushed approach to its formation. Insider sources have indicated that the Prime Minister's Office, through his press secretary Alistair Campbell, had given Tony Banks's Office just three days to establish the Task Force and had largely directed its remit and the appointment of the Chair.

The Task Force was effectively attempting to embrace all the established national organisations in football, from fans, to players, to administrators. While this may have demonstrated an admirable democratic concern for consultation, it also established huge obstacles to effective decision-making from the outset. It was, above all, an unwieldy structure which would prove difficult to organise efficiently and in which organisational loyalties would tend to dominate. Further, its representative nature meant that other people, with whom Mellor had a much better relationship, had not been included (generally, the 'lead figure' in each organisation had been appointed by the Minister for Sport) and so there was a sense in which David Mellor wanted his own people on board, rather than those given to him by a government attempting to keep everyone happy.

Thus, very soon after the formation of the Full Task Force, its format was revised to encompass a second body, the Football Task Force Core Working Group. This body was much more David Mellor's baby, although with the agreement of Tony Banks: it was a tighter grouping of just ten individuals, each allegedly chosen on 'individual' rather than 'organisational' criteria, and given the task of undertaking the main volume of work – evidence-collecting and report-drafting. The Working Group comprised David Mellor; Richard Faulkner (former Football Trust and Vice-Chair); David Davies (FA); Peter Leaver (Premier League); Peter Lee (Football Trust); Eleanor Oldroyd (BBC); Uriah Rennie (Premiership Referee); Sir Roland Smith (Chairman of Manchester United plc); Robbie Earle (Wimbledon FC); and myself. Sir John Smith, former Deputy Chief Constable of the Metropolitan Police, was also added as a special adviser.

The Working Group met for the first time at the end of August 1997 at David Mellor's house with subsequent meetings held at the Football Trust. From very early days it was decided that the issues of racism and disabled access were to be dealt with first, representing areas where it was believed there would be a broad agreement between the parties, with the commercial concerns to come later. It was also agreed that the Working Group would take evidence both at its meetings at the Trust and in a series of regional visits.

These day-long visits – initially to be the preserve of the Working Group, but quickly adapted to include the interests on the Full Task Force – were divided into two parts: during the day appointments were held with clubs, local authorities, fans' groups and other bodies; and in the evening open public forums were staged where individual fans could ask questions of those on the panel and raise their concerns. On one level, it must be stressed that these represented a unique process of consultation of a kind never before undertaken. They had a democratic ethos in which as many organisations as possible were given appointments and as many fans as possible were encouraged to attend and give their views to the Task Force members directly. No other government task force, or any previous administration has undertaken such a consultation with the world of football. In short, it represented one of the biggest 'open surveys' of football ever. However, it was not without its problems, as I shall outline below.

Administration and cost

Other more practical issues included the administration and funding of the Task Force. The Football Trust, itself in the process of being reformed, agreed to host the Task Force and gave initial pump-priming to cover the costs of meetings. The government, belatedly, agreed to provide £100,000 to cover the work of the body (rather than the £200,000 initially asked for by the Working Group), which had to pay for travel and accommodation for all members, including ten regional visits, as well as a full-time administrator and some proposed commissioned research. A suggestion to get *pro bono* work from financial and legal firms with whom members had close ties was rejected for fear of jeopardising the body's independence. This may appear surprising in hindsight, given that other interests were subsequently allowed to run rampant, but it also reflected the Labour Government's concern to avoid allegations of commercial interests influencing policy. In subsequent months, the timetable, which was initially set at five months but quickly extended, required additional resources to be made available.

Progress

At the time of writing the Task Force has been in existence for 19 months. It has undertaken ten regional visits to the main cities in England and has held a number of evidence-gathering sessions in London. It has met with 14 Football in the Community Schemes, 28 local authorities, 30 professional clubs, ten county FAs, 73 football supporter groups, ten community organisations, three women's and girls' teams and a variety of football researchers. Three reports have been produced: *Eliminating Racism From Football*; *Improving Facilities for Disabled Supporters*; and *Investing in the Community*. The fourth, which will encompass the commercial areas of the remit and the representation of supporters, is currently under negotiation within the Task Force. Recommendations have included, respectively, alterations to racist chanting legislation and initiatives to attract ethnic minorities to football; increasing the numbers and quality of disabled spaces at football grounds; and a 5 per cent levy on television income to the Premier League to fund grass-roots football. Although the Task Force has no statutory powers, the reports have all been welcomed by the Minister for Sport and some areas have been enacted. For instance, most recently it has been declared that clubs seeking public assistance in rebuilding stadia must comply with Task Force recommendations on disabled facilities[14] and alterations to the *Football Offences Act 1991* to make racist chanting an individual offence are under way.

Kicking uphill: problems with the Football Task Force

However, a number of issues and problems have emerged during the Task Force's work which raise questions about its ability to significantly reform English football, and about the approach of New Labour to the governance of football.

Administration and organisational problems

Questions about the government's genuine commitment to investigation and change were immediately raised by the setting of such a tight timetable – an initial completion date of the end of 1997, within only five months. This was soon revised and a much vaguer, longer timetable was put in place which is still ongoing. The desire to deal with the racism and disabled access reports quickly demonstrated a failure either to understand the breadth of interest and research undertaken in these areas or, for some, the complexities of the issues involved. The need to organise dual sets of meetings for the Working Group and Full Task Force, involving a host of organisations and individuals, also caused delay.

Whilst the principle of the regional meetings was sound, they, too, experienced problems. The initial intention was to have eight, all completed by early May 1998. Lobbying from geographical areas not originally included (East Anglia and the South Coast) added more work and, along with postponements, the programme was not completed until October 1998. Further, two reports had been almost completed by the time most of the visits took place, yet interested parties on those issues were still being consulted, taking up valuable time after the reports had been written.

The regional meetings also suffered at times from administrative problems (postponements had a detrimental effect on attendance, for instance) and bad timetabling (the Liverpool visit was first scheduled for the anniversary of the Hillsborough Disaster and then for an evening when Everton were competing in the FA Youth Cup in front of nearly 20,000 spectators). There was also a cavalier approach to any notion of methodology in evidence-gathering, exacerbated by an inconsistency in attendance of Task Force members, itself a result of the heavy commitment the visits represented. There was also a disproportionate amount of time given to some organisations over others – inexplicably clubs were seen individually and fans groups seen collectively – all of which lessened the impact of the visits. Having said that, some useful consultation was undertaken despite the problems, as the impressive list of organisations consulted indicates.

Although there is not sufficient space to explore these issues fully here, some administrative and funding concerns seriously exacerbated problems the Task Force already faced. The central role of the Football Trust in the Task Force's administration became particularly problematic at some stages, given that its reformed structure meant it was now funded by the Premier League, FA, PFA and Sports Council, and not from government and football pools company sources as previously (see chapter 1 for further details), thus compromising its independence. Furthermore, the Task Force also became subject to chronically unprofessional delays. Re-interpretation of Group agreements and alterations in the Task Force's work (such as an idiosyncratic approach to commissioning research) both reduced further its reputation as a body to be taken seriously and increased cynicism among fans anxious for meaningful change.

Whilst these concerns were problematic, however, they were not as fundamental as other key issues which emerged.

Membership

The formation of the Working Group was itself a recognition by the Chair of the main Task Force body that for it to undertake such a heavy volume of work with some 15 organisations on board was not realistic. The feeling was that this was unwieldy, involving almost every vested interest in the game which, if a consensus was to be achieved, raised the prospect of almost continuous, time-consuming diplomatic negotiations. Given that David Mellor had antagonised some sections of the football fraternity through his newspaper column and radio show, achieving consensus was, from the outset, going to be doubly difficult.

The Working Group itself clearly contained a number of anomalies. It included members of organisations already on the Task Force; it included actual members of the Full Task Force; and whilst attempts were made to explain it as a 'group to undertake the ground work, through taking evidence, analysing it and forming preliminary conclusions to be presented for consideration by the full membership',[15] it clearly already had an uneasy and fluid relationship with the Full Task Force. Furthermore, despite the attempt to bill it as a group of individuals, organisational loyalties and affiliations were never far from the surface. The Working Group still represented an attempt to keep a variety of interests in the game 'on board' and members were continually referred to as representatives of 'their' organisation even when it was inappropriate. By way of example, I myself resigned from the Football Supporters Association (FSA) National Committee in August 1998 as it was neither appropriate for me or the FSA to have me continually referred to as the FSA representative.

Membership became an issue both for the Task Force as well as some of the organisations involved with it. For example, it is reported that the appointment of David Davies attracted the hostility of some within the FA. It was widely recognised that the chief executive's department and the Public Relations department were rivals of a sort, and certainly had different agendas – something which has most vividly been illustrated with the resignations of Graham Kelly and Keith Wiseman from the FA over allegations of dubious conduct with regard to a financial loan made by the FA to the Welsh FA in return for support in UEFA elections – and Pat Smith (FA deputy chief executive), who deputised for Kelly at some meetings, withdrew her participation. My own position as (then) an FSA Committee member also raised problems: within the FSA there was a concern that I had been picked because of my FSA role, yet with no obligation or mandate to represent it; and rival fans groups, particularly the National Federation of Football Supporters Clubs (NFFSC), protested at my involvement at all.

Furthermore, membership raised major questions more generally about how individual members were expected to conduct themselves. Were members expected to speak, act and present themselves in public as members of the Working Group, potentially to the detriment of their organisations' interests? What leeway would be given to differences of opinion being aired in public? To what extent could the government really expect those who represented such specific interests in football as Sir Roland Smith (chairman of Manchester United plc) to contribute to much more general concerns in football without reference to their own agendas (particularly, in Sir Roland's case when they were busy negotiating with Rupert Murdoch for the sale of Manchester United to BSkyB)? Furthermore, given that no one was to be paid for their work on the Task Force, the level of commitment to it was a problem on a number of levels. For some, attendance became haphazard (e.g. Robbie Earle, due to playing commitments); for others it meant an overbearing workload alongside other full-time jobs (as in my own case); and for the Chair it meant that his own opinions were, quite reasonably, continually aired on his radio show and newspaper column, although distinctions sometimes became rather too blurred.

This problem was exemplified in one example, in the summer of 1998, when PFA chief Gordon Taylor launched an attack on David Mellor following an article Mellor had written for the *Evening Standard* which criticised players' commitments to community work. Taylor refuted the lack of commitment calling for Mellor's sacking in a letter to the Prime Minister and then, when it was revealed that the article was based on figures supplied to the Working Group by the PFA itself, he criticised the use of confidential submissions in articles for the media. Whilst one can sympathise with Taylor's concern to protect his members' interests and reputation, it also highlighted the difficulties for those in the Task Force with other, legitimate public roles. This argument re-surfaced in January 1999 with the publication of the Task Force's *Investing in the Community* report, which led to Taylor's resignation from the Task Force.

Perhaps more problematically, it highlighted the difficulties inherent in the Task Force, in terms of expecting representatives of football organisations to act against their own perceived best interests and for the good of football as a whole. New Labour's Third Way – relying on the 'community' to reach compromise and change – was hardly likely to succeed in the football arena where there are not only huge sectional differences of opinion, approach and interest, but where there are severe factional political infighting battles within some organisations. Vice-Chair Richard Faulkner has asserted that:

> the ability of the Task Force to bring together representatives from all areas of football, acknowledge individual concerns and bring about agreement on difficult issues has been one of our greatest – and most unexpected – strengths.[16]

However, like turkeys not voting for Christmas, radical change was always going to be unlikely, given the decision-making structure of the Task Force.

Thus, on one hand, the government wanted the Group to undertake the task of a commission – a collection of appointees to 'think the unthinkable' and make policy recommendations; yet on the other, they would not pay individuals so they could give up their other interests to concentrate fully on the task in hand. Indeed the government still wants, at the time of writing, to achieve a consensus among football's notoriously divided organisations on issues such as the role of plcs in football. Furthermore, the twin-track organisational structure not only caused confusion, but gave all football's organisations (in the Full Task Force) the ability to veto any of the Group's recommendations. David Mellor's declared hope that there would be an '*esprit de corps*' within the body rapidly began to look like a matter of hope rather than reality.

Remit

If the membership and organisation of the Task Force had flaws which might wound prospects for a new governance of football, the nature of the remit did not help either. David Mellor perceptively described the remit as the outcome of throwing a handful of pieces of paper with issues on them up into the air and seeing which ones landed first.

There didn't appear to be any coherence to them – a couple of perceived 'easy' targets (racism and disabled access), media priorities (merchandise, players as role models) and some commercial concerns. Furthermore, the remit was certainly not the result of consultation with the bodies in the game as to what they thought were the key issues. So the participating bodies were to be involved in a process of discussing issues in football which they had not chosen and may not have even considered to be key problems or priorities. The remit was certainly not the result of either research or consultation with fans as to what *their* priorities were.

The government clearly wanted to 'do something' about football and be seen to be backing the ordinary fan – Tony Banks declared on several occasions that he 'hadn't set up the Task Force for its recommendations to sit on the shelf' – and had hinted at exactly what it wanted achieved in the *Charter for Football*. In line with its Third Way approach, though, it also wanted the recommendations to appear as a result of consultation and consensus, as the product of the Task Force, rather than be seen as the government imposing its will on a reluctant industry. This wish implied that it had to let the Task Force proceed with its work and come to its own conclusions, yet paradoxically, providing such a specific agenda smacked of government prescription.

The remit itself was a curious amalgam of *Charter* commitments, new issues and compromises by Labour once in office. The rejection of any role in investigating a new formula for administering the game and reforming the FA and the absence of an investigation into television's role in football, drastically weakened the Task Force's scope and potential to deliver meaningful recommendations. Given developments such as the TV-driven European Super League and the Office of Fair Trading's investigation into the Premier League's collective selling of television rights, both during the life of the Task Force, such restrictions on its scope did, and still do, question its relevance to the future governance of the game.

Given that one of Labour's motivations for introducing the governance of football on to the policy agenda was the public disquiet at the widening gulf between rich and poor, and given television's central role in this process, it is all the more surprising that neither the role of television finance, nor the governance structures of football, were on the agenda for the Task Force. Although events such as BSkyB's bid (in Autumn 1998) to take over Manchester United did arguably fall under a consideration of plcs – it was only possible because United were listed on the Stock Exchange – the remit failed to recognise the central role of television finance. Further, given its specificity, the remit also failed to recognise that a large proportion of shareholders may also be fans – a theme developed elsewhere in this book (in chapter 11, for example). Such shortcomings may have been the result of New Labour's desire to avoid controversy and conflict with global media interests such as those controlled by Rupert Murdoch's News International group, but in doing so they illustrated an appalling lack of understanding of the football industry, its finance, structure and future.

The changes between Labour's initial interest in the game, in the shape of the *Charter for Football*, and its activities in office, in the shape of the Task Force, are instructive. The former was concerned with structure, organisation, ownership and control; the latter with achieving consensus and improving the image of the game. The pursuit of the 2006 World Cup is almost certainly part of this calculation, something which Tony Banks has put considerable energy into. Issues such as a possible return of terracing, as well as biting the bullets of television's involvement in football and reform of the game's administration, both threatened breaking the fragile consensus around 2006. This concern with image rather than substance was exemplified by the government's reaction to violence in France during the 1998 World Cup: whereas fans had been courted in the run-up to the election, the Labour administration could hardly be differentiated from its Tory predecessors in its condemnation of fans in Marseilles when organisations such as the FSA were trying to protect the innocent. Exemplifying this problem was the Department of Media, Culture and Sport's (DCMS) refusal to help fund the FSA's Fan Embassy during the 1998 World Cup in France, an initiative which was in reality a very unglamorous, uncontroversial and practical measure with a proven track record of reducing problems at grounds. The DCMS position was in response to the FSA's refusal to publicly back the government's advertising campaign encouraging fans not to travel to France without a ticket. The FSA believed the campaign was irrelevant and a waste of money given the late hour at which it was due to run.

However, two other issues illustrated more than any others the problems of the Task Force's remit and membership during its lifetime: terracing and the attempt by BSkyB satellite television company to take over Manchester United.

Terracing

The Task Force was established to confront issues of importance for supporters, the result of a Labour election manifesto pledge by Tony Blair that 'Labour is determined to get a fair deal for fans to improve the way in which football is run'.[17] The problem with such commitments is what to do when you strongly disagree with what fans want to discuss.

As mentioned above, Tom Pendry had raised the prospect (and hopes) of the government reconsidering the all-seater requirement introduced after the *Taylor Report*, albeit with new, stronger safety guidelines. Evidence from the continent suggested that this was feasible at the highest level, with both Bayern Munich and Borussia Dortmund building new stands with safe terraced areas capable of being converted to seated areas when needed (for example, for UEFA matches). Supporters' groups had long maintained that some fans wanted to stand, that it was possible to have limited, low-level standing areas and that to group those who want to stand with those who want to sit merely caused extra problems. I and others warned the Task Force that this would become an issue – much to their consternation and initial disbelief – and that the government should consider including it as an area of the remit.

The issue came to a head at Manchester United where strong-arm tactics were used by Special Projects Security, the security firm employed by the club, to forcibly eject fans standing in some sections of Old Trafford. The running public relations disaster for the club was perhaps one motive for chief executive Martin Edwards to go on record saying that he supported a reintroduction of terracing at Old Trafford. When the Task Force held its first regional meeting at Leicester, calls for the reintroduction of terracing were supported 4 to 1 at the public meeting. At Manchester, the entire gathering was utterly dominated by support for the issue. At Sheffield and Birmingham further support was expressed. No issue other than ticket pricing produced such concerted support from fans in the regional visits.

Tony Banks had initially, and unbriefed, been conciliatory to the idea. This was soon 'stamped on', to use his own words, by the Labour Party hierarchy and any chance whatsoever of the government letting the Task Force consider terracing was subsequently dismissed. Political sensitivity for the Hillsborough families was cited, but can hardly have been the real reason when the same government was about to refuse a reopening of the Hillsborough Inquiry. It was clear in the first few months of the Task Force that standing was an issue which should have been investigated, something backed by every supporters organisation but, again, a concern with image overrode either common sense or any semblance of democracy by letting fans determine the agenda. So sensitive was the issue that it was conveyed to the author that any support for terracing had to be given as an individual and no perception that the issue had any Task Force support could be allowed.

What this also illustrated was that whilst the actual content of both remit and discussions were somewhat haphazard, they were kept within strict boundaries which the government deemed acceptable. Debates were always closely monitored by the Department of Culture,

Media and Sport officials, advice given as to the desired direction, and drafts of reports checked before release so as not to embarrass the government. It was not prepared to accept anything which might upset its public relations 'apple cart' – such as terracing – and that meant circumscribing fans' wishes on what could be discussed. In actual fact, the government could have made good use of a discussion of safe standing areas: it would have highlighted innovative British technology and expertise in crowd control; it would have opened up a solution to the ticket price problem; and it would have appeared that they were listening to fans' concerns rather than trying to silence them. The terracing issue illustrated that for New Labour, there was some very old-fashioned controlling going on.

BSkyB and Manchester United

BSkyB's attempted bid to take over Manchester United clearly had major implications for the future structure of ownership in the game and its governance. The bid threatened to make the gap between rich and poor in the Premiership widen further and arguably was the first step to removing decision-making on the future of the game from football and placing it in the hands of television corporations. What is more, such a bid was only possible because Manchester United had been floated on the Stock Exchange.

One area of the Task Force's remit was, 'to reconcile the potential conflict between the legitimate needs of shareholders, players and supporters where clubs have been floated on the Stock Exchange'. The battle for ownership of England's biggest club between large shareholders, the board and the monopoly supplier of live Premiership football on television on the one hand, and supporters groups and small shareholders on the other, could hardly have been more relevant. Indeed, the public outcry which accompanied the bid and which forced its referral to the Monopolies and Mergers Commission was based around key Task Force concerns, such as the neglect of fans, the broader public interest and the threat that posed to the break-up of the Premier League and further fragmentation of football (see chapters 1, 5 and 6).

What is more, the Premier League's restrictive practices court case was looming at the time, and the bid clearly had implications for that. Indeed, the RPC case was arguably out of the Task Force remit, given previous indications from government that the role of television in football was not to be considered. Yet arguments about the effect a break-up of collective bargaining for TV rights would have on fragmenting the game, widening the gap between the élite and grass-roots, and its negative effect in a strategic long-term sense, prevailed.

The Football Task Force was unequivocal in its opinion on football's access to television money in its report, *Investing in the Community*:

> English football depends on redistribution of income . . .
> English football's ability to invest in its own future is critically
> linked to there being no break-up in the present collective
> bargaining arrangements . . . The Football Task Force is united
> in its belief that this outcome would have a negative impact on
> English football.[18]

It is all the more incredible, then, that not only did the Task Force make no comment to the Minister for Sport, the Secretary of State for Trade and Industry, the Office of Fair Trading or the Monopolies and Mergers Commission, against the BSkyB take-over, but that such a statement was ruled *ultra vires* by the DCMS civil servants.

I attempted to get a Task Force statement against the take-over on two occasions. The first,[19] when the case was still being considered by the OFT, was supported by an extraordinary cross section of opinion on the Task Force, including the FA, the PFA, the League Managers Association, supporters groups, the Local Government Association and individuals. Yet a combination of Premier League opposition and a DCMS ruling prevented it being made. A statement from those in agreement was made, which had to make clear that this was 'a collection of individuals who happen to be on the Football Task Force'!

The case was an amazing illustration of the shortcomings of the Task Force: its remit became a flexible beast to suit powerful interests on the body, enabling them to control the agenda when their future was under threat in the restrictive practices court. So a case as fundamental to the future of the game and as central to one area of the remit as the BSkyB take-over was blocked on the behest of those same interests. Furthermore, for a body seeking progress by consensus, opposition to the take-over had been demonstrated by all sections of the game on the Task Force; but the clear will of the majority was overridden. In short, the Task Force's remit was inadequate as it was susceptible to interpretation and therefore to becoming a tool for certain interests, and the membership of the Task Force allowed those powerful interests in the game to dominate and effectively veto the wishes of the majority.

Conclusions: the Third Way to the football regulator?

The Football Task Force can be accused of many things: a concern with media priorities; a desire for a consensus while allowing the powerful to dominate; a belief in consultation but coupled with a strong desire to limit any controversial messages; a lack of strong, knowledgeable political leadership to force change; a desire to do 'something' for 'the people' (or at least be seen to be doing so); a rambling inconsistency on occasion; and an inability not to be side-stepped by events elsewhere (such as the BSkyB take-over attempt), even when all these issues are within the power of the government to address within the Task Force's remit, staffing and resourcing. In addition, however, there are two concluding issues which will determine how successfully its work will be viewed. One is what kind of example it sets as a Third Way approach to policy formulation. The other, and most important, is what effect it will have on football in terms of its remit, recommendations and the regulation of the game.

An example of the Third Way?

In many ways it is right to argue that the 'Task Force itself is a striking example of New Labour politics, perhaps even of the elusive Third Way'.[20] An ex-Tory Chair; a left-wing minister; the inclusion of all bodies into the process; a desire for the 'community' to find solutions, in this case the 'football community'; a high media profile; public consultations; yet all closely overseen by the party's spin doctors – former Minister for Trade and Industry and media manager-supreme Peter Mandelson could not have scripted it better. However, it also entails a number of tenets of the Third Way approach which have raised serious problems.

The Task Force was not set up within a government department, or as a civil service institution, so that its decisions would appear as 'community' decisions. Yet, contradicting this is evidence that the government has drawn strict parameters for its work.

There has been a desire to achieve change by consensus and consultation as reflected in the make-up, organisation and scope of the task force. But this has raised a problem in terms of dealing with the conflicts of interest inherent in a sport increasingly overrun by commercial interests. The Task Force has arguably been inherently flawed from the outset because of this. Issues of basic conflict of interest within the game have kept arising throughout its lifetime: the Premier League and the Office of Fair Trading; the European Super League; BSkyB's attempted take-over of Manchester United and the wider involvement of television in football. It has so far not only proved inadequate to deal with these issues, but by and large has sought to avoid them. Furthermore, rather than achieving a consensus, it has ended up tussling with the notion of an independent regulator for football who would impose reform and order on the game, evidence if any were needed that the game has great difficulty in reforming its own governance structures.

In some senses the experience of the Task Force merely illustrates the weakness of the Third Way approach: it seeks to involve all interested parties in decision-making, whereas arguably they should be the subjects of evidence presentations, and it attempts to achieve a consensus when there is clearly anything but. Given the government's desire to retain some control of the agenda and outcome, the manner in which it was established and the issues it was presented with, there is a strong argument to say in this instance that the Third Way approach has always been flawed. However, it is the idea that powerful interests in football will readily agree to subsume their own interests to those opinions which they perceive as diametrically opposite which is its biggest weakness.

Football's regulation: a new governance for the game?

Arguably, like the government itself, too many matters relating to the Football Task Force are really about image, or timidity in the face of big business. Even when there is demonstrable public support, the structure of the body and its philosophy of achieving consensus between conflicting interests within the game stands in the way of radical proposals. The main commissioned research on fans for the Task Force illustrated that 79.2 per cent were against media companies owning clubs; 85.7 per cent supported a code of conduct; and 63.7 per cent wanted it enforced through a new, independent regulator.[21] This mandate has been further supported during the Task Force's regional visits, and the work of the body has been underpinned by enthusiastic support from fan groups and individuals who have given their time freely.

Yet the prospects for such radical intervention seem slim. The restrictive practices court case and the MMC report on the BSkyB take-over of Manchester United, along with the reform of the Football Association, may ultimately have much more to say about the future of the people's game than nearly two years of Task Force work. If they do, then it will have been deemed to be a failure.

However, it is the case that the reports already published make a reasonable attempt to confront some serious issues in the game – the recommendations on racism and improving facilities for the disabled have encompassed many of the wishes of both ethnic minority and disabled supporters groups. The report on community policies includes a commitment by the Premier League to provide at least 5 per cent of television income to the grass-roots in football and to improve clubs' roles within their communities. In all three reports, some sections include material which offers hints as to the tone of the final report: the *Improving Facilities for Disabled Supporters* report included a recommendation that disabled fans' ticket prices should be related to the ability to pay, with clear implications for all ticketing policy; and support for football's community schemes included a recommendation that mechanisms enabling fans to be represented on club boards and the independent funding of supporters organisations be examined.[22]

On the other hand, judgement will be reserved until the acid test of the publication of the Task Force's Final Report. Will it recommend in the ticketing remit that concessions be universally available, including for the low-waged and students, and that there be uniformity in allocation, distribution and pricing of tickets for home and away fans – both major issues for supporters? Will it commit to no price increases above the rate of inflation? Will it provide for funding of fans' organisations and allow for them to be meaningfully represented at all levels in the game, including the FA Council? Will it place restrictions on the ownership of clubs and encourage fan ownership? Will it rule that media corporations are unsuitable owners of football clubs? All these are yet to be answered at the time of writing, but should serve as the benchmark for the Task Force's achievements.

Perhaps most crucial, though, is the question of whether the Task Force will lead to a new regulatory structure for football. The history of the governance of football is that the clubs will not undertake change which they perceive to be against their own (short-term) interests unless they are forced to do so. This was certainly the case with provision of safe grounds in which spectators could watch the game. It is almost unforeseeable that there will be any universal change in practice amongst football clubs on the recommendations of the Task Force unless these recommendations are backed by some independent force. For example, there has been little evidence of any progress a year after the report on racism in football was made. So far the threat of withdrawal of Football Trust money from lower clubs has been one stick; and a minor legislative change in policing racist abuse is another;[23] but an overall recommendation to the government to force change on clubs and football authorities has not yet been made.

Yet there is considerable argument, combined with the public support outlined above, which supports the establishment of a strong independent regulator. Lord Justice Taylor's Report into the Hillsborough stadium disaster in 1990 was a watershed for English football. In it he said that:

> The picture revealed is of a general malaise or blight over the game due to a number of factors. Principally these are: old

grounds, poor facilities, hooliganism, excessive drinking and poor leadership (para. 26).[24]

As David Conn argues in chapter 2, whereas football has arguably dealt with the first four of these concerns in the top two divisions at least, with the assistance of considerable subsidy from the public purse (see also chapter 1), the question of leadership and the governance of the game has not been adequately addressed. This was recognised in Labour's *Charter for Football* which called for a thorough reassessment of the administration of football. Further, Taylor argued:

> As for the clubs, in some instances it is legitimate to wonder whether the directors are genuinely interested in the welfare of their grass-roots supporters. Boardroom struggles for power, wheeler-dealing in the buying and selling of shares and indeed whole clubs sometimes suggest that those involved are more interested in the personal financial benefits or social status of being a director than of directing the club in the interests of its supporters (para. 53).

Although there have been improvements in some instances, in many cases at club level these concerns persist (see chapters 1 and 2) and whatever the weaknesses of the body, the Task Force has been charged with providing answers.

Football has always been a heavily regulated industry (for good reasons which are addressed in many of the chapters in this book), overseen by its governing body, the FA, with clubs required to meet a number of criteria. Football, particularly the FA, have allowed the effectiveness of this regulatory function to slide into decay in the last decade or more, with its focus increasingly concentrated on the international team and tournaments, its role as the national rule-making body and as the primary enforcer of player discipline. This decline in the quality of the regulation of individual clubs has happened at a time of increased commercial activity and the formation of holding plcs to own football clubs, the formation of the Premier League (ironically driven by the FA partly to gain greater control over the game!), massive increases in ticket prices and a crisis in the lower divisions. Sir John Smith's recommendations for addressing the problem of financial irregularities at clubs highlighted the neglect of regulation in the financial sphere and argued that the FA must reassert its role in this area as the game was rocked by a series of money scandals (on which, see the chapters by Conn and Hamil). Although some efforts have been made to address the issue, the appointment of a Compliance Officer whose primary remit appears to have been drawn quite tightly around the issue of player discipline (with responsibility for the investigation of financial irregularities left ill-defined) and the 'cash for votes' scandal at the FA which led to the resignation of Graham Kelly and Keith Wiseman, have raised questions about the gravity with which the FA is addressing the need for reform in this area.

In reality, as other chapters in this book illustrate, football has been a special legislative case for many years because it is a special type of business. Football shares a number of characteristics with other regulated industries: each club is arguably a monopoly; it is a national and local asset; its recent restructuring has reduced the level of regulation to the benefit of corporate financial interests; it suffers from the 'fat cat' syndrome, as David Conn argues; it has demonstrably failed to properly serve its customers on many occasions; and it has failed to ensure, as the gambling and racing industries are required to, that its businesses are managed by 'fit and proper' people.

One proposal which I drafted for the Task Force was that a semi-independent regulator is established within the structure of the FA, but with an independent chief executive with the power of veto over its future remit and those who work for it.[25] This proposal would ensure that the regulation of financial, legal and commercial activities of clubs is seen as independent from vested interests within football's governance, and ensure that there is a 'critical distance' between regulation and the FA's (and the Premier and Football Leagues') own activities within the game, especially competition organisation, thus avoiding any conflict of interest. Furthermore, such a regulator would establish a code of conduct for football clubs; establish binding rules for clubs; set performance targets for football clubs on a variety of issues, including those on the Task Force's remit; call any club to account at any time for alleged breaches of the code or rules; gain access to any evidence from clubs, including financial and ticket records; carry out spot checks; issue reports on the performance of clubs in relation to the code of conduct and make recommendations, in conjunction with clubs, for any failure to meet standards; undertake a series of measures where the regulator has the power to *enforce* rules, including imposition of new club governance structures, fines and point deductions.

Although such a system would leave some areas of football's governance to the clubs and restrict the scope of the regulator to 'naming and shaming' those that don't meet the code of conduct requirements, its evidence-gathering powers would make its power of influence considerable. Furthermore, on some crucial areas, it would have the power to enforce change. These areas could include: financial matters along the lines proposed in Sir John Smith's report *Football: Its*

Values, Finances and Reputation;[26] a new 'Rule 34' (see chapters by Conn, by Michie and Ramalingam, and by Michie and Walsh) including rules on ownership, plcs and corporate and media take-overs; a pricing structure for football; representation of fans at club and governing body levels; and funding of fans' organisations.

The extent to which the Football Task Force follows such a model and the weight it gives to crucial indices of 'independence' and 'enforcement' is likely to be the determining factor in evaluating the Task Force's lasting contribution to the development of governance structures in football. As a wider comment on the country and its government, the Task Force should take note of Arthur Hopcraft's words:

> The way we play the game, organise it and reward it reflects the kind of community we are.[27]

Notes

[1] I must also thank Matthew Brown for comments on an earlier draft of this chapter, which have been included.

[2] The extent of politicians' newly publicised interest in football was neatly illustrated in Bull, D. and Campbell, A. (eds.) (1994) *Football and the Common People*. London: Juma.

[3] *Independent on Sunday*. 1995, 15 January – and quoted above in the introduction to this book.

[4] Labour Party (1996) *Charter for Football*. London: Labour Party.

[5] NNC, a company based in Sale, Cheshire, had developed a computerised Crowd Monitoring System by 1990, just after the completion of the Taylor Inquiry. Although tested at Old Trafford and during New Year's Eve celebrations in Trafalgar Square, it has never been given the chance to be endorsed by football as a whole.

[6] For example see *Sports Events (Sale of Alcohol) Act* 1985; *Football Spectators Act* 1989. For a discussion of civil liberty implications for fans, see Brown, A. 'Football Fans and Civil Liberties', *Journal for Sport and the Law*. Vol. 1 No. 2. July 1994.

[7] Brown, M., *Chelsea Independent*, 1998.

[8] The Office of Fair Trading is currently in the restrictive practices court accusing the Premier League of operating a cartel in its collective sale of TV rights; and the Monopoly and Mergers Commission investigated (and recommended against) the take-over of Manchester United by BSkyB television.

[9] Football Task Force press release, 30 July 1997.

[10] Glanville, B. 'An own goal by Labour'. *The Times*, 29 July 1997.

[11] Littlejohn, R. 'Mellor's meddling can only result in own goal'. *Daily Mail,* 29 July 1997.

[12] Dunn, M. 'Government has ignored us, says FA chief Kelly'. *Daily Express*, 19 July 1997.

[13] Varley, N. 'Fans fast to make Mellor demands'. *The Guardian*, 29 July 1997.

[14] 'New Stands At Football Grounds To Include Disabled Facilities Or Lose Out On Grants'. *DCMS* press release, 11 February 1999.

[15] Football Task Force press release, 29 August 1999.

[16] Faulkner, R. (1999). 'The Football Task Force – past, present and future', address to *SMI – Football Finance IV*.

[17] Editorial, *The Times*, 29 September 1997.

[18] Football Task Force (1999). *Investing in the Community*: 7.3–7.6

[19] This began at a meeting of the Working Group on 22 September 1998.

[20] Brown, M. *Chelsea Independent*, 1998.

[21] Williams, J. and Perkins, S. (1999). *Ticket Pricing, Football Business and 'Excluded' Football Fans*. Leicester: Leicester University: Tables 2.43, 2.45 and 2.46.

[22] For details of the Task Force's recommendations so far, see: Football Task Force (1998). *Eliminating Racism From Football*, London: DCMS; Football Task Force (1998). *Improving Facilities for Disabled Supporters*, London: DCMS; Football Task Force (1999). *Investing in the Community*, London: DCMS.

[23] The *Football Offences Act* 1992 is to be amended to outlaw an individual, as opposed to a group, chanting racist abuse.

[24] Inquiry by the Rt. Hon. Lord Justice Taylor (1990). *The Hillsborough Stadium Disaster: Final Report*. CM962. London HMSO.

[25] Brown, A. and Taylor, P. (1999). 'Notes on the Regulation of Football – Rationale and Outline', paper presented to Football Task Force Working Group, 26 February 1999.

[26] Smith, Sir J. and LeJeune, M. (1998). *Football: Its Values, Finances and Reputation*. The Football Association.

[27] Hopcraft, A. (1968). *The Football Man*. London: Sportspages.

4. The BSkyB Bid for Manchester United Plc

Simon Lee

All the passion of a banknote

It is apt that the tenth anniversary of Hillsborough should coincide with the conclusion of two deliberations which will profoundly affect English professional football during the first years of the new millennium. The government's response to the Monopolies and Mergers Commission's (MMC) recommendations, following its scrutiny of the BSkyB bid for Manchester United, and the outcome of the Office of Fair Trading's (OFT) restrictive practices court case against the alleged cartel formed by the Premier League in its negotiations and deal with BSkyB and the BBC, threaten to unleash an even more frantic wave of commercial machinations upon English football.

In his final report into the Hillsborough stadium disaster of 15 April 1989, Lord Justice Taylor identified five factors responsible for 'a general malaise or blight over the game' of English football (Home Office, 1990, para. 26). Four of these five factors (old grounds, poor facilities, hooliganism and excessive drinking) have been largely eliminated from at least the upper echelons of English professional football in the intervening years. Unfortunately, poor leadership remains a blight on the English game. It is worth recalling the late Lord Taylor's thoughts on this subject:

> As for the clubs, in some instances it is legitimate to wonder whether the directors are genuinely interested in the welfare of their grass-roots supporters. Boardroom struggles for power, wheeler-dealing in the buying and selling of shares and indeed of whole clubs sometimes suggest that those involved are more interested in the personal financial benefits or social status of being a director than of directing the club in the interests of its

supporter customers. In most commercial enterprises, including the entertainment industry, knowledge of the customer's needs, his tastes and his dislikes is essential information in deciding policy and planning. But, until recently, very few clubs consulted to any significant extent with the supporters or their organisations (Home Office, 1990, para. 53).

A decade on from Hillsborough, the welfare of football supporters and their legitimate right to be consulted as major stakeholders in the English game remains largely unrecognised in the governance of professional football. The explanation for this oversight is simple. In January 1990, the *Taylor Report* entreated that 'now is the moment for the fullest reassessment of policy for the game' (Home Office, 1990, para. 58) but in its aftermath there was no fundamental reassessment of the future direction and governance of English professional football. The subsequent decade has been characterised instead by increasingly frantic 'wheeler-dealing' and the shameful pursuit of 'personal financial benefit' by many football club chairmen and their fellow 'fat cat' directors. In a move entirely redolent of the political economy and values inspired by Thatcherism, the major clubs have broken away from their Football League brethren to create the FA Premier League in order to enable themselves to appropriate a much larger share of English professional football's income. In keeping with Thatcherite values, 'the widening gap (between the Premier League clubs and the rest) was dignified with a philosophy: "market forces", a philosophy that abandoned the limited notion of redistribution from the richer clubs to the poorer which had characterised the development of the game during its modern history' (Conn, 1997:152).

The language of football is one of revenue streams, brand loyalty and inelastic demand for tickets irrespective of the price charged or the televised saturation coverage of games. In short, 'football has changed, from something which belonged to its people, to a business' where 'today's FA Carling Premiership car parks are exhibitions of ostentation, field studies of inequality' (Conn, 1997:27,152). For its part, England's premier club, Manchester United, has been tamed 'into the corset of a middle-class "entertainment industry"' (Conn, 1997:46). Alex Ferguson recently described the level of support at Old Trafford as 'awful . . . more like a morgue than a football match' (*United Review*, Vol.60, No.16), a sad but apt reflection on a ground now overflowing with the passive, passionless presence of an armchair-, replay- and pundit-educated generation. But Manchester United is not the only major club whose soul has been corrupted by this commodification of the culture of English football.[1] The flotation of

Newcastle United showed 'football's true face in the '90s, all the passion of a banknote' (Conn, 1997:62). Indeed, that the dividend from this transaction should be a capital gain of around £100 million to Sir John Hall, one of Mrs Thatcher's most ardent advocates, and not a single major trophy won for supporters whose great-grandparents last saw the First Division trophy paraded in Newcastle in 1927, is an appropriate commentary on the values and motive force of the Premier League.

From gap, to chasm, to abyss

The condition of contemporary English professional football and its governance are testament to the extent to which it has embraced the values of Thatcherism. Since the early 1980s, the richest English clubs have attempted to secure a larger share of the game's income, initially by threatening the creation of a 'Super League' in 1981 and temporarily settling for an agreement which enabled them to keep all gate receipts from home fixtures and no longer having to share them with visiting clubs. When a further attempt was made to break away in 1985, the top clubs were kept in the fold by the pompously named 'Heathrow Agreement', the First Division being awarded 50 per cent of all TV and sponsorship revenue, a larger share of voting rights in Football League decisions and a cut in the end-of-season gate levy to 3 per cent. These demands were made in the wake of the Bradford and Heysel disasters but added to the trend towards redistribution of football's revenue in favour of the richer clubs (Conn, 1997:140). Subsequently, further threats of a breakaway were diverted by the then 'Big Five' clubs (Manchester United, Liverpool, Everton, Arsenal and Tottenham Hotspur) being able to negotiate their own television contract with ITV. This resulted in their receiving 50 per cent of English football's £44 million income from television, but nevertheless still having to share the other half with the Second Division (25 per cent), and the Third and Fourth Division (25 per cent split between them). When the breakaway from the Football League finally occurred in 1991, the creation of the Premier League was not based on purely commercial grounds since it had been calculated that the existing structure of English professional football could generate £112 million income per year if properly marketed (Conn, 1997:145). The motivation instead was the desire of the leading English clubs to secure control of a larger share of the rapidly growing revenue from television contracts, as was proven with the signing of the five year £304 million deal between the Premier League clubs and BSkyB.

The development of English football in the 1990s has therefore mirrored wider society in its departure from post-war notions of progressive taxation and redistribution towards an enterprise culture which has often confused the opportunistic pursuit of individual self-interest for entrepreneurial innovation and risk-taking (Lee, 1997a). The pace at which societal inequalities in income and wealth accelerated under the Thatcher and Major Governments has been extensively documented (Hills, 1998; Child Poverty Action Group, 1996). Although average incomes grew in Britain by around 40 per cent between 1979 and 1994–95, the richest tenth of the population saw their income grow by 68 per cent, while the poorest tenth saw their income fall by 8 per cent (including housing costs). In fact, the overall distribution of income had rapidly diminished in post-war Britain, and the onset of Thatcherism saw an exceptional growth in income inequalities, both in historic and international terms (Hills, 1998:5). Will Hutton has depicted the resulting income distribution in terms of 'The thirty, thirty, forty society', where only a 'privileged' 40 per cent of the population enjoy security and affluence while the remainder experience marginalisation, insecurity and poverty (Hutton, 1995:106–8). In English football, the inequalities in income and wealth are even starker. The August 1998 Deloitte & Touche *Annual Review of Football Finance* documented how, 'The gap between the Premier League and Football League is turning from gap, to chasm to abyss' (Deloitte & Touche, 1998:7).

The Premier League's turnover (up 34 per cent to £463.9 million in 1996–97) now constitutes no less than 68.7 per cent of English professional football's total income. Thus, English football, according to Hutton's framework, could be characterised as a 69/31 society where the richest 20 clubs receive more than twice as much as the poorest 72. However, within that gross figure of inequality is concealed the fact that the top five finishers in the Premier League in 1996–97, namely Manchester United, Newcastle United, Arsenal, Liverpool and Aston Villa, had a combined turnover greater than all the 72 clubs in the Football League (Deloitte & Touche, 1998:5). The £23.2 million average turnover of the 20 Premier League clubs is 4.2 times greater than the average turnover of the First Division clubs. Driven by the increases in television revenue, the profitability gap between the average operating profits of the Premier League clubs and the First Division clubs has grown from £3.8 million in 1995–96 to £4.8 million in 1996–97 (Deloitte & Touche, 1998:7). Furthermore, Manchester United's 1996–97 revenue of £87.9 million meant that it alone had received no less than 13 per cent of English professional football's gross income and 19 per cent of the Premier League's revenue. Thus, English football could be described as the 13, 54, 31 society where one rich Premier League club now receives nearly half the income received by no fewer than 72 other professional clubs in the Football League – less a case of 'All for one, and one for all', than 'All for one, and all for one'. As a result of the increasing purchase of players from overseas, and reflecting the trade deficit suffered by the national economy, English football suffered a net outflow of revenue overseas of £100.4 million in 1996–97, following an outflow of £78.4 million in 1995–96 (Deloitte & Touche, 1998:23). Net transfer spending has been most prevalent among Premier League clubs seeking to avoid relegation and First Division clubs seeking promotion. The outflow of income from clubs in the Premier League to those in the Football League via transfer deals was only £14.5 million in 1996–97, compared to £25.2 million the previous year. A loss of £28 million in 1996–97 meant that the Football League had made an aggregate operating loss of £118 million in the five years to 1996–97. In the same period, the Premier League has made an operating profit of £260 million (Deloitte & Touche, 1998:11). There appears to be a 'trickle down' effect, but mirroring the wider development of British society, it is one of percolation of poverty rather than the distribution of wealth.

Greed is good: the governing principle of English football

During the 1990s, driven and epitomised by the creation of the Premier League, the traditional, amateurish and increasingly archaic associational model of governance of English professional football by the FA and the Football League has been challenged and displaced by a principal-agent or financial model of corporate governance (Keasey, Thompson and Wright, 1997:3).[2] Driven by their desire to gain a tighter control over, and a larger share of, football's fastest growing income stream, i.e. income derived from satellite, terrestrial and (impending pay-per-view) television contracts, the directors of Premier League clubs have embraced a shareholder-centric, short-termist form of corporate governance which unashamedly assumes that profit-maximising behaviour provides the best means for welfare maximisation, i.e. the good of their respective clubs. A series of Premier League club chairmen and their merchant banker advisers have advocated stock-market flotations as the best means of modernising football stadia and investing in world-class players. This Anglo-American model of governance has been criticised for being excessively concerned with the short-term maximisation of profit, itself the consequence of capital market failure, and the award of excessive remuneration for directors (Hutton, 1995). Critics have also pointed to the fact that investment in stadia modernisation has normally been undertaken (partly with public funds) prior to stock-market flotation, and that share issues have principally been vehicles for a few rich individuals to make spectacular capital gains at the expense of their clubs' longer term competitiveness. Indeed, flotations have only been possible by virtue of the clubs first becoming subsidiaries of non-footballing companies, thereby rendering inapplicable Rule 34 (a) (v) of the FA which states that 'if a club is wound up, its property must be distributed to other local sporting clubs' (Conn, 1997:165–6). At the level of the ordinary football supporter, the corporate rebranding of English clubs has sought to replace the traditional collective intensity, passion and camaraderie experienced by English football supporters on the terraces with an all-seated, passive and individualised experience where the possession of an extensive (and expensive) collection of replica shirts, club merchandise and a satellite dish have become the benchmarks by which an increasingly middle-class audience has expressed its transient enthusiasm for football (Lee, 1997b).

As an alternative to the principal-agent model, the stakeholder model of governance has contended that participation and accountability should be defined more widely than the maximisation of shareholder or owner value and that governance should explicitly recognise and defend the welfare of other groups or stakeholders which have a long-term association with the corporation (Hutton, 1995, 1997; Kelly, Kelly and Gamble, 1997). This model of governance is held by its advocates to be both more equitable and socially efficient than the principal-agent model because it is based on relationships of trust and co-operation (Fukayama, 1995). Critics of the stakeholder model have argued that it is intrinsically incompatible with corporate objectives, and undermines both private property and accountability (Willetts, 1996; Sternberg, 1998). However, English football is a sport that has only recently embraced corporate values and whose continuing health, as the organisation of American football on redistributive principles demonstrates, requires a pattern of governance, participation and accountability which defies the norms of the principal-agent model of corporate governance and which ensures competition between teams in a viable league structure. If ever a business warranted the concept of stakeholding, then a football club would appear a prime candidate given the unique combination of emotion and finance which supporters invest in their clubs.

The relationship between supporters and their respective football clubs is primarily an emotional bond, frequently a matter of lifelong personal allegiance which transcends the impersonal experience of individual consumption and market transactions which the principal-agent model embraces. In England, the importance of football teams to their communities has long been seen as an important source of collective, often civic, identity and pride (Russell, 1997). Identity lies in what the members of a particular community share 'not individually but collectively, not privately but publicly', a fact which has given identity 'an inescapable institutional focus' (Parekh, 1994:501–2). In England, football grounds have provided the primary and perhaps the only institutions where civic identities have been celebrated en masse by the local population on a regular basis. In an overly centralised British state, which has been reluctant to devolve genuine political power to sub-national English political structures, but instead has devolved managerial and administrative responsibility for the implementation of difficult and unpopular decisions to local authorities (Lee, 1999), football clubs have taken on an additional significance in the expression of civic identity. Thus, for many English people, football has been the source of:

> a sense of belonging at the ground, at the game, standing together in communal support for these clubs. In a world which had undermined the old certainties, of community, religion, ritual, football provided all three around its central, indefinable magic (Conn, 1997:132).

This has been ever more so in the materialistic, secular 1990s, and may in part explain the sudden attraction of football to an atomised middle class in search of some form of collective identity and security to transcend their essentially individualistic lifestyles. As recent events in Chester, Brighton, Portsmouth and Oxford vividly demonstrate, this unique status of football in England has been reflected in the sometimes desperate attempts mounted by supporters and the wider community to maintain their clubs in the ranks of the 92 professional clubs, a number far in excess of anything sustained elsewhere in continental Europe.

Unfortunately, the potential of stakeholding for involving supporters in the governance of their national sport was never tapped by the old associational pattern of governance practised by the FA and Football League, and more recently has been actively resisted by the majority of the new corporate élite. Shareholding supporters at the vast majority of clubs remain marginalised and virtually excluded from the corporate governance of their clubs. Given that, prior to the BSkyB bid, shareholder supporters owned no less than 23.4 per cent of the shares in Manchester United, giving them a larger stake in the club than any of the directors or any single institutional shareholder, it might have been thought that they would merit a seat on the board of directors to ensure that their interests were represented in the management and governance of the club (SUAM, 1998). However, this is a demand which has been constantly resisted since the club's flotation in 1991. Mark Goyder, an Arsenal fan who also happens to be the founder of the Centre for Tomorrow's Company, an institution concerned with issues of corporate governance, has suggested that shareholder-fans are confronted by a 'double jeopardy' because 'you buy shares in the club and they do horrible things to you, and because they do horrible things to you, your share price falls' (cited in Harverson, 1998a). The shareholder-fan fulfils the role of shareholder, customer and supporter, three roles rolled into one which Goyder contends should warrant a special dialogue between clubs and their shareholder-fans and special governance structures for football clubs. And yet, Charlton Athletic remains the sole English Premier League club with a shareholder-fan on its board to represent the 17 per cent of shares held by 3,000 Charlton supporters (Harverson, 1998a).

Manchester United: in a financial league of its own

The prominence of short-termist, especially shareholder, financial interests in the governance of English professional football has been most vividly illustrated by the cynical transformation of England's largest club into a global corporate brand (Szymanski, 1998). At present, Manchester United is in a league of its own when it comes to the finances of English football. The club generates £78 of turnover per spectator entering Old Trafford, well ahead of Newcastle United's £51 and Liverpool's £44. In June 1998, United's share value represented 42 per cent of the £985.1 million of the 18 English football clubs with a share listing. Its net assets of more than £72 million accounted for nearly 30 per cent of the Premier League's assets (Deloitte & Touche, 1998: 5, 7, 39). Old Trafford's current ground capacity of 55,300 (soon to rise to 67,400) and its supply of 34,600 season-tickets is nowhere near sufficient to satisfy the demands of its more than 100,000 members. There are more than 200 registered branches of the official supporters' club in 24 countries (but the club refuses to recognise any others because of its incapacity to meet demand for match tickets). There are also an estimated 17,000 unofficial websites about the club world-wide. The official Manchester United magazine has sustained a monthly print run of more than 100,000.

Manchester United plc's turnover in 1996–97 was £87.9 million, almost 20 per cent of the Premier League's gross turnover of £455 million (up 32 per cent on the previous year) and more than double the turnover of Newcastle United, its closest financial rival (by size of turnover). United's £27.6 million pre-tax profits helped to reduce the Premier League's overall deficit in 1996–97 to £9.5 million after transfer deals (*The Guardian*, 16 April 1998). Because United's response to the implications of the Bosman ruling was to extend and improve the contracts of some of its major stars, its wages bill (already the largest in the Premier League) rose by an explosive and inflationary 70 per cent to £22.5 million. However, both supporters and the City regarded this as a sound investment in the club's future which still meant that, at 26 per cent, United was the Premier League club devoting the smallest share of its turnover to its players' contracts. More recently, United's financial performance has been less impressive. In the financial year to the 31 July 1998, on a static turnover of £87.9 million, United's pre-tax profits fell from £27.6 million to £14.1 million following net transfer spending of £15.5 million (the acquisition of Jaap Stam, Dwight Yorke and Jesper Blomqvist). More significantly, although television revenues increased by £3.6 million to £16.2 million, income from merchandising fell by 16 per cent to £24.1 million. This was attributed to an overall decline in the market for replica shirts as fashion items, a trend purportedly exacerbated by United supporters waiting for the arrival of yet another new home strip. The rampant wage inflation of recent years continued with the club's overall wage bill rising 23 per cent to £26.9 million (*Financial Times*, 29 September 1998).

In presenting its annual results in the year to July 1997, the club chairman Professor Sir Roland Smith announced that a new subsidiary, Manchester United International, had been established with a view to opening 150 shops around the world within three years to sell club merchandise and memorabilia. Merchandise sales during the year had declined from £29 million to £24 million, which Smith attributed to the Asian financial crisis. However, many supporters closer to home would attribute a large part of this decline to their refusal to purchase club merchandise that had dropped the words 'Football Club' from the club badge. To many supporters, this decision, which transformed a proud football crest into just another corporate logo, appeared more than any other to symbolise the emasculation of the club's very identity and raison d'être by corporate greed (*The Guardian*, 29 September 1998). In a similar vein, the club had also decided to take a 25 per cent share of the £5 million hotel development at Waters Reach, Trafford Park. This has raised the spectre among supporters of a further loss of tickets to a new and highly lucrative extension of the corporate hospitality market.

In September 1997, United announced that it was to launch its own subscription television channel in partnership with BSkyB and Granada. Describing the launch of MUTV as a 'major milestone',

Martin Edwards also stated that he would be happy for the club to break away from the Premier League and go it alone following the expiry of the existing contract with BSkyB and the BBC in 2001.[3] In the interim, Edwards stated that the club needed 300,000 of its claimed 3 million supporters to subscribe to MUTV for it to make a profit. Edwards statement pointed the way towards the possibility of a future breakaway league but again demonstrated the contrast between commercial logic and the traditions of the English game. It might make eminent short-term commercial sense for the top ten English clubs to form their own breakaway league (possibly including Glasgow Rangers and Celtic) and to negotiate their own television contracts. However, it is extremely doubtful whether supporters would wish to watch (either as paying supporters or pay-per-view subscribers) the fixtures of a contrived league abstracted from the game's historic roots.

From FC to plc to 'Rupert's Rovers'

When Martin Edwards agreed to sell his remaining shares in Manchester United plc as part of the £623.4 million BSkyB bid for the club, his decision appeared to be the final betrayal of a legend sacrificed upon the altar of a single family's financial ambition (Crick and Smith, 1989). It may originally have cost Martin Edwards's father Louis as little as between £31,000 and £41,000 to secure personal control of Manchester United Football Club. Subsequently, in the late 1970s, in the face of annual losses and because dividends were restricted to a maximum of 5 per cent of the face value of each share, the Edwards family decided to increase vastly the number of shares through a rights issue which would give every shareholder the right to buy 208 £1 shares for every share held. Since this exercise did not involve an injection of external investment, this appeared to be a device for increasing dividend payments, and was bitterly opposed by other shareholders, including Sir Matt Busby and the club secretary Les Olive. In advance of a rights issue which they were planning in 1977, the Edwards family bought up more shares to increase their shareholding to 74 per cent. The £600,000 invested in the share issue by Martin Edwards constituted 'the sum total of his "investment" in United, ever'. The Edwards family's total investment was only £740,000. Whereas only £312 was distributed to shareholders in 1978, following the rights issue, the board announced a dividend of £50,419 in 1979 which rose to £151,284 in 1981, the maximum allowable when the FA increased the maximum dividend to 15 per cent of share value (Conn, 1997:36).

When Manchester United was floated on the London stock-market in 1991 at the now paltry value of £47 million, Martin Edwards reduced his shareholding in the club to 28 per cent, realising £6 million from a sale of 1.7 million shares. Subsequently, further share sales have enabled the Edwards family to raise a total of £28 million, while generating an annual income of around £1 million from Martin Edwards' salary and the dividends from his remaining shareholding, valued at more than £80 million by the terms of the BSkyB bid. Edwards had been approached in mid-June 1998 by Mark Booth, the chief executive of BSkyB, with the view to the sale of Edwards' shares as part of a take-over bid. If the take-over proceeded, Edwards would join the board of BSkyB and Booth would in turn join United's board. As the BSkyB offer increased from 217.5 pence per share to its eventual 240 pence, valuing the club at £623.4 million, there was an absence of unanimity among the United board about how to respond to the offer.[4] Initially, the offer was opposed by several board members, including Greg Dyke, a non-executive United director and chairman of Pearson Television who ironically had negotiated TV contracts between ITV and the Football League in his earlier guise as head of ITV Sport. Dyke was reported to have argued that United had a strong future as an independent club, not least because of the onset of pay-per-view TV and because the OFT might win its restrictive practices court case against the Premier League, thereby allowing United to sell its television rights to the highest bidder (*Financial Times*, 16 September 1998). However, once the BSkyB offer reached 240 pence per share, Dyke found himself in a minority of one and therefore decided that further resistance was futile, although he decided to donate the £60,000 profit he would make on his own 80,000 shares (the difference between the BSkyB offer price and the share price beforehand) to Manchester-based charities.

Dyke was not alone. Philips and Drew Fund Management, the club's largest single institutional shareholder with more than 4 per cent of shares, stated that it was 'slightly disappointed' given that it felt United 'had a very strong future if it remained independent' (*Financial Times*, 10 September 1998). The revelation by Sam Chisholm, the former chief executive of BSkyB, that Rupert Murdoch had been prepared to pay double the £304 million it paid in 1992 to win the rights to screen live Premiership football (Conn, 1997:21) is indicative of the degree to which the fate of BSkyB had become inextricably linked, if not ultimately dependent, on its relationship with sports broadcasting, especially live coverage of English football. In 1992, BSkyB had paid £304 million for the exclusive rights to screen Premiership matches. By 1997, the commercial dividend had been a 333 per cent increase in BSkyB's turnover, transforming its profitability from 1992 losses of £47 million into profits of £62 million in 1993, £170 million in 1994, £237 million in 1995, £315 million in 1996 and £374 million in 1997 (Conn, 1997:21).

The commercial logic underpinning BSkyB's bid was self-evident. If it could acquire United for around only £200 million more than the value of the club's shares prior to its bid, BSkyB would have cheaply won control not only of the world's most profitable football club but also the club with the largest global fan base. If a European Super League was established or further reforms of existing UEFA competitions undertaken, BSkyB would be at the heart of the negotiations. At the same time, BSkyB would also ensure itself a prime position in the Premier League clubs' negotiation over pay-per-view TV and the next domestic TV contract beyond 2001. Under the existing television contract, the Premier League would allocate 50 per cent of the revenue between its 20 clubs. A further 25 per cent would be allocated on the basis of merit at the end of each season – the top club receiving the largest share. The remaining 25 per cent would be allocated on the basis of the number of appearances on television. In practice, this already meant that the largest clubs received the lion's share of the television revenue. However, if the Restrictive Practices Court was to rule that the Premier League had acted as an illegal cartel in its negotiation of TV contracts with BSkyB and terrestrial television channels, a BSkyB-owned United would then no longer have to share its revenue. It would be free to secure an even larger share of English football's TV income by exploiting potential demand for pay-per-view from United's global fan base.

Ownership and control of Manchester United would provide BSkyB both with an insurance policy against the uncertainties surrounding the future development of broadcasting in Europe and a means to expand demand for subscriptions to its channels world-wide. BSkyB had been profitable with its domestic subscription confined to less than 20 per cent of the population. It was the desire for a greater share of television revenue which drove the creation of the Premier League. It would be ironic, but perhaps in some sense poetic justice, if the League in turn was undone by the same base commercial greed. Furthermore, if the competition authorities decided that there were sufficient anti-competitive grounds for blocking the BSkyB bid, rather than simply laying down some preconditions for the bid's approval, Murdoch could point to the precedents established in other countries for the media ownership of major sports clubs. For example, Murdoch's own News Corporation had previously bought the Los Angeles Dodgers baseball team, together with shares in the New York Knicks basketball and New York Rangers ice hockey teams, along with further options on the Los Angeles Lakers basketball and Kings ice hockey team. In the field of football, the French pay-per-view broadcaster, Canal Plus, had bought into Paris St Germain while in Italy, Silvio Berlusconi, the media mogul, owns AC Milan (Harverson, 1998b). In any event, it appeared that the BSkyB bid might have seriously undervalued Manchester United, especially in the context of the OFT court case. Prior to the BSkyB bid, Warburg Dillon Reed had valued the club at £780 million, or 300 pence a share, 25 per cent more than BSkyB's £623.4 million, or 240-pence-per-share offer (*Financial Times*, 23 October 1998). David Brooks, an analyst at Nomura, stated that, 'My gut feeling is that I can't believe other companies will allow BSkyB just to walk off with the crown jewels' (*The Guardian*, 10 September 1998).[5] But despite media reports that Salomon Smith Barney, an American investment bank, had contacted HSBC, United's financial advisers, with a view to making a rival bid (*Financial Times*, 14 September 1998), it soon became apparent that such a bid was unlikely, at least until the government's position on competition rules had been clarified.

The Sky's the limit: a TV cuckoo in football's nest

On 7 September 1998, Peter Mandelson, the (then) Secretary of State for Trade and Industry, announced that the BSkyB bid would face scrutiny by the director general of the OFT to establish whether the bid should be referred to the Monopolies and Mergers Commission (MMC). In the immediate aftermath of Mandelson's decision, and in the face of opinion surveys showing 95 per cent opposition among United supporters to the BSkyB bid, Mark Booth and Martin Edwards signed an open letter to supporters in which they claimed that BSkyB understood that United was not just another business but 'part of the cultural fabric of Manchester and the nation' and, therefore, the existing management would be left to run the club (*The Times*, 10 September 1998).[6]

Edwards asked supporters, 'Before you string me up, give things a chance . . . I am not about to do anything that destroys the health and tradition of this club. If I do then I deserve to be strung up.' Furthermore, Edwards reminded supporters that the new owners were 'an £8 billion company and that gives us the kind of money we never had' (*The Times*, 10 September 1998). The implication was that BSkyB would buy big to maintain United's success on the field, but supporters remained sceptical of Murdoch's intentions. The spectre of players being sold to alleviate potential cashflow problems in other parts of the Murdoch empire loomed large. For his part, Booth insisted that BSkyB were 'not going to move the ground, pick the team, change the name, hike the ticket prices or change the club in any way that is not consistent with its traditions'. To supporters, this spin on events appeared to overlook the fact that Booth was to join the United board and Edwards join the BSkyB board – hardly a case of the corporate *status quo ante*.

Government ministers and opposition politicians were united in their hostility to the announcement of the bid. Tony Banks, the Minister for Sport, reacted to the BSkyB bid by contending that it could not 'be treated as if it were just a normal take-over of one publicly quoted company by another'. If the biggest football club in England was bought by the biggest broadcaster of live football, 'then clearly the implications for commercial policy are profound'. In Banks's judgement, there were 'concerns held across government about the dangers inherent in allowing football clubs to be bought up as commercial commodities'. His only surprise was that such a bid had not happened earlier given that 'as soon as football clubs become plcs, they find themselves subject to predatory take-overs'. However, football clubs could not 'be treated like products in a marketplace as allegiances to them are based on cultural affinities' (*Financial Times*, 26 October 1998). If clubs were allowed to own more than one team, Banks thought there was a danger that, when those teams met in competition, a commercial view might dictate which team won the match. The vice-chairman of the Conservative Party's parliamentary media committee, Roger Gale, asserted that it was not 'the place of media empires to own football clubs. What it means is that Murdoch will have a vote at the Premiership negotiating table. It is a way of buying a vote around that table.' This view was shared by a spokesman for the OFT who stated that 'it is possible there could be competition implications, but there might be a restrictive agreement, in which case we would challenge it' (*The Times*, 7 September 1998).

David Mellor, chairman of the government's Football Task Force (but in this instance responding personally), contended that it would be 'an act of cardinal folly' for the Manchester United board to accept a take-over by Rupert Murdoch. For Mellor, the stark choice facing the club was between being 'a pawn in a global media power play by Rupert Murdoch, who hardly knows where Manchester is', or still being 'part of the great city of Manchester – a football club where a clear bond of trust continues to exist between its supporters and the club' (*The Guardian*, 9 September 1998). Furthermore, Mellor suggested that the take-over made a more compelling case for a special regulator for football, an issue which he claimed the Football Task Force would address in the coming months. Reaction to the bid from within English football was equally hostile. For Gordon Taylor, the general secretary of the Professional Footballers' Association (PFA), Rupert Murdoch constituted nothing less than 'a TV cuckoo in football's nest' (*The Guardian*, 16 September 1998). Addressing the 1998 Trades Union Congress, Taylor argued that the government should introduce new and strict competition laws to prevent television moguls from transforming Manchester United into 'Rupert's Rovers', thereby protecting the integrity of English sport from business monopolies. Taylor warned that 'football is the people's game, but the umbilical cord between fans and clubs is being brutally severed'. Indeed, he added that the Labour Government should remember its roots and cease to placate big business interests. Sport could only survive in a competitive environment whereas, Taylor contended, business always sought to remove competition and therefore 'the two worlds do not fit easily together' (*The Guardian*, 16 September 1998).

Resistance to the BSkyB bid among United supporters was led by the Independent Manchester United Supporters Association (IMUSA), (an organisation in which the author must declare an interest, being an IMUSA member), and by the quickly formed Shareholders United Against Murdoch (SUAM). IMUSA organised a rally at Manchester's Bridgewater Hall which was paid for by a donation of £10,000 from Roger Taylor, the drummer from the rock group Queen. Unfortunately, although this meeting did provide an important rallying point for those seeking to oppose the bid, the rally itself failed to fill the hall's capacity, a fact not lost on David Mellor who subsequently used his Radio Five 6.06 phone-in show to question the opposition of United supporters to the bid.[7] SUAM was established by several United supporters who also happen to be influential people in journalism (Michael Crick, SUAM's founder, a reporter on the BBC's *Newsnight* programme and the author of many books, including biographies of Michael Heseltine, Jeffrey Archer and a seminal work on the history of Manchester United); business (Richard Hytner, former chief executive of the Henley Centre for Forecasting and now head of the Publicis advertising group); and academia (Jonathan Michie, Sainsbury Professor of Management at Birkbeck College, University of London). The fact that, unlike many other supporters' organisations, SUAM had been founded by people with knowledge of the operations of the media and the City of London, meant that it was able to fight a very effective guerrilla campaign against the BSkyB take-over. One of its first actions was to draw the attention of the Take-over Panel to the fact that the offer document sent to United shareholders was arguably misleading because it failed to inform them that they had the right to reject BSkyB's offer (*Financial Times*, 24 October 1998). Although SUAM failed to persuade the Panel that misleading information had been circulated to shareholders, it was able to raise sufficient funding to be able to send its own mailing to the club's 30,000 shareholders and also circulate a document to institutional shareholders which contended that the BSkyB bid had undervalued United (SUAM,1998).

The triumph of the patron-client model of corporate governance over the stakeholder model was vividly demonstrated at the November 1998 annual Manchester United plc shareholders' meeting. SUAM members Michael Crick and Jonathan Michie led a sustained attack by shareholders for more than two hours against the board's decision to recommend acceptance of the BSkyB offer. Michie asserted that 'it is in the best interests of this company and this football team for the club to remain independent', but this contention was rejected by both Martin Edwards and Sir Roland Smith, the club's chairman. They claimed that the club's prospects would be enhanced if it became part of the BSkyB group because it would have access to the latter's capital and media expertise. Indeed, Smith perversely argued that, 'You know what we're proposing is a good thing because everybody is opposed to it', to which the response from one shareholder was, 'Bollocks' (*Financial Times*, 20 November 1998).

New Labour's footballing inheritance

For most of the 1980s, the culture of English football remained refreshingly untouched by the values of the share-owning, property-owning enterprise culture, even if the built environment surrounding many grounds was being transformed (often not for the better) by the wider social and economic restructuring inflicted upon England by Thatcherism. Without doubt, 'In the Thatcherite lists of "them and us", football was firmly "them".' (Conn, 1997:111.) Although she 'handbagged' many other English institutions during the 1980s, Margaret Thatcher was simply not interested in football. The plurality, diversity and strength of local English identities which football demonstrated could play no part in, and indeed contradicted, the certainty of Thatcher's own conception of British national identity.

If Conservative politics affected football culture, then it was through the medium of the Thatcher Government's law and order agenda. Conservative politicians, including Luton Town's former chairman, David Evans, used football opportunistically to promote an agenda that included increased police powers of surveillance.[8] The 1989 Football Spectators Bill proposed the introduction of identity cards and a Football Licensing Authority to be headed by a chief executive, John de Quidt, a civil servant experienced in the art of putting down prison riots (Conn, 1997:113). The national identity card scheme was never implemented, having been rendered redundant by the onset of all-seater stadia, closed-circuit television inside grounds and individual club membership schemes. If the terraces had provided a welcome but often dangerous refuge from Thatcherite reforms during the 1980s, the same cannot be said for the increasingly all-seater stadia of the 1990s. Supporters of English Premier League teams have found themselves increasingly regarded by their clubs, not as supporters *per se* but as consumers, investors and shareholders. Supporters of First Division but especially Second and Third Division teams have found their clubs increasingly financially marginalised and, in many cases, their very survival threatened.

Unlike its Conservative predecessors, New Labour had chosen not to adopt such a passive attitude towards the English game. Instead it has seen political advantage in associating itself with the upper echelons of the professional game that had enjoyed a renaissance in popular culture during the early 1990s. During the 1997 General Election campaign, Tony Blair, a self-confessed Newcastle United supporter, enjoyed photo-opportunities with Alex Ferguson and Kevin Keegan. Building on the *Football Charter* drawn up in Opposition, New Labour's General Election manifesto promised to bring an end to the policy of selling off playing fields (to which the lamentable Test match performance of the England cricket team will serve as a lasting testament to a lost generation) and to 'provide full backing to the bid to host the 2006 football World Cup in England' (Labour Party, 1997:30). However, any expectation among supporters that the change of government would usher in a radically different approach to the governance of English football was soon dissipated. The newly instituted Football Task Force was given a wide-ranging remit to examine issues (racism, access for the disabled, supporter involvement in the running of their clubs, and ticket and merchandise pricing) but no powers other than moral suasion to raise its status beyond that of 'the political equivalent of the mid-field player who does a lot of unselfish, off-the-ball running – a lot of energy expended but ultimately a minimal contribution to the game's overall shape and direction' (Lee, 1997b:47).

The potential political embarrassment which the BSkyB bid, and the Government's reaction to it, might cause were vividly illustrated when a House of Commons Early Day motion signed by 39 Labour MPs, four Conservative and three Liberal Democrats, and stating that the bid would 'create an unacceptable situation', was signed by Gerry Sutcliffe and Ian Pearson, parliamentary private secretaries to Treasury ministers, thereby breaking with customary parliamentary convention (*Financial Times*, 26 October 1998). Among the other signatories of the motion were Joe Ashton, the chairman of the parliamentary football committee and Rhodri Morgan, the chairman of the House of Commons Public Administration select committee. The motion also stated that allowing BSkyB to take-over United would 'create an unacceptable situation' where BSkyB would own Europe's largest football club and be the largest purchaser of televised football, a move 'which would not be in the best public interest of fans, clubs or television viewers and sport in general' (*Financial Times*, 23 October 1998). Claiming that their motion was 'not a protest against Mr Murdoch, but reveals widely felt concerns about a concentration of ownership', the MPs urged Peter Mandelson not only to establish an inquiry into the funding of football by television but also to refer the bid to the MMC without waiting for the verdict of the OFT's investigation. In a similar vein, the Foreign Office minister and Greater Manchester MP, Tony Lloyd, had earlier expressed his own concern that a BSkyB-controlled and Murdoch-backed Manchester United might 'get a degree of control which is unhealthy for the ordinary supporter'. (*Financial Times*, 8 September 1998.)

The BSkyB bid also confronted Peter Mandelson, the Secretary of State for Trade and Industry, with a potential source of huge personal and political embarrassment. His alleged friendship with Elizabeth Murdoch, Rupert Murdoch's daughter and managing director of Sky Networks, had been extensively documented prior to the bid. Sky Networks had been a major investor in the troubled Millennium Dome project. A web of intrigue had surrounded the relationship between New Labour and the Murdoch media empire since July 1995 when Tony Blair had flown to Australia to meet Murdoch in person. Following that meeting, the Murdoch press had turned against and away from the Major Government towards active support for Tony Blair. A vivid example of the lengths which the government would go to cultivate its media contacts was provided on 17 July 1998 when Gordon Brown flew all the way to Sun Valley, Idaho, just to give a speech to a News International Conference. Reassuring his corporate audience of New Labour's good intentions towards the corporate world, Brown began by contending that 'successful economies in a global marketplace will need more competition, more entrepreneur-ship, more flexibility to adapt. Countries that do not have this are already suffering lost markets, stagnation and economic decline.' Brown sought to define a 'new politics of opportunity and responsibility, characterised by the maximisation of economic stability, the promotion of opportunity for all and the reduction of welfare dependency'. The old mantras of 'Keynesian fine-tuning and rigid application of fixed monetary targets', which had been designed for 'sheltered national economies' had 'now broken down in our modern, liberalised and global capital markets' (Brown, 1998).

At an international level, Brown's speech was in keeping with a broader trend in politics which has seen politicians opportunistically seize upon globalisation as an alibi for inaction, in economic and industrial policy terms, on the grounds that the state is powerless in the face of increasingly integrated global markets and their most important manifestation – the multi-national corporations (Weiss, 1998).[9] Indeed, from May 1995, the OECD member states had attempted to negotiate a Multilateral Agreement on Investment (MAI) which, if its completion had not been scuppered by the sudden and unexpected withdrawal of the French Government in October 1998, would have led to a new regime for investment under which the capacity of national governments to regulate corporations would have been dramatically reduced and, by the same token, corporations' responsibilities, in the field of labour and environmental standards in particular, would have been dramatically reduced.[10] At the domestic level, Brown's speech coincided with the publication of the results of the government's year-long Comprehensive Spending Review which, in the case of the DTI, had reaffirmed the degree to which New Labour had largely accepted rather than fundamentally challenged the political economy of its Conservative predecessors. The government's subsequent White Paper on Competitiveness, *Our Competitive Future: Building the Knowledge-driven Economy*, did claim to have defined a 'new model for public policy' in which the role of the government's industrial policy would be 'making markets work better' through the promotion of innovation and entrepreneurship (DTI, 1998:13). In reality, in terms of corporate governance, this was little more than a restatement of the agenda most coherently spelt out in the January 1988 White Paper, *DTI – the Department for Enterprise* (DTI, 1988) which had based the Thatcher Government's industrial policy on open markets and the enterprise of individual entrepreneurial initiative (Lee, 1998a).[11] The government's (1998) White Paper did draw attention to the 1998 Competition Act which 'outlaws cartels and the abuse of a dominant market position'. The government also stated that it had 'no plans at present to change the merger regime' but would publish a consultation paper in early 1999 on the case for reform (DTI, 1998:51).

The problem is that there may be a conflict between the desire to promote competition and innovation by new market entrants, which could justify ending the Premier League's 'cartel', and the likelihood that ending the 'cartel' might place certain clubs, not least Manchester United, in a position where, even if it did not occupy a 'dominant market position', it would nevertheless have the autonomy to generate a disproportionate share of football's income while still operating within the collective structure of a football league system – both domestic and European. Before his resignation, Mandelson had argued that competition policy should be taken out of politicians' hands, in a manner similar to the removal of operational control over monetary policy to the unelected Monetary Policy Committee. At the same time, although a new 'Combined Code', based on the report from the Hampel Committee on Corporate Governance, had been appended to the Listing Rules of the London Stock Exchange from 31 December 1998 (Clarke, Conyon and Peck, 1998), the Code had done little to redress the imbalance in corporate governance between the rights and representation of the interests of major individual and institutional shareholders, and those of smaller shareholders, whose individual shareholding may be insignificant but whose collective shareholding (as in the case of Manchester United) might be significant.

In his evidence to the House of Commons Trade and Industry Select Committee on the 4 November, when questioned about his stance towards the concentration of media power, such as that generated by the BSkyB bid, Mandelson stated that he was satisfied that the bid did raise competition issues, notably 'the possible unfair advantage that BSkyB would be able to obtain through ownership of Manchester United Football Club over other broadcasters', although he acknowledged that the director general of the MMC had also stated that there were other public interest concerns legitimately raised by the bid. Mandelson did not take the opportunity to indicate whether he recognised these concerns. Instead, he stated that he was satisfied the new competition regime established by the government, soon to be codified in the 1998 Competition Act, coupled with existing specific broadcasting legislation, provided 'sufficient control in this area'. Furthermore, he did not think that 'there would be justification for different prohibitions for different industries' for 'to start picking and choosing and applying different sorts of legislation provision to different industries and different markets will first of all be very difficult to carry out but also will get you into all sorts of difficulties and complications from which it will not be easy to extract yourself' (TIC, 1998:Q.43–46).

The unique nature of the BSkyB bid, and the problems it posed for the competition authorities in the UK, was demonstrated when, in an unprecedented move, the MMC published the range of issues which it would be examining. The MMC asserted that it had taken this step in accordance with the government's open government policy 'in order to allow others to make representations to the commission' before the submission of its report to the Department of Trade and Industry on 12 March 1999 (*The Guardian*, 10 December 1998). The reaction from the club to this move by the MMC was to dismiss its significance by suggesting that the club had already addressed many of the salient issues and none should prevent the take-over. In a similar vein, BSkyB stated that it had 'clear and convincing responses' to all the issues raised by the MMC. However, Michael Crick, on behalf of SUAM, noted that the MMC appeared 'to be taking a very wide interpretation of what public interest means' (*Financial Times*, 10 December 1998).

English football: a team game?

English football's governing associations are in trouble. The outcome of the OFT's case against the Premier League currently being heard in the restrictive practices court could be of equal significance to the future of English professional football as the government's blocking of the BSkyB bid. Having encouraged clubs to break away from the Football League to create the Premier League in 1991, the Premier League has been faced with the genuine possibility that, should the OFT case be upheld, England's élite clubs might themselves soon choose to break away from the Premier League to participate in alternative competitions, such as the putative European Super League. The Premier League has therefore mounted a vigorous defence against the OFT. Prior to the start of the court case, it pledged that live coverage of Premier League football would be 'platform universal', i.e. available on terrestrial television, as well as other television media, from 2001, if it was allowed to negotiate the next contract with the broadcasters (*Financial Times*, 23 December 1998). Mike Lee, the Premier League's spokesman, has argued that, '[Collective bargaining] is the product of a democratic agreement' since the 20 clubs sell their television rights collectively because that is what they want (*The Independent*, 12 January 1998). The Premier League has asserted that it is only the game's governing body which takes into account all aspects of the game, not least the need to schedule fixtures in different competitions and to accommodate the interest of all the League's clubs. In practice, the League's real concern is that one exercise in the narrow pursuit of financial self-interest is in danger of being supplanted by another narrower project.

The OFT's rival contention is that the current arrangements result in the screening of only 60 live matches per season out of a total of 380 Premier League fixtures, and therefore supporters are denied the chance to see their clubs on television on a more regular basis, while other broadcasters are being prevented from providing that service to those supporters. Furthermore, the OFT does not believe that the removal of the arrangements would change the role of the Premier League significantly, create chaos or deny clubs their current financial and amenity benefits. Most importantly, the OFT does not believe that 'the redistributive arrangements provided for by the current agreements are the only means of securing such claimed benefits' (OFT, 1999). It argues that there could be a very different redistributive settlement, irrespective of whether the Premier League's television contracts are negotiated collectively or individually, if the clubs were to recognise their obligations to their brethren in the Football League and beyond.

Among those who have supported the Premier League's defence are the Football Task Force. In its most recent report, the Task Force has contended that between 1997 and 2001 the Premier League will be spending £50 million or around 5 per cent of its income outside the Premier League. However, this transfer of revenue is largely dependent on the level of transfers from the Football League to the Premier League – currently a diminishing asset because of the perception of better value from money from abroad, especially post-Bosman. The Task Force wishes to see an equivalent sum invested in 'grass-roots facilities and projects' as opposed to the Football League, noting that one unidentified city council in the north-west has a £2.8 million backlog in maintenance at its 38 sports sites. It is not just the grass roots but the actual subsoil of English football which has been allowed to deteriorate (Conn, 1997:254-279). The sale of an estimated 5,000 playing fields and the often squalid condition of the remainder is in part testament to the recent priorities of national government, local authorities and schools when confronted with the constraints of public spending and the national curriculum. It also reflects the FA's historical reliance upon local authorities for the provision of pitches to satisfy the requirements of its 43,000 amateur clubs. What the Task Force has highlighted is a long-standing shortfall in capital investment in the infrastructure of the amateur game in England which is unlikely to be remedied either by the terms of the Comprehensive Spending Review (CSR) for the Standard Spending Assessments of English local authorities or by the maintenance of the 16.66 per cent share of National Lottery funding for sport (DCMS) – given the many other and higher priorities for funding from these two revenue sources (Lee, 1998b; 1998c). Many struggling English amateur clubs will have seen a certain irony in the fact that the alleged loan of £3.2 million which led to the resignation of both the chairman and chief executive of the FA was intended for investment in the grass roots of Welsh football.

The Task Force has also called for more community schemes which mobilise football to tackle social exclusion for, at present, it claims players' contractual obligations to the community are often 'more honoured in the breach than the observance' (*The Independent*, 12 January 1999). This report has vividly demonstrated the limitations of the Task Force's role in the governance of football. It has resorted to exhortation because moral suasion is its only weapon against the Premier League clubs. In a world of public limited companies and football club subsidiaries, it has no other leverage. At the same time, the strident tone of the criticisms of professional footballers by the Task Force's chairman and his downplaying of the significance of the community schemes run by the PFA, led to the resignation from the Task Force of Gordon Taylor, the PFA's general secretary. Taylor has spoken of David Mellor's 'vindictiveness towards players' and his failure to recognise the £500,000 annual contribution by the PFA to its Football Club and Community Programme (*The Guardian*, 9 January 1999). Coupled with the resignation of Graham Kelly and Keith Wiseman from the FA, this row demonstrates the extent to which English football is now lacking authoritative leadership at precisely the time when its structures are confronted by some of their most major challenges. Having attempted on three previous occasions during the past decade to streamline its procedures, and having been obstructed by its 91-member Council or its shareholders, the FA will soon attempt to launch its own modernisation for the fourth time.

The Third Way or Third Division for football's governance?

English football urgently needs a more effective process of governance. However, given its passive stance towards take-overs and consolidation in the electricity generation and water industries (e.g. the PowerGen take-over of East Midlands Electricity and the Enron take-over of Wessex Water) and its guarded and diluted proposals for addressing public concern about the performance of the privatised railways and other utilities, the government has demonstrated that it does not have the stomach for stronger regulation. Recent attempts to define the Third Way have confirmed the marginalisation of the concept of stakeholding in the government's thinking (Blair, 1998; Giddens, 1998). However, the most important reason why the Blair Government is unlikely to intervene to challenge the privileged role of big business in an increasingly corporate-driven future for English professional football is that it would mean challenging the privileged role of big business in the whole New Labour project, not least the rebranding of British national identity.

When New Labour fashioned the Department for Culture, Media and Sport (DCMS) from the old Department of National Heritage, the Culture Secretary Chris Smith described it as 'a department of the future' which would enable the British people to discover 'a new sense of our culture and our identity' (DCMS, 1997a). Indeed, Smith has subsequently suggested that cultural activity is a key to a new sense of identity for the British people 'of who and what we are [and] to set a sense of direction for our society which would otherwise be impossible'. Indeed, the redefinition of British identity will enable the British people to be reconciled with Economic and Monetary Union and devolution (Smith, 1998:22–23). The creation of the DCMS has been part of the rebranding of Britain, a project encapsulated in Mark Leonard's pamphlet, *Britain TM*, which portrays Britain as a corporate trademark in urgent need of modernisation. Thus British national identity, or rather UK plc (for national identity is equated with the corporate identity of the multinational) is to be 'rebranded' to reflect Britain's, or rather London's, renaissance (for Britain is in reality the metropolis, or more specifically its dynamic cultural, media-based and financial service industries) as the coolest capital in the world (Leonard, 1997:12). Chris Smith has himself referred to how, 'The recent Demos work is frightening in the evidence it amasses, about the way in which as a nation we look backwards – and the impact this has on others' view of us, as well as on our own view of ourselves' (DCMS, 1997b). In reality, far from being the heavyweight and scholarly tome Smith implies, *Britain TM* is nothing more than a mere wafer-thin, 75-page pamphlet from a metropolitan think-tank, Demos. The only frightening aspect of it is the arrogance with which it seeks to impose an inherently and unashamedly top-down project upon the nations and regions of Britain – an exercise subsequently repeated for the European Union (Leonard, 1998).

England plays no part in this rebranding exercise. At club level, English football reflects the expression of a diversity of local English identities rather than a singular British identity. At national level, as Euro '96 and the recent World Cup demonstrated, the England team provides an alternative focal point for English rather than British national identity. Neither manifestation of English football culture sits comfortably with the Blair Government's rebranding of Britain, especially at a time when devolution for other parts of the UK could fan the flames of English nationalism (Lee, 1999). Under New Labour, the DCMS, the department primarily responsible for the Government's contribution to the governance of English football, is preoccupied by a culture-led exercise in British rebranding. It has studiously avoided any references to England or English identity. Sport has become the Cinderella activity of the DCMS as demonstrated by the fact that, after 18 months in office, the government has yet to deliver its strategic vision for sport. Furthermore, funding for sport under the DCMS's Comprehensive Spending Review settlement is set to increase from a mere £49 million in 1998–99 to £52 million in 2001–2, an increase of only £6 million out of a total increase in DCMS spending of £290 million (DCMS,1998). Despite being essentially an English department, because it co-ordinates policies for England and its regions which have long been devolved to the Scottish, Welsh and

Northern Ireland Offices and which are now accountable to directly elected structures, the DCMS has confined the development of a distinctively English agenda to a commitment to tidy up the landscape of unelected quangos which administer sport (and culture too) in the England regions so as to create clearer financial accountability (Lee, 1998c). Consequently, the DCMS has adopted an essentially passive and reactive stance towards developments in English football, as its relaxed attitude towards the recent negotiations over the future ownership of Wembley has demonstrated.

Neither of the competition authorities nor BSkyB would have needed to have been involved in the future governance of English football, had either the FA and Football League (or those associations in tandem with the Thatcher and Major Governments) launched the fundamental reassessment of English football which the late Lord Taylor had called for in 1990. The vacuum which was left by their respective inaction and non-intervention has been filled by the Premier League and BSkyB. For their part, the football authorities are now belatedly showing signs of action, closing the stable door not only after the horse has bolted but after the stables themselves have been redeveloped into exclusive private apartments for a rich élite. The Premier League is vigorously defending the OFT case and pleading that it has acted in the general interest of its member clubs. It has, but its motives acted against the wider interest of English football as a whole. The Premier League is now in danger of being supplanted by a further exercise of corporate self-interest. Whatever the manifest shortcomings of the private associations which have governed English football in the past, one cannot escape the fact that government has a vital role to play in corporate governance because 'it is the only power in any land which can strike a balance between the conflicting wishes of competing interests' and is ultimately the creator of the framework within which these interests compete (Charkham, 1995:2). Thus, the fact that corporations now increasingly control football, and have managed and rebranded it as a commercial venture, is not a spontaneous act of nature which the state is powerless to prevent. The government's blocking of the BSkyB bid for Manchester United was a welcome demonstration of the state's continued power over such processes. It is to be hoped that the government's response to the final reports from the Football Task Force will build on this initial result.

Notes

[1] Commodification has been defined as 'the process by which more and more goods, services or human relationships become tradeable in a market and produced for profit'. (Abercrombie, 1996:110).

[2] Corporate governance has been defined as 'the mechanisms by which companies are controlled, directed and made accountable'. (Clarke, Conyon and Peck, 1998:22). The principal official reports on corporate governance have been delivered by Cadbury (1992), Greenbury (1995) and Hampel (1998). For a cross-national comparison of patterns of corporate governance, see Charkham (1995).

[3] Although under the current BSkyB deal, Premier League clubs receive £247,593 for each of their guaranteed minimum three live appearances per season on Sky, this sum is widely regarded by media analysts as derisory compared with the projections for income which United might derive from pay-per-view, especially if the club was free to negotiate its own television deal.

[4] Based on existing share prices at the time of the BSkyB bid, it was calculated that (at least notionally) BSkyB could have bought up to seven other Premier League clubs for its £623.4 million investment in Manchester United. These other clubs were Liverpool (then capitalised at £144 million), Newcastle United (£104 million), Aston Villa (£73 million), Tottenham Hotspur (£64 million), Leeds United, owned by Leeds Sporting (£50.6 million) and Charlton Athletic (£17.4 million). (*The Times*, 10 September 1998.)

[5] On the 21 September, BSkyB announced that it had irrevocable undertakings or owned a total 25.75 per cent of United shares (*The Times*, 22 September 1998). By the end of October, BSkyB had secured effective control over the club by virtue of its having received acceptances from shareholders representing 33.5 per cent of the shares, including irrevocable undertakings to accept the offer from United directors to augment the 11 per cent of shares it had already bought or was in the process of acquiring on the open market.

[6] The propaganda war to persuade supporters of the club's best intentions was soon initiated. At the first home game following the announcement of the BSkyB bid, the match programme carried the news that a £30 million redevelopment of Old Trafford was to take place to enable the capacity to be raised from its present 55,300 to 67,400. Work would begin on the addition of an extra tier of seating to the Scoreboard End of the ground in May 1999, to be followed by the addition of an extra tier at the Stretford End by August 2001. Supporters' attention was also drawn to the forthcoming £15 million investment in a new training complex at Carrington

and also a *Sunday Mirror* survey which showed that the club's admissions prices remained among the cheapest in the Premiership. United's season tickets were rated the seventh cheapest. (*United Review*, vol.60, no.4, 12 September 1998).

[7] When the Football Task Force had held one of a series of roadshows in Manchester, Mellor was reported to have cried off through ill-health from attending a meeting dominated by demands from supporters for the reintroduction of terracing, not least at Old Trafford. Fortunately, Mellor sustained a miraculous recovery to fulfil a speaking engagement the evening after the roadshow.

[8] In the aftermath of the Miners' Strike and the News International printworkers' dispute at Wapping, supporters found themselves increasingly subjected to new police tactics and powers developed to control pickets and urban rioters. For example, the tactic of turning back coach loads of pickets en route to working pits during the miners' strike was later deployed on several occasions to prevent supporters attending potentially explosive end-of-season fixtures.

[9] Hirst and Thompson have rejected the thesis that the contemporary world economy is more open and integrated than ever, pointing to the nature of the world economy between 1870 and 1914. Furthermore, because of it being the source of laws and regulations, they have asserted that the nation state has a vital role to play in the governance of markets at not only the national, but also the international, supranational and global levels. (Hirst and Thompson, 1996:192).

[10] For an analysis of the MAI negotiation and the Blair Government's policy towards it, see TIC (1998).

[11] For an analysis of the implications of the Comprehensive Spending Review for the DTI, see Lee (1998a).

References

Abercrombie, N. (1996). 'Cultural Values and Commodification: The Case of the Publishing Industry', in A. Godley and O. Westall (eds), *Business History and Business Culture*. Manchester: Manchester University Press.

Blair, T. (1998). *The Third Way: New Politics for the New Century*. London: Fabian Society.

Brown, G. (1998). 'Speech by the Chancellor of the Exchequer Gordon Brown to the News International Conference', *HM Treasury news release 117/98*. 17 July.

Cadbury, A. (1992). *Report of the Committee on the Financial Aspects of Corporate Governance*. London: Gee Publishing.

Charkham, J. (1995). *Keeping Good Company: A Study of Corporate Governance in Five Countries*. Oxford: Oxford University Press.

Child Poverty Action Group (1996). *Poverty: The Facts*. London: Child Poverty Action Group.

Clarke, R., Conyon, M. and Peck, S. (1998). 'Corporate Governance and Directors' Remuneration: Views from the Top', *Business Strategy Review*, Vol.9, No.4, pp. 21–30.

Conn, D. (1997). *The Football Business: Fair Game in the '90s?* Edinburgh: Mainstream Publishing.

Crick, M., and Smith, D. (1989). *Manchester United: The Betrayal of a Legend*. London: Pan Books.

DCMS (1997a). 'Chris Smith welcomes new name for his Department', *DCMS press release 178/97*. 14 July. London: Department for Culture, Media and Sport.

DCMS (1997b). 'Creative Futures: Culture and our Sense of Identity', *DCMS press release 50/97*. 19 September. London: Department for Culture, Media and Sport.

DCMS (1998), 'A New Approach to Investment in Culture', *DCMS press release*. 14 July. London: Department for Culture, Media and Sport.

Deloitte & Touche (1997). *Deloitte & Touche Annual Review of Football Finance*. Manchester: Deloitte & Touche.

Deloitte & Touche (1998). *Deloitte & Touche Annual Review of Football Finance*. Manchester: Deloitte & Touche.

DTI (1998). *Our Competitive Future: Building the Knowledge-driven Economy*. Cm.4176. London HMSO.

Fukayama, F. (1995). *Trust: The Social Virtues and the Creation of Prosperity*. London: Hamish Hamilton.

Giddens, A. (1998). *The Third Way: The Renewal of Social Democracy*. Cambridge: Polity Press.

Greenbury, R. (1995). *Directors' Remuneration: Report of a Study Group Chaired by Sir Richard Greenbury*. London: Gee Publishing.

Hampel, R. (1998). *Committee on Corporate Governance: Final Report*. London: Gee Publishing.

Harverson, P. (1998a). 'Logic of Manchester United's latest fan'. *Financial Times*, 7 September.

Harverson, P. (1998b). 'Fair share ruled out for football fans'. *Financial Times*, 12 December.

Hills, J. (1998). *Income and Wealth: The Latest Evidence*. York: Joseph Rowntree Foundation.

Hirst, P. and Thompson, G. (1996). *Globalization in Question: The International Economy and the Possibilities of Governance*. Oxford: Polity Press.

Home Office (1990). *The Hillsborough Stadium Disaster. Inquiry by the Rt. Hon Lord Justice Taylor: Final Report*. London HMSO.

Hutton, W. (1995). *The State We're In*. London: Jonathan Cape.

Hutton, W. (1997). *The State to Come*. London: Vintage.

Keasey, J., Thompson, S. and Wright, M. (1997). 'Introduction: The Corporate Governance Problem – Competing Diagnoses and Solutions', in K. Keasey, S. Thompson and M. Wright (eds), *Corporate Governance: Economic and Financial Issues*. Oxford: Oxford University Press.

Kelly, G., Kelly, M. and Gamble, A. (1997). *Stakeholder Capitalism*. London: Macmillan.

Labour Party (1997). *New Labour because Britain deserves better*. London: The Labour Party.

Lee, S. (1995). 'Imagining England', paper presented for a workshop on 'Englishness and Questions of National Identity' at the 1995 Political Studies Association Annual Conference, York University. 20 April.

Lee, S. (1996). 'A Corner of a Foreign Field: Football Violence and English National Identity', paper presented at the 'Fanatics! Football and Popular Culture in Europe' Conference. 12 June.

Lee, S. (1997a). 'Competitiveness and the Welfare State' in M. Mullard and S. Lee (eds), *The Politics of Social Policy in Europe*. Cheltenham: Edward Elgar.

Lee, S. (1997b). 'Grey Shirts to Grey Suits: The Political Economy of English Football in the 1990s', in A. Brown (ed.), *Fanatics: Power, Identity and Fandom in Football*. London: Routledge.

Lee, S. (1998a). 'Necessity as the Mother of Intervention. The Implications of the Comprehensive Spending Review for the Department of Trade and Industry', paper presented at 'The Third Way to Spend?' conference, Hull University. 11 November.

Lee, S. (1998b). 'Cool Britannia, Frozen England? The Implications of the Comprehensive Spending Review for the Department for Culture, Media and Sport', paper presented at 'The Third Way to Spend?' conference, Hull University. 11 November.

Lee, S. (1998c). 'English Questions Unanswered? The Implications of the Comprehensive Spending Review for England and the English Regions', paper presented at 'The Third Way to Spend?' conference, Hull University. 11 November.

Lee, S. (1999). 'The Competitive Disadvantage of England' in K. Cowling (ed.), *Industrial Policy in Europe*. London: Routledge.

Leonard, M. (1997). *Britain TM: Renewing our Identity*. London: Demos.

Leonard, M. (1998). *Making Europe Popular: The Search for European Identity*. London: Demos.

Major, J. (1992). *Trust the People: Keynote Speeches of the 1992 General Election Campaign*. London: Conservative Political Centre.

OFT (1999). 'Premier League Court Case Starts', *Office of Fair Trading press notice 1a/99*. 6 January.

Parekh, B. (1994). 'Discourses on National Identity', *Political Studies*, Vol. XLII, pp. 492–504.

Perryman, M. (1997). *Football United: New Labour, The Task Force and the Future of the Game*. London: The Fabian Society in association with When Saturday Comes.

Russell, D. (1997). *Football and the English: A Social History of Association Football in England 1863–1995*. Preston: Carnegie Publishing.

Smith, C. (1998). *Creative Britain*. London: Faber and Faber.

Sternberg, E. (1998). *Corporate Governance: Accountability in the Marketplace*. London: Institute of Economic Affairs.

SUAM (1998). United Shareholders warn City 'Bid Sells United Short', *Shareholders United Against Murdoch*. 20 October.

Szymanski, S. (1998). 'Why is Manchester United So Successful?', *Business Strategy Review*, Vol.9, No.4, pp. 47–54.

TIC (1998). *The Work of the Department of Trade and Industry. Oral evidence to the House of Commons Trade and Industry Select Committee, Session 1997–98. HC1138.* London HMSO.

TIC (1999). *Multilateral Agreement on Investment. Third Report from the House of Commons Trade and Industry Select Committee, Session 1998–99. HC10.* London HMSO.

Weiss, C. (1998). *The Myth of the Powerless State: Governing the Economy in a Global Age.* Oxford: Polity Press.

Willetts, D. (1996). *Blair's Gurus: An Examination of Labour's Rhetoric.* London: The Centre for Policy Studies.

5. Football and Broadcasting and the MMC Case

Jonathan Michie and Christine Oughton

In September 1998 British Sky Broadcasting Group made a formal offer to acquire Manchester United. The bid, which amounted to an attempt by Britain's dominant pay-TV sports broadcaster to control Britain's leading football club, rang warning bells amongst BSkyB's competitors and Manchester United's shareholders and fans. The former feared that it would consolidate BSkyB's already dominant position in the market for live football broadcasting and make it even more difficult for others to make inroads into the industry. The latter felt that Manchester United's interests would become subservient to BSkyB's broadcasting interests, as the club would become a bargaining and marketing tool for a broadcasting company intent on enhancing its dominant position in the pay-TV market. The Director General of Fair Trading agreed that both the fans and BSkyB's competitors were right to be worried and, on his advice, BSkyB's proposed acquisition of Manchester United was referred to the Monopolies and Mergers Commission (MMC) for investigation under the Fair Trading Act 1973.

The MMC was charged with the task of investigating the proposed acquisition and determining whether it might be expected to operate against the public interest. It is normal for the MMC to consider public interest concerns but unusual for the Office of Fair Trading (OFT) to *require* this in the referral. This unusual step no doubt reflected the unprecedented number of submissions received by the OFT, overwhelmingly opposed to the take-over. The MMC set up a panel of five experts drawn from the members of the commission, chaired by Dr Derek Morris, the overall chairman of the MMC. During the next four and a half months, the panel investigated the proposed acquisition taking evidence from over 350 parties.

On 12 March 1999, the MMC delivered its findings and report[1] to Stephen Byers, the Secretary of State for Trade and Industry who four weeks later, on 9 April 1999 announced his decision to block BSkyB's proposed acquisition of Manchester United based on a full acceptance of the findings of the MMC.[2] In his announcement to the Stock Exchange Mr Byers said:

> Having considered the [MMC] report, advice from the Director General of Fair Trading and also taking into account further representations which have been received, I have decided to accept in full the unanimous recommendations of the MMC . . . The MMC's findings are based mainly on competition grounds, where they concluded that the merger would adversely affect competition between broadcasters. But they also examined wider public interest issues, concluding that the merger would damage the quality of British football. I accept these findings.[3]

In this chapter we outline and assess the issues raised by the BSkyB/Manchester United case and discuss their implications for the future of British football. We start by considering the nature of the football industry. An appreciation of this, and of the peculiar 'brand loyalty' of the consumers (fans), is important to a proper understanding of the effect that the acquisition of football clubs by broadcasting companies would have on the public interest. We then analyse the anti-competitive effects that the attempted acquisition would have had on the broadcasting and media markets before going on to consider broader public interest concerns relating to the quality of British football.[4]

The nature of the football industry

The nature of the footballing industry, with its local and community involvement, and fan loyalty, creates public interest concerns and also makes the industry peculiarly vulnerable to anti-competitive behaviour. Before detailing the grounds on which the attempted acquisition of Manchester United by BSkyB would have acted against the public interest it is important to appreciate several things: firstly, the unique nature of the footballing industry, secondly the rather different notion of the 'firm' that is appropriate for an analysis of this industry than is the case when analysing most other industries, and thirdly, the peculiarities of this industry's customers – the football fans.

Regarding, first of all, the nature of the football industry, while it has become fashionable to refer to the range of stakeholders that a firm or industry has beyond its shareholders, the importance of these other stakeholders – and in particular the local communities – in the case of football is absolutely vital.[5] While anti-competitive practices should be opposed whatever the industry, the precise way in which such practices operate varies from industry to industry, and so an appreciation of the impact of these practices in the case of the acquisition of a football club by a media company is assisted when the nature of the footballing industry is understood.

Secondly, regarding the 'firms' involved in the industry, the importance of the football club to the local community – and conversely the importance of the local community as a key stakeholder in the football club – has been reflected in the fact that the firms that own and control football clubs have generally been dedicated to this task. There are of course football-related activities in addition to the operation of the actual football club, but this does not detract from the fact that the main line of business of the firm is not media or other interests but, rather, the football club. In addition, while wealthy individuals have often bought football clubs, these individuals have tended to be supporters of that club, and have not used the club to promote their own business operations to the disadvantage of other firms competing in whatever markets their own business operates.

Thirdly, as Hamil argues in chapter 1, the relation of the customer – in this case, football fans – to the product and hence to the company, is rather different from that which pertains to other industries. In most industries, if a firm's product is not sufficiently competitive in terms of price and other factors, consumers will be lost to rival firms. In the case of football, the customers tend not to switch allegiances so easily (either between clubs or sports). This creates a situation analogous to one of local monopoly discussed below. It is true that fans can continue to support the club and may be able to consume the product through pay-TV (current practice in the UK allows one to subscribe to BSkyB, for example who hold the exclusive rights to broadcasting Premiership matches live), rather than paying through the turnstile at the ground. But this is a rather limited form of competition, since it does not involve the consumer switching from one team to another, and in any case, even this limited degree of competition between outlets would have been eliminated entirely in the case of Manchester United if the attempted acquisition had been allowed to proceed.

The special nature of the football industry thus not only creates particular public interest concerns, it also influences the way in which specific restrictions on competition operate in this market.

The particular and peculiar nature of the football industry, and the concomitant necessity for regulatory intervention, has long been recognised. It led, for example, to the Football Association's Rule 34 aimed at preventing the commercial exploitation of clubs, and more recently to the establishment by the government of the Football Task Force.

The peculiar nature of the football industry can, finally, be illustrated with reference to one of the consequences that the attempted acquisition would have had which has not, as far as we are aware, been commented on to date in public discussion, namely that several thousand shareholders who have a keen and passionate interest in the future success of the company in which they have a stake (as owners as well as supporters) would have been forced by law, against their will, to part with their shares. This is a rather dramatic reversal of the whole impetus of government policy over several years now, across both Conservative and Labour Governments, to encourage wider share ownership. Indeed, one of the main arguments used in favour of floating Manchester United Football Club as a plc was precisely to encourage wider share ownership. BSkyB made clear that their aim was to acquire the 90 per cent of shares which would have allowed them, by force of law, to require all remaining shareholders – which in the case of Manchester United plc consists of several thousand fans – to then part with their shares in their club. As one shareholder put it at the November 1998 Manchester United plc AGM, his share certificate is displayed proudly on his wall at home; if the acquisition had proceeded he would not have replaced it with a share certificate in BSkyB.[6]

Anti-competitive threats and restrictions on competition

BSkyB's bid raised three separate areas of concern regarding anti-competitive threats and restrictions on competition.

The market for watching Manchester United

There is a large market for watching Manchester United. This market is part of the wider market for watching football, which in turn is part of the general market for watching sport, itself a part of the broader market for entertainment. While there are therefore related and segmented markets, there is no doubt that there is a distinct market for watching Manchester United, for which a match between, say, Coventry and Wimbledon (two other Premiership clubs) is not a close substitute. There are two outlets for this market for watching Manchester United – either attending the ground (which is sold out to capacity – currently 55,300, although there are plans to expand this to 67,400 over the next two years) or else watching games live on television. The sales via these two outlets are organised and priced by separate companies, namely Manchester United and BSkyB respectively. Had the attempted acquisition been successful it would have created a monopoly provider for the two outlets. This would have resulted in at least two anti-competitive threats.

Firstly, the monopoly provider would be able to decide on price rises for the two outlets simultaneously. And although, as with any monopolist, there would be a point beyond which price rises became unprofitable, the monopoly provider would no longer be as concerned at the prospect of a price rise shifting some customers to the other outlet of watching the match on television.

Secondly, there would have been a wider danger of this restriction on competition leading to an abuse of the resulting market power, with behaviour detrimental to the interests of attending fans, such as altering the day of the week, and time of day, when matches are staged.[7] This is already done to some extent, in the interests of maximising viewing figures, but at least there is a strong countervailing force in that the interests of the attending fans are represented by a company (Manchester United) separate from the broadcaster.[8]

Anti-competitive practices and restrictions on competition

BSkyB has a huge financial interest in the televising of live Premiership football. The attempted acquisition would have weakened the competitive position of BSkyB's broadcasting rivals and would have strengthened BSkyB's already dominant position in pay-TV. The football club in question would have been owned by one of the broadcasting companies and would inevitably, therefore, have been used to distort the bargaining process, creating restrictions on competition.

If the attempted acquisition had proceeded then in any subsequent negotiations over the rights to televise football, there would have been a change in the balance between the TV company on the one hand and the football clubs on the other: BSkyB and its rival broadcasters would have been on one side of the bargaining table, and on the other side would have been the clubs, with BSkyB owning and representing the biggest and most powerful of these.[9]

The interest of all football clubs is to reach agreement with whichever broadcasting company offers the best deal. With the attempted acquisition, other broadcasting companies would have been put at a competitive disadvantage vis à vis BSkyB. Manchester United could have been used to push for an acceptance of the BSkyB offer. They might have done this even if the deal had not been in the interests of the football industry taken as a whole, provided it was in the interests of their parent company, BSkyB.

Manchester United's vote – and more importantly, its power and influence – would have been used to favour a deal with BSkyB rather than with BSkyB's competitors.[10]

In addition to representing a distortion of the competitive process to the detriment of other broadcasting companies, such a situation could also have posed an anti-competitive threat to other football clubs in the Premiership (and might in addition have had a deleterious effect on clubs outside the Premiership). If the merger had gone ahead and the restrictive practices court were to have brought an end to the current bargaining arrangements, then other broadcasters would have been at a competitive disadvantage vis à vis BSkyB in attempting to secure television rights, since the biggest and most popular club would already be owned by one of the other broadcasting companies. This would no doubt have provoked those other broadcasters to buy up top football clubs themselves (such as Newcastle, Arsenal, Liverpool and Chelsea). Whether the BBC would have been permitted to defend itself in this way is, however, rather doubtful. Neither would such a reaction be something to be welcomed; on the contrary, it would replicate many of the anti-competitive dangers described in this chapter, and would further divide the Premiership between the few top clubs on the one hand and the rest of the league on the other.

In addition, the position of other football clubs vis à vis BSkyB would have been affected by BSkyB's ownership of one of the clubs. Had the attempted acquisition been reported as Manchester United acquiring BSkyB then this would no doubt have raised objections from the other clubs, that the main broadcaster was to be owned by one of the clubs. BSkyB ('owned' under this scenario by Manchester United) would even have the right to move the dates and times of crucial games to be played by Manchester United's rivals in the title race. This is just one of the perhaps more minor ways in which vertical integration between a broadcaster and a football club could be abused, the more general implications of which we now turn to.

Abuse of vertical integration

The attempted acquisition would have decreased competition through the vertical integration of the supplier (Manchester United) and broadcaster of Manchester United football matches (BSkyB). In the event of Premier League clubs negotiating television rights individually, Manchester United would then be 'negotiating' with its owners – a most extreme case of exclusive trading. There is reason to be concerned that such vertical integration might even have operated against the interests of Manchester United itself. If BSkyB required the participation of Manchester United to launch a European Super League or any other such venture, there would have been a risk that the club might have been forced by their parent company to break away from the Premiership if that was what was required to accomplish the parent company's media goals.[11]

The vertical integration of BSkyB and Manchester United would have created three additional anti-competitive threats.

Firstly, in 2001 when the other broadcasters will have to compete with BSkyB over the rights to televise live Premiership matches, whether the clubs are still negotiating collectively or not (following the outcome of the case before the restrictive practices court), BSkyB would have been in a position to offer more than its rivals. If collective selling continues, a proportion of BSkyB's offer would have returned directly to the vertically integrated company while in the latter case all of the money would so return. In the case of collective selling, it is important to realise that the proportion of the money that would have returned to BSkyB, *via* its ownership of Manchester United, would have been greater than 5 per cent[12] as even under the present agreement, matches involving Manchester United are shown more often and attract more viewers than matches involving the average Premiership club. Indeed, in the 1997–98 season Manchester United appeared in 12 of the 60 matches broadcast live by BSkyB, and those matches accounted for 25 per cent of the total number of viewers for all 60 matches. If in the future any element of pay-per-view were to be introduced whereby revenues relate to audience figures, this proportion would, therefore, be greater than Manchester United's current share of 7.7 per cent (see chapter 6, Table 1).

Secondly, such vertical integration would risk the natural competitive processes in both industries – broadcasting and football – being distorted through cross subsidies. The likely direction would be for the broadcaster to cross-subsidise the football club, since the competitive advantage this would give the football club against the competitor football clubs would be expected to produce a subsequent pay-off to the broadcaster, as success on the field led to increased viewing figures, including through pay-TV.[13] Such cross-subsidy would lead to growing inequality and competitive imbalance; these effects would have been exacerbated if the BSkyB bid had proceeded and subsequently triggered other bids by broadcasters for Premier League clubs. There is also the possibility that the cross-subsidy danger could work the other way, with the broadcaster using profits from the football club to allow the broadcaster to undercut its rival TV companies for a time.[14]

Thirdly, the attempted acquisition would have represented a form of vertical foreclosure, impeding competition. The market for football broadcasting and packaging is increasingly a market for ideas in which diversity and creativity matter. Such a market is best served by being fragmented, allowing new entrants to innovate and compete. Vertical integration restricts such processes. Indeed, the attempted acquisition would have been a move against the trend, deliberately promoted by government, to encourage out-sourcing from broadcasters to other content providers.

Public interest concerns and the quality of football

The bid by BSkyB to acquire Manchester United represented a serious threat to the interests of football in Britain as a leisure activity as well as a business sector. It is important to maintain – and indeed strengthen – the current links between the various sectors of the football industry. The majority of Premiership players start their careers in the lower divisions, including in non-league football. The majority also end their careers there, either as players, managers, or in some other football-related occupation. There are therefore strong bonds within the game. These links are vital to the continued health of the sector, and in the long term even to the success of individual Premiership clubs despite the fact that over the short and medium term their profitability could be boosted by neglecting such links. It is important to stress two points here.

Firstly, rich individuals have bought clubs in the past, and clubs have also been floated as plcs. The attempted acquisition was quite different from all previous take-overs or flotations, in that it would have left the football club as only a small part of the parent company's operations and in addition, the main interest of that parent company (BSkyB) – namely broadcasting – would have been other than football, and yet at the same time there would have been a strong incentive to use the footballing part of the business in the interests of the parent company. The importance of the link between the football club and other footballing clubs in England would have become, at best, less important in the eyes of the relevant shareholders (namely shareholders in BSkyB).

Secondly, the attempted acquisition should not be considered in isolation. If this acquisition had been allowed to proceed it would likely have provoked subsequent take-overs of other major Premiership clubs. Such a process would have been inimical to the long-term development of the game as a whole. It could even have led towards a formal breakaway of such 'super clubs' from the rest.

There is also the local monopoly aspect of football clubs that needs to be taken into account. Football fans almost invariably support only one team and this support is translated commercially through attending matches and watching or listening to them through TV and radio, and through purchasing associated goods and services. Such consumers (fans) cannot easily switch their consumption to another football club. Support and loyalty creates a lock-in to one club. Thus, the owners of football clubs are, in effect, local monopoly suppliers of a unique product and this raises major regulatory concerns. There have been various factors preventing the abuse of this monopoly power in the past, including the FA's Rule 34. The attempted acquisition would have represented a serious risk that this monopoly power would be exploited against the public interest.

Some further discussion should perhaps be given regarding this point, that each club is, to a large extent, a local monopoly. As mentioned above, this is due to the nature of football support, with clubs relying on local support and this in turn resulting in fan loyalty to the local club. This monopoly power derives both from geographical locality and from the nature of fan loyalty.[15] In other sectors of the economy (such as the water industry) such local monopoly would be seen as sufficient reason for direct regulation. In the case of the football industry this has not, to date, proved necessary as there has been a general recognition both of the above facts and also, therefore, of the importance of not over-exploiting this monopoly power. There is serious reason to doubt whether BSkyB would have exhibited the same degree of self-restraint. There was thus serious reason to suspect that an abuse of monopoly power would have resulted. As indicated above, the attempted acquisition would have diminished what restraining influences there are at present, such as the choice between attendance at the ground on the one hand, and paying for a BSkyB subscription to watch Premiership games live on television on the other.

The MMC's findings

The MMC broadly accepted the points made above and recommended against the merger – a recommendation that the government accepted. In announcing his decision, the Secretary of State for Trade and Industry stated that:

> the proposed merger may be expected to reduce competition for the broadcasting rights to Premier League matches. This would lead to less choice for the Premier league and less scope for innovation in the broadcasting of Premier League football. The MMC also concluded that enhancing BSkyB's ability to secure rights to Premier League matches in the future would reduce competition in the market for sports premium television

channels. This would in turn feed through into reduced competition in the wider pay-TV market.[16]

On the question of wider public interest concerns the commission concluded that the merger would adversely affect football:

> We have concluded that the merger would reinforce the existing trend towards greater inequality of wealth between clubs, weakening the smaller ones. We have also concluded that the merger would give BSkyB additional influence over Premier League decisions relating to the organisation of football. On both counts the merger may be expected to have the adverse effect that the quality of English football would be damaged. This adverse effect would be more pronounced if the merger precipitated other mergers between broadcasters and Premier League clubs.[17]

The commission also concluded that there were no suitable or credible undertakings to address these concerns and that the only way of dealing with the full range of public interest concerns was therefore to prohibit the merger. It will be clear from our arguments above and from several of the other chapters in this book that, in our view, the findings of the MMC and the subsequent decision by the government were correct and in the best interests of football. This decision now needs to be built upon, firstly to prevent any other media company–football club mergers, and also to prevent greater inequality of wealth between clubs being caused by the uneven distribution of broadcasting revenues and the over-commercialisation of the game generally. It is to be hoped that the industry will instead be properly regulated.

Notes

[1] Monopolies and Mergers Commission (1999) *British Sky Broadcasting Group plc and Manchester United PLC: A report on the proposed merger.* Cm4305. TSO, London.

[2] Under current legislation, if the MMC (now the Competition Commission) recommends that a merger be blocked, the final decision rests with the Secretary of State for Trade and Industry who can overrule the MMC's recommendation and allow the

merger to go ahead. However, the power to overturn a 'blocking' recommendation by the MMC has rarely been exercised and Mr Byers had previously announced his intention to remove political discretion from these decisions.

[3] Department of Trade and Industry (1999).

[4] This chapter draws on our submission to the MMC (Michie *et al*, 1998) made jointly with Keith Cowling, Simon Deakin, Laurence Harris, Michael Kitson, J. Stan Metcalfe, Malcolm Sawyer, Ajit Singh and Roger Sugden, to whom we are therefore grateful. We are also grateful to Gordon Borrie, Sean Hamil, Alan Hughes and Geoffrey Whittington for advice on the drafting of the submission.

[5] In the 1992 Fulham FC *v* Cabra Estates plc case, the Court of Appeal expressed the view that the company (Fulham Football Club) was more than the sum of its 'members' (i.e. shareholders), and on these grounds blocked the sale of the football club's ground.

[6] Of course, several such shareholders might well have refused to surrender their shares even when required to by law; the point is that their share certificates would have simply become null and void, with the investment lost.

[7] This would be particularly detrimental to travelling fans who might have already made travel arrangements, including the purchase of aeroplane or rail tickets which may be wholly or in part non-refundable.

[8] The fact that Rupert Murdoch has a major interest in broadcasting live Premiership matches in Asia, through his Star TV company (which at present is still making a loss, with the offer of live Premiership matches being thought to be a potentially important mechanism for moving into profit, as with BSkyB's move from loss to profit after securing the exclusive rights to broadcasting live Premiership matches), raised particular concerns regarding the time of day at which such matches might be played, had BSkyB come to own Manchester United.

[9] Manchester United's £90 million turnover and £26 million profit are the biggest of any football club in the world.

[10] BBC, the ITV companies and so on.

[11] In 1998, Manchester United and the other clubs involved in discussions regarding a European Super League were threatened by the Premiership with expulsion. (Manchester United denied they were involved in any discussions, although this denial turned out to be false).

[12] Five per cent, since Manchester United is one of twenty clubs in the Premiership.

[13] Such cross-subsidy would have quite different implications from the case of money being put into a football club by, for example, a rich benefactor; in the case of the attempted acquisition of Manchester United by BSkyB a cross-subsidy of Manchester United might have been pursued not just to favour Manchester United against other football teams, but also because this would have then given BSkyB an advantage over

the other broadcasting companies.

[14] For example during a temporary, anti-competitive price war.

[15] Gerry Boon of accountants Deloitte & Touche has referred to the demand inelasticity from this brand loyalty: 'That means you can put the prices up but the demand doesn't change. They still buy the product.' (cited in D. Conn, *The Football Business*, Mainstream Publishing, 1997, p.155). Manchester United could probably continue to sell all tickets – even on an advanced season ticket basis – for all home games even if they increased prices by say 50 per cent, to around £30 a ticket. This would bring in more than £500,000 additional revenue per game, totalling more than £10 million a year, representing a massive increase in annual profits. Average admission price increases of over 30 per cent were introduced for the 1991–92 season (*Manchester United PLC Prospectus*, 1991).

[16] Department of Trade and Industry (1999). Press Release: *Stephen Byers Blocks BskyB/Manchester United merger*, p. 2. London: Department of Trade and Industry.

[17] Monopolies and Mergers Commission (1999) *British Sky Broadcasting Group plc and Manchester United PLC: A report on the proposed merger*, p. 50 Cm4305. London: TSO.

References

Conn, D. (1997). *The Football Business*. Edinburgh: Mainstream Publishing.

Department of Trade and Industry (1999). *Press Release: Stephen Byers Blocks BSkyB/Manchester United Merger*. London: Department of Trade and Industry.

Michie, J. *et al* (1998). *Evidence for the Monopolies and Mergers Commission on the Proposed Acquisition of Manchester United PLC by British Sky Broadcasting Group plc*. Mimeo, Birkbeck College, London (Summary published in MMC Report, 1999).

Monopolies and Mergers Commission (1999). *British Sky Broadcasting Group plc and Manchester United PLC: A report on the proposed merger*, Cm4305. London: TSO.

6. Revenue-sharing from Broadcasting Football:

The Need for League Balance

Jeanette Findlay, William L. Holahan, and Christine Oughton

The nature of the game

One of the features of football that distinguishes it from other industries is that the supply of the product – entertainment via football matches – depends on the prearranged agreement of all the clubs in a league to offer a series of joint products (matches) throughout the season as part of an organised competition for the league title. Hence, the game is as much a product of the league, as it is a product of the individual clubs. This raises a number of questions about the organisation and regulation of football and the role of football leagues. In this chapter we look at various aspects of the current system of league organisation and regulation and consider how changes to this system are likely to affect the future of the game. In particular, we focus on three aspects of live television broadcasting of league matches.

Firstly, we aim to shed light on the motives for revenue-sharing within football leagues. Revenue-sharing is commonplace in sports leagues and football is no exception. It is therefore important to understand why leading clubs find it in their interests to redistribute income to lagging clubs.

Secondly, we consider the likely effects of moving from a system of collective league bargaining and associated revenue-sharing to a system where each individual club sells the right to broadcast its matches individually. And finally, we consider the incentives for revenue-sharing in a system of vertical integration, where all aspects of a club's activities – from the pitch to the television screen – are owned and controlled by a broadcasting company.

Each of these possibilities takes on particular significance at this time as debates about the future organisation of football are taking place against the backdrop of the work of the Football Task Force, the case brought by the Office of Fair Trading (OFT) against the Premier League in the Restrictive Practices Court (regarding collective league bargaining over the sale of broadcasting rights) and the wake of the Monopolies and Mergers Commission (MMC) report on the attempted take-over of Manchester United by BSkyB.

It is our contention that these three aspects of football organisation and regulation are inextricably linked and therefore any attempt to reform the current system of regulation needs to deal simultaneously with rules regarding the sale of broadcasting rights, revenue-sharing and ownership structures. Our discussion of these issues is organised as follows. We start by looking at the motives for revenue-sharing, the current rules for revenue-sharing in the Premier League, and the impact of revenue-sharing and league balance on television-viewing audiences for live Premier League matches. Secondly, we focus on the system of collective league bargaining, the link between league bargaining and revenue-sharing, and the likely impact of the break-up of collective league bargaining on league balance and the future organisation and performance of the Premier League. Thirdly, we turn our attention to the possibility of vertical integration between broadcasting companies and football clubs and consider the implications for the future of the Premier League. Finally, we suggest a number of areas for regulatory reform to take the game forward in an era in which revenue streams from broadcasting are likely to continue to increase.

It's good to share: a balanced league is a prosperous league

Sports leagues have an inherent tendency to become dominated by a handful of leading clubs that compete for the league title with a tail of less successful clubs that make up the league. A key factor that determines the overall success of a league is *league balance* or *competitive balance*. If the gap between the dominant and lagging clubs in the league becomes too large then a significant number of league matches become too predictable and the absence of strong competition leads to unexciting games that attract few spectators. It is not difficult to see that in an unregulated league there is a tendency for imbalance to develop. The leading clubs have larger gates, charge more for individual seats, sell more merchandise and can command higher prices for the broadcasting rights to their matches. These revenues can be reinvested via the purchase of the best players which serves to maintain and enhance the leading clubs dominance. This inherent tendency to league imbalance results in one of the peculiar economic problems facing sports leagues (Neale, 1964, Fort and Quirk, 1995), namely that while in most industries competitors are not adversely affected, and are even likely to benefit if rivals perform badly or go to the wall, this is not so in sports leagues. In the case of football where the product supplied is the joint product of the clubs that compete in the league, a certain number of competitors is required for the league to function at all. The bankruptcy of competitor clubs in a football league can undermine the league. Likewise, if a group of clubs choose to leave the league it can seriously weaken the economic prospects of those that remain. In order for the league to prosper and attract maximum numbers of spectators and viewers there must be a certain number of clubs and a certain degree of competitive balance between those clubs.

The problem for sports leagues is that unbalanced competition can set up virtuous and vicious circles at the top and bottom of the league that undermine the league's existence in three inter-related ways. First, in an unbalanced league viewing figures, and hence the revenue from broadcast matches, are not maximised because many of the matches in the league lack competitive edge and become predictable and boring. Second, a number of clubs in the bottom half of the league face the risk of bankruptcy which in itself threatens the existence of the league. And, third, lack of league balance means that the league can become unstable and vulnerable to competition from rival leagues or to breakaway groups forming new 'super' leagues where (initially) balance may be more equal.

It is for these reasons that most sports leagues operate regulatory systems that aim to promote league balance by redistributing revenues from stronger to weaker teams. The important point to note is that redistribution can be advantageous even for the leading clubs because it enhances competitive balance, makes for more exciting matches and increases revenue streams – in effect the leading clubs get a smaller share of a bigger pot so their total income can increase.

In the early days of television broadcasting all income was divided equally between the 92 clubs that made up the Football League. However, as David Conn explains (chapter 2), as the money coming into football grew, the leading clubs successfully argued for a bigger share of the bigger pot. The move away from equality culminated in the formation of the Premier League in 1992. The Premier League now negotiates the sale of the rights to broadcast its matches independently of the rest of the Football League. As a result, the gap between the Premier League and the Football League has widened considerably in recent years (on which see chapter 4).

Within the Premier League a system of match and revenue-sharing operates. Under the current agreement each club is guaranteed to appear in at least three live match broadcasts and revenue is shared according to a 50:25:25 per cent rule, whereby 50 per cent of the revenue from broadcasting is divided equally, 25 per cent is allocated as a Facility Fee in payment for the number of screened matches in which each team appears and the remaining 25 per cent is allocated as a Merit Award reflecting the final positions of the clubs in the league at the end of the season. This system of revenue-sharing is far from equal, in contrast with systems elsewhere, for example in the US National Football League 95 per cent of revenues are shared equally. Nevertheless, it does ensure that clubs at the bottom of the league are guaranteed some revenue from Facility Fees and Merit Awards in addition to their equal share of half of the total revenue. Figures on the allocation of revenues from live broadcasting are shown in Table 1 for the 1997–98 season.

Table 1. The Distribution of Revenue from Live Broadcasting 1997–98 Season

	Merit Award	Facility Fee	Equal Share	Total Income	Share of Revenue
	£	£	£	£	%
Arsenal	3,250,000	3,030,984	3,040,278	9,321,262	7.8
Manchester Utd	3,087,500	3,030,984	3,040,278	9,158,762	7.7
Liverpool	2,925,000	2,525,820	3,040,278	8,491,098	7.1
Chelsea	2,762,500	2,273,238	3,040,278	8,076,016	6.8
Leeds Utd	2,600,000	1,768,074	3,040,278	7,408,352	6.2
Blackburn	2,437,500	1,515,492	3,040,278	6,993,270	5.9
Aston Villa	2,275,000	1,262,910	3,040,278	6,578,188	5.5
West Ham	2,112,500	1,262,910	3,040,278	6,415,688	5.4
Derby County	1,950,000	1,262,910	3,040,278	6,253,188	5.2
Leicester	1,787,500	1,010,328	3,040,278	5,838,106	4.9
Coventry	1,625,000	1,262,910	3,040,278	5,928,188	5.0
Southampton	1,462,500	1,010,328	3,040,278	5,513,106	4.6
Newcastle Utd	1,300,000	1,515,492	3,040,278	5,855,770	4.9
Tottenham	1,137,500	1,262,910	3,040,278	5,440,688	4.6
Wimbledon	975,000	1,010,328	3,040,278	5,025,606	4.2
Sheffield Wed.	812,500	757,746	3,040,278	4,610,524	3.9
Everton	650,000	1,515,492	3,040,278	5,205,770	4.4
Bolton	487,500	1,262,910	3,040,278	4,790,688	4.0
Barnsley	325,000	757,746	3,040,278	4,123,024	3.5
Crystal Palace	162,500	1,010,328	3,040,278	4,213,106	3.5

Source: the Premier League

It can be seen that in the 1997–98 season each club was guaranteed broadcasting revenue from live matches of at least £3.9 million, comprising an equal share of £3 million, a minimum payment for Facility Fees of £757,746 and a minimum merit award of £162,500. The revenue-sharing rules mean that Crystal Palace, who finished bottom of the league and appeared in only five live matches, still received live broadcasting revenue equal to £4.2 million.

While revenue-sharing within the Premier League is far from equal – the share of the leading club is more than twice that of the bottom club – the figures mask the fact that significant revenues are, in effect, redistributed from the leading to the lagging clubs. The scale of the redistribution can be gauged by analysing the viewing figures for different teams and comparing these with revenue shares. The entertainment value of football matches varies considerably according to a number of factors, including: the quality of the teams; the extent to which the teams are competitively balanced; the size of each club's fan base and the strength of fans' support or the degree of 'fan equity'. (See chapter 1).

What this means is that the units of entertainment, and hence the number of viewers, varies from match to match. A leading club such as Manchester United will supply more units of entertainment and therefore attract more viewers for each match that it is involved in than a club in the bottom half of the league, such as Southampton. Moreover, the units of entertainment supplied by Manchester United matches will vary according to the quality of the opposing team, the degree of competitive balance between the two protagonists and the particular circumstances of the league. A match between Manchester United and Arsenal will provide more units of entertainment than a match between Manchester United and Everton, partly because of the overall quality/ranking of the teams, and partly because of the degree of competitive balance between the teams and the unpredictability of the outcome. In addition, the same pairing between Manchester United and Arsenal will supply different units of entertainment, and therefore different viewing figures, according to the points difference between the two clubs at the time the match is played (competitive balance) and the importance of the match in determining the outcome of the league championship.

In short, the viewing figures for any particular match are strongly influenced by two key factors, the quality of the two clubs and the degree of competitive balance. An increase in either of these two factors will increase the entertainment value of a match and will therefore increase viewing figures and revenues. It is this positive impact of competitive balance on viewing figures and revenues that provides the economic incentive for leagues to adopt redistribution rules designed to enhance league balance and increase revenue streams.

It follows that maximising the units of entertainment generated by league matches requires an optimal mix of quality and competitive balance. The league can be balanced in a downward direction by reducing the quality of the leading clubs but *negative league balance* is clearly not desirable. Alternatively, *positive league balance* may be attained by balancing the league in an upward direction by ensuring that quality of play is preserved while simultaneously redistributing income from the leading to the lagging clubs. Clearly, to preserve and enhance quality of play *and* competitive balance, revenue re-distribution should ideally take place against a background of increasing revenue.

The emergence of new and expanding markets for live broadcasting and other means of dissemination have opened up the possibility of increased revenue streams. While this has the potential to bring great benefits to the game, raising the stakes means that regulation and redistribution are more necessary than ever. In particular, it should be noted that under the current distribution rules, increases in total revenue widen the absolute gap between the richest and poorest clubs. This is likely to enhance the quality of play of the leading clubs but reduce competitive balance. Similarly, any move to reduce the revenue stream to the Premier League would result in negative league balance as overall the league becomes poorer but the absolute gap between the richest and poorest clubs is reduced. The objective of leagues should be to promote both quality and *positive* competitive balance since it is the combination of both of these factors that maximises entertainment value and thus viewing revenues. When revenue streams are increasing, as they have been over the past decade, progressive redistribution rules are necessary to maintain and promote league balance.

Not enough redistribution

Information on the extent of redistribution in the Premier League can be derived by looking at the relationship between matches, units of entertainment (viewing figures) and revenue shares of leading and lagging clubs. In the 1997–98 season, Manchester United appeared in 12 out of 60 live TV Premier League matches, representing 20 per cent of matches and 10 per cent of appearances by Premier League clubs – given that two clubs appear per match. However, in terms of viewing audiences, matches involving Manchester United accounted for over 25 per cent of total TV viewers for all live matches. In contrast, at the other end of the league table Crystal Palace appeared in 8.3 per cent of live broadcasts but these matches accounted for only 7.1 per cent of viewers. The dominance of the top five Premier League clubs can be seen by looking at their share of matches and viewers. In the 1997–98 season the top five clubs appeared in 60 per cent of matches and these matches accounted for over 70 per cent of all viewers.

Comparison of these figures with the allocation of revenue from broadcasting makes it clear that there is a subsidy from the leading clubs in the league, especially the top five, to the rest. For example, Manchester United's matches accounted for 25 per cent of all viewers but the club only received 7.7 per cent of revenue. The top five clubs' matches accounted for 70 per cent of all viewers but these clubs only received 35.6 per cent of total revenue.

Despite the equalising effect of the current regulatory system for the allocation of live appearances (at least three per club) and broadcasting revenues (on the 50:25:25 per cent rule), the tendency to imbalance can be seen in the financial and sporting performances of the clubs within the Premier League. The top five clubs in the Premier League (ranked according to their league position at the end of the 1996 season) accounted for 68.4 per cent of the total operating profits (£53,221 million before transfers) generated in the Premier League in 1996. Hence success, on and off the field, tend to go hand in hand (see Dell'Osso and Szymanski, 1991 and Kay, 1993, both of which show that there is a strong relationship between competitive success on the field and spending on players which, in turn, is closely associated with the financial performance of clubs). Five clubs in the Premier League made pre-transfer operating profits of over £5 million; five clubs made pre-transfer profits of between £2 and £5 million, seven clubs made operating profits of between £1 and £2 million, and three clubs made losses (Deloitte & Touche, 1998, note that these are pre-transfer fee figures; post-transfers, 14 clubs made losses). In the absence of revenue-sharing rules within the Premier League, the number of clubs sustaining losses would have been greater and the profitability of the leading clubs higher.

Taking all of these factors into account it can be seen that there is redistribution in the Premier League but that it has not been sufficient to protect the league from the risks of fragmentation, near-bankruptcy (of some clubs) and potential breakaway groups. When redistribution is inadequate, leagues become increasingly unbalanced and the leading clubs effectively end up subsidising the lagging clubs. In addition, viewing figures are not maximised and clubs at the top may be tempted to leave the league to form a new super league that holds the prospect of greater competitive balance, larger audiences, larger broadcasting revenues and, initially, less need to subsidise lagging clubs.

However, the search for league balance via top-slicing to form new leagues is a *will-o'-the-wisp*. The formation of the Premier League has led to league fragmentation and increasing imbalance between the Premier League and the rest, as well as to fragmentation and imbalance within the Premier League. League balance can only be attained and maintained in the long run by effective redistribution. What is needed is a thorough investigation into the impact of broadcasting revenues on *positive* league balance under different redistribution rules. In many ways these issues should have been at the centre of the Football Task Force's work but, as Adam Brown notes (chapter 3), broadcasting revenues were not part of the Task Force's brief.

Collective bargaining, competitive balance and collective outcomes

Our foregoing discussion has shown that systems of collective league bargaining and associated redistribution rules can enhance the degree of competitive balance, increase the units of entertainment offered by the league and so increase revenue. It should be noted that while collective league bargaining can increase revenue streams to a league, this does not necessarily imply that the league is exercising monopoly power since redistribution within a league can also serve to increase competitive balance and thus the entertainment value of matches – viewers pay more but for better quality games.

In the UK the current system of collective league bargaining has been the subject of legal action brought by the Office of Fair Trading against the Premier League. Here, we consider a number of points that are relevant to this case. The first thing to note is that the removal of the Premier League's right to negotiate would not necessarily lead to an increase in economic welfare as the market for broadcasting is highly concentrated (see Motto and Polo, 1997, for detailed figures on this). In the UK, prior to BSkyB's entry into the market in 1992 a bi-lateral monopoly existed between the league and BBC/ITV who acted in unison (Baimbridge *et al*, 1996). When BSkyB entered the market the agreement between the BBC and ITV broke down and all three broadcasters competed for the contract, which was won by ITV in 1988 and by BSkyB in 1992 who has owned the exclusive rights ever since. It is now unclear as to whether the terrestrial channels (in particular the BBC) can afford to compete with BSkyB and it is likely that in the next negotiations for the rights, the league will bargain with two key players (ITV and BSkyB).

The important point, however, is that since there is a lack of competition on both sides of the market, the act of making one side of the market more competitive while the other side retains market power may not lead to any overall improvement. The likely effect of removing the right of the Premier League to negotiate collectively is to shift the balance of power in favour of broadcasters who already exert considerable market power, and to shift the balance of wealth and power between the clubs in favour of the top clubs. This shift in bargaining power will reduce the revenue stream to the Premier League and result in negative league balance, but by itself it will have little effect on consumer choice or the price of viewing matches. What it is likely to mean is that BSkyB will have more bargaining power to buy up the rights to screen those matches that will maximise its viewing figures and the broadcaster will not be constrained by an agreement to show the matches of lagging clubs that attract fewer viewers. Consumer choice on BSkyB is likely to be reduced, while other broadcasters may buy the rights to the matches BSkyB chooses not to screen (provided scheduling problems can be overcome).

In this regard there are interesting parallels to be drawn with the US experience. Prior to 1962 the National Football League (NFL) in the US faced a court-ordered injunction that forbade the league to engage in national television negotiations (Fort and Quirk, 1995, p. 1290). This injuction was lifted in 1962 when Congress exempted league-wide national television contracts from anti-trust legislation and the league signed national contracts, first with CBS and then with all three major television networks – these national contracts were accompanied by a system of revenue sharing within the NFL. At the time of the shift from individual to collective league bargaining, income to the NFL from the sale of television broadcasting rights increased in nominal terms by 33 per cent from $3.5 million to $4.7 million (Fort and Quirk, 1995, p. 1290). However, the extent to which this reflects monopoly power or other effects due to increased league balance or increased demand for televised sport is uncertain. What is clear is that in the 31 years between 1962 and 1993 there have been five other occasions where increases in television revenues exceeded 33 per cent which suggests that the switch to collective bargaining did not result in exceptional increased revenue.

An important difference between the UK and the US cases is that in the UK the Premier League sells live broadcasting rights exclusively to one broadcasting company. This may be compared with the situation in the US where exclusivity is not granted to any one broadcasting company. Rather, as Fort and Quirk note, 'in the 1993 season, the league had national TV contracts worth about $950 million per year with all three major networks' (Fort and Quirk, 1995, p. 1291). Given that one of the public interest concerns of the OFT is with consumer choice and wider access, it would seem appropriate that the exclusivity of the current UK system is examined in its own right since, as the US experience illustrates, it is exclusivity rather than collectivity that provides monopoly rights in broadcasting. Removing exclusivity would not only widen access to the public good aspects of football, it would also generate more competition in (football) broadcasting.

A second important point springs from the institutional constraints that serve to limit competition. At present BSkyB has exclusive rights to screen 60 matches per season averaging between two to three matches a week. These matches are normally not played on a Saturday (last season there were three exceptions) so that they do not detract from gates at the grounds. If the OFT's action in the Restrictive Practices Court succeeds and the system of exclusive rights remains, individual clubs will compete with each other to fill a limited number of live match slots (at present two to three a week). Moreover, in a situation where the clubs are competing with each other over broadcasting revenue there would be every likelihood that the Premier League's system of match sharing and revenue sharing would break down. From the broadcaster's perspective, viewing figures would be maximised by screening matches between (or involving) the top five clubs in each of these two to three slots. Hence, there would be a strong incentive for a broadcaster with exclusive rights to target these clubs in order to maximise sales/viewers. Given the present institutional constraint of two to three matches per week (not played on a Saturday), it is likely that clubs outside the top five would be excluded in their own right. If more matches are to be screened under the present system of exclusive live broadcasting rights then more matches would have to be shifted from Saturday kick-offs to mid-week slots which will change the character of the game and impact negatively on gates at the grounds. Research by Baimbridge *et al* (1996) has shown that live transmission of Monday evening matches by BSkyB has resulted in a significant decline in demand at the grounds. Screening live matches on a Saturday would introduce greater consumer choice on television but it would also mean that gates at the grounds would fall further with consequent adverse effects. This is the situation in Italy where gates have fallen dramatically and Juventus is currently considering knocking down its stadium to build a smaller one. In football, as in other sports, the crowd is part of the spectacle and the prospect of playing in front of near empty stadia is not one that should be encouraged by regulatory authorities.

As a third and related point it can be seen that removing the league's right to negotiate collectively is likely to lead to greater competitive imbalance. The current agreement for redistribution from the leading to the lagging clubs would cease and the leading clubs and broadcasters would face strong financial incentives to screen those matches that maximised viewing figures which would yield even higher revenues to the top clubs. Under such a system the gap between the leading and lagging clubs would widen, the stability of the league would be further threatened by increased league imbalance and there would be the real prospect of top clubs breaking away from the Premier League to participate in a British or European Super League of leading clubs where competitive balance might (initially) be more equal.

Finally, there is the question of the extent to which the system of collective league bargaining allows the Premier League to exercise monopoly power and extract monopoly rents. To answer this question it is instructive to look at the profitability of the League. If the League were making excessive profits this would provide indicative evidence that the arrangement was acting against the public interest. However, an examination of the profitability of the league in the last two years for which accounts are available suggests that profitability is not strong. In 1996 and 1997 the Premier League made operating profits before transfers of £53.2 million and £86.3 million, respectively. With turnover (excluding transfers) of £339 million in 1996 and £463 million in 1997, this means that the league's profit margin (before transfers) was 15.7 per cent in 1996 and 18.6 per cent in 1997 (Deloitte & Touche, 1998). These margins do not appear to be excessive by comparison with profit margins in other industries. Moreover, post-transfer, pre-tax profits were negative in both 1996 (–£65.7 million) and 1997 (–£4.4 million) (Deloitte & Touche, 1998). Since transfer fees represent a real cost to the industry it would appear that the clubs in the league are not benefiting excessively from the current institutional arrangements, in fact the combined profits of the League net of transfers are negative! What may be the case is that any rent the League extracts is, in turn, extracted by the players. But changing the negotiating system of the League is unlikely to change this fact. The end of collective bargaining by the Premier League will lead to the top clubs becoming richer and will mean that they can afford to bid more for top players. Furthermore, there is an international market for football players and in the absence of international regulation, unilaterally removing one country's ability to bid in that market will simply mean that the best players will be attracted elsewhere.

Controlling football from pitch to screen: vertical integration between broadcasters and football clubs

Here we apply our foregoing analysis to related aspects of the question of merger between a dominant football club and a dominant sports broadcaster. Of course, this case has particular interest in the wake of the Monopoly and Mergers Commission (MMC) report on the proposed merger between Manchester United and BSkyB. It is not our purpose here to review all the arguments concerning that case; rather we concentrate on aspects relating to broadcasting, revenue-sharing and league balance.

The report of the MMC was submitted before the Restrictive Practices Court decision and hence it was not known what regulatory arrangements would be in place for the sale of TV rights. If the current position of collective league bargaining remains there would have been two main effects. Firstly, BSkyB's dominant position in sports broadcasting would be enhanced as it would have had access to insider information and would effectively have sat on both sides of the negotiating table. Although Manchester United only has one vote in the league its influence is wider because it can threaten to leave the collective negotiating process should the other clubs not support its preferred option. This threat is credible both because Manchester United is one of the leading 'subsidisers' in the league and because the club could earn significantly more in revenue if it sold the rights to its matches independently. Clearly, Manchester United representatives do not have to be in the room when the decision is being made to wield influence over other clubs. Rather, Manchester United has bargaining power regardless of whether it is present during the meeting or not. Secondly, there is the related possibility that BSkyB would have extracted part of the income from the league by using its control of Manchester United to bid less. This would have reduced the total amount available to the league and resulted in negative league balance.

If the current system of collective bargaining by the league were scrapped, many of these arguments would continue to apply, but in the case of vertical integration between a leading club and a dominant sports broadcaster, the arguments take on greater weight. By owning Manchester United, BSkyB would effectively have controlled 25 per cent of the viewing market. Moreover, the merger would increase the chances of Manchester United pushing for the formation of a new super league because the commercial interests of Manchester United would have become subservient to those of BSkyB, whose marketing interests would best be served by the formation of a British or European 'super league' with increased viewing audiences. (On the implications of BSkyB's attempted acquisition bid see the chapter by Jonathan Michie and Christine Oughton and the chapters by Jonathan Michie and Andy Walsh; Jonathan Michie and Shay Ramalingam; and Rob Branston, Keith Cowling, Nestor Duch Brown, Jonathan Michie and Roger Sugden).

A European or British 'super league' is a way of increasing league balance (in the short run) and thus of raising demand for match viewing without the use of redistribution. Hence, BSkyB would find a 'super league' to be in its short-term financial interests. The remaining national clubs outside the 'super league' would lose access to premier class revenue streams and the quality of national leagues would decline as the clubs find they have less revenue with which to buy players. Fragmentation between leagues would increase and in the absence of effective and progressive redistribution, any 'super league' would also become increasingly imbalanced in the short to medium term.

The way forward: stronger regulation and greater redistribution

In the absence of redistribution, sports leagues have an inherent tendency to become dominated by a handful of leading clubs with a tail of lagging performers that make up the league. In order to ensure adequate competition it is necessary for there to be a certain degree of co-operation between the leading and lagging teams in the league. Such co-operation is beneficial in that it generates a greater degree of competition between teams, which raises the overall demand for match viewing and increases revenue streams. This explains why leading clubs are prepared to redistribute income to lagging clubs.

Our analysis also sheds light on why leading teams in the Premier League and Scottish Premier League may find it in their short-term interests to join a European super league. A league that consisted of the very best clubs in Europe is likely to be initially more balanced than current national premier leagues and is therefore likely to increase demand while at the same time reduce or eliminate the subsidies paid by leading national clubs. However, it is also likely to reduce the degree of competition in national leagues and undermine the quality of play by top-slicing revenue streams and reducing the income available to the remaining clubs. Any move to a European super league that is unaccompanied by regulatory measures to transfer resources from the super league to national leagues will undermine the quality of national leagues. Moreover, without progressive redistribution rules the super league itself will become unbalanced. In short, there is every prospect that the fragmentation that has already emerged in football will increase. These dangers are likely to be greater if the system of collective bargaining by the league were brought to an end or if a situation of vertical integration between a leading club and a leading sports broadcaster were established.

The system of collective league bargaining that operates in the Premier League is functional in that it provides a mechanism for match- and revenue-sharing. Any attempt to remove collective league bargaining is also likely to signal the end of match and revenue-sharing and lead to greater competitive imbalance. At the same time it will increase the bargaining power of dominant broadcasters. Rather than removing the collectivity of the Premier League it would be more appropriate to end the system of granting exclusive live broadcasting rights to a single broadcasting company. Collectivity without exclusivity would have the advantage of opening up the market for broadcasting without undermining the system of redistribution that underpins the collective nature of the product supplied by the League. In contrast, exclusivity without collectivity will allow monopoly power in broadcasting to continue: current viewing figures suggest that a broadcaster would only need to contract with, or own a handful of leading clubs to control 70 per cent of the market for live Premier League football.

In conclusion, the emergence of the market for live broadcasting offers potential benefits in the form of increased revenue streams for football clubs and wider viewing access for football fans. However, the peculiar economics of sports leagues together with concentration in the market for broadcasting and attempts by broadcasters to control leading clubs combine to threaten to undermine these benefits and the future of the game. There is an urgent need to examine both the impact of broadcasting revenues on league balance and fragmentation under different distribution rules, and systems of corporate governance in football. If national governments and sports associations such as the Football Association wish to ensure a healthy future for national league football then they should work together with European and international bodies to design and implement appropriate regulatory measures.

References

Baimbridge, M., Cameron, S. and Dawson P. (1996). 'Satellite television and the demand for football: a whole new ball game?' *Scottish Journal of Political Economy*, Vol 43:3:317–333.

Cameron, S. (1997). Regulation of the broadcasting of sporting events, *Institute of International Affairs*, September, pp. 37–41.

Dell'Osso, F. and Szymanski, S. (1991). 'Who are the champions? (An analysis of football and architecture)'. *Business Strategy Review*, 2/2, Centre for Business

Strategy: London Business School, 113–30.

Deloitte & Touche (1998) *Deloitte & Touche Annual Review of Football Finance*. August.

Fort, R. and Quirk, J. (1995). 'Cross-subsidization, Incentives, and Outcomes in Professional Team Sports Leagues'. *Journal of Economic Literature*, XXXIII, September, 1265–99.

Kay, J. (1993). *Foundations of Corporate Success*. Oxford University Press, Oxford.

Motta, M. and Polo, M. (1997). 'Concentration and public policies in the broadcasting industry: the future of television'. *Economic Policy*, Vol. 25, October, pp. 293–334.

Neale, W. C. (1964). 'The peculiar economics of professional sports'. *Quarterly Journal of Economics*, LXXVII:1.

Sloane, P. (1997). Editorial: 'The economics of sport: an overview'. *Institute of International Affairs*, September, 1–6.

7. Is Paul Ince an Asset or a Liability?

Accounting and Governance Issues in Football

Jonathan Michie and Shraddha Verma

In business generally, it has become popular for managers to refer to their workforce as 'their greatest asset'. Management gurus have stressed similar ideas for some time now. And there is a solid body of academic research suggesting that a company's workforce is indeed becoming an increasingly important factor in corporate success. 'Human capital theory' stresses the parallels between investment in fixed capital on the one hand, and investment in people through training on the other. 'Human resource management' has replaced traditional industrial relations. And the 'new growth' literature stresses the role of investment in people and ideas – and achieved 15 minutes of fame when Gordon Brown sang the virtues of 'post-neo-classical new growth theory'. Where was Gordon Brown's populist spin doctor Charlie Whelan when we needed him?

But if the most valuable assets of a company are indeed its workers, how is this reflected in the company's accounts which, after all, are supposed to indicate the value of a firm's net assets? The answer is that in general, despite the rhetoric, firms do not include their workers within their balance sheet. All this is going to have to change in the case of one category of firm, namely football clubs. New accounting rules will require clubs to include players in the balance sheet.

This appears a sensible move. The issue of whether, and if so how, company accounts should refer to the value to the business of the people who work there, does seem to be of particular relevance to football clubs with regard to their players (as opposed to other people who work at the club, who will not, of course, need to be included in the balance sheet). This is especially so for those that are publicly limited companies. Firstly, because the above sort of statements – regarding the most valuable assets of the business being their workers – are undeniably true for football clubs and their players. In most cases these companies will have total – never mind just net – assets of at most a few tens of millions of pounds. This will be largely the football ground, or at least the land on which the ground is built – where the prospective buyers would in many cases include the likes of Sainsburys and Tesco, looking for new superstore sites. But in many cases the club might be able to sell a single player for over £10 million, with just a handful of their top players possibly bringing in more than the whole of the club's fixed assets, as listed in the balance sheet.

This remains the case even after the Bosman ruling. Jean-Marc Bosman was a footballer for RFC Liège in Belgium. The club refused to release him even at the end of his contract. He finally (after five years) won his case in the European Court of Justice in 1995. The Court ruled that the club had acted in restraint of his freedom of movement as an EU citizen (since RFC Liège's refusal to release him, in particular to the French club Dunkerque, prevented him from taking a job across an EU border). The ruling established that once a player's contract with a club has come to an end, the player can move to any other club with no transfer fee having to be paid to the club from which the player is moving. (For a discussion of the implications of this case for accounting for football players, see Morrow, 1997).

Despite this, clubs have continued to be prepared to pay transfer fees higher than ever to other clubs in order to attract players before their contracts have expired. Thus Manchester United paid £12 million to Aston Villa in the summer of 1998 for the transfer of Dwight Yorke, who had two years of his contract still to run. Even before the Bosman ruling, clubs would sometimes wait until players who they were pursuing were out of contract. This was because although the player's club could still ask for a transfer fee, this was generally much lower in such circumstances. This, for example, is what Manchester United did to secure the transfer of Peter Schmeichel from Brondby when that club had initially demanded a transfer fee that Manchester United had regarded as excessive. Conversely, clubs sometimes waive their rights to a transfer fee even though a player is still under contract and hence a transfer fee would still be payable to the club. This, for example, is what Manchester United agreed to do for the same player, Schmeichel, when he moves on in the summer of 1999. The effect of this is to increase the financial package that the player is able to demand for himself.

Even when a transfer fee is paid, this same sort of process may be involved to some degree, as for example with the sale by Manchester United of Mark Hughes to Chelsea. Mark Hughes made explicit his desire for Manchester United to set the transfer fee as low as possible, so that of the total amount that any club or clubs might be prepared to pay for his services, more would go directly to him rather than to his old club. Finally, the opposite sort of process can occur when players in effect subsidise their move by waiving a part of what would normally be due to them, calculated as a proportion of the transfer fee. This reduces the gap between what the player's existing club insists on receiving on the one hand, and what the prospective club is prepared to pay. This in effect is equivalent to an estate agent reducing their commission fees on the sale of a property in order to reduce the gap between what one party is demanding and the lower amount being offered by the prospective purchaser. This was done, for example, by Jaap Stam to overcome the deadlock in the negotiations over his transfer to Manchester United in the summer of 1998.

This chapter asks how, then, should clubs account for the value of their players within their financial statements? The new accounting rules issued by the Accounting Standards Board are compulsory for all clubs. But as indicated below, there are many different approaches which can be taken to implementing such rules in practice. There may turn out to be some variation between clubs in how they actually interpret and apply the new rules. Indeed, this may be an area where a new regulator might intervene to insist on a more consistent set of accounting procedures than would otherwise emerge, much as the existing regulators such as OFTEL do, when they require companies to produce a set of regulatory accounts in addition to those that the companies are in any case obliged by law to produce.

We also touch on a number of other accounting and corporate governance issues that are of particular importance to the business of football, albeit also having a wider interest and importance. The most important of these in our view is the inadequate state of British company law in relation to take-overs. Faced with a take-over bid, company directors are, it would appear, unable to take any account of the long-term interests of the company of which they are a director, and instead are obliged to look only at the price being offered per share. Thus at the November 1998 Manchester United AGM, Greg Dyke was asked why he had voted to recommend the BSkyB bid to shareholders (despite the widespread reports that he personally was opposed to the take-over). The director reported that he had taken legal advice throughout and that he had been advised that it was his fiduciary duty to recommend the offer if the price was a good one.

Finally, the flotation of football clubs on the Stock Exchange has led to a rather unique situation. Thousands of individuals own shares in a company not just because they regard it as a good financial investment – indeed, in some cases they buy the shares despite the fact that they do not so regard it – but rather because they have a keen personal interest in how the company is run. What is surprising, in this context, is what little thought appears to have been given as to how the views of these shareholders can best be taken into account.

Accounting for football players

The balance sheets for most football clubs – including those that are plcs – have not up until now included the assets the clubs have in the form of the value of the players. But they are of value, both in the sense of either generating revenue or having a transfer value.

This omission has been due partly to the fact that there are problems of 'capitalising' human assets in general. These relate to issues of how to deal with valuation, depreciation and so on. It would be impossible to generalise these arguments for all 'intangible' assets, which is perhaps part of the reason why there have not been more attempts until now to tackle the issue of valuing players in the balance sheet – there are accounting issues that need to be addressed.

For example, a player may be an asset, for the reasons just mentioned. He may help generate revenue. And it may be that he can be sold. On the other hand, a player may also be a liability, not just for the obvious reasons, as alluded to in our chapter title, but also because the club may be contracted to pay him – possibly very high wages – for several years to come. To have a top player on just a game-by-game contract is extremely rare. Indeed, in this as in so many other respects, Eric Cantona may well have been unique.

'My greatest assets are my workforce'

Interest in human-resource accounting developed in the 1960s and research into issues such as developing models for valuing human resources and analysing attempts to set up human-resource accounting systems in companies was undertaken until the late 1970s. Research into human-resource accounting then rather declined, with only limited interest being shown in this area. However, the recent enthusiasm for 'human-resource management', 'investing in people' and so on has seen bodies such as the European Union and the Organisation for Economic Co-operation and Development identifying intangibles and employees as important for national competitiveness and hence important areas for further analysis and investigation.

So the decision to account for football players rather goes with the flow, in valuing one's workforce. On the other hand, the case of footballers is rather unique. In the case of football clubs, this particular subset of the workforce may be the most important and expensive asset the company has, with clubs paying large transfer fees to acquire players. Up until now, most clubs have 'expensed' these transfer fees in the profit and loss account in the period they were incurred. It has now been decided that this is not an appropriate accounting treatment since the transfer fees are paid to acquire footballers for more than just one accounting period.

When deciding how to account for football players, two main issues need to be addressed. Firstly, do football players fulfil the accounting criteria to be classified as assets of the football clubs? And if so, how should they be accounted for? An asset is defined – in the draft statement of principles (a conceptual framework being developed by the accounting profession) – as 'the right to future economic benefits arising from past transactions and enforceable by the entity'. Tangible fixed assets are further defined in Financial Reporting Exposure Draft (FRED) 17 on fixed assets as 'assets that have physical substance and are held for use in the production or supply of goods and services, for rental to others, or for administrative purposes on a continuing basis'. Intangible assets are defined in Financial Reporting Standard (FRS) 10 on goodwill and intangible assets as 'non-financial fixed assets that do not have physical substance but are identifiable and are controlled by the entity through custody or legal rights'.

Using the above definitions, can football players be classified as intangible assets for accounting purposes? Football players are certainly acquired to help generate future economic benefits for the football clubs, generally on a continuing basis – that is, for more than one year. The benefits that they are contracted to generate are intangible – a contribution to the footballing success of the club. They sign contracts which legally bind them to a particular club and these contracts are legally enforceable by the clubs. Players who have a contract with a club cannot leave that club or play for anyone else without the permission of the club. This was illustrated when Pierre van Hooijdonk did not want to play for Nottingham Forest at the start of the 1998–99 season, and was widely reported as criticising the club and his fellow players.

Due to the contract he had signed, he could not play for any other club without permission from Nottingham Forest or without being sold by Nottingham Forest. Neither event was forthcoming. In the end he had to return and play for Nottingham Forest, even though his subsequent goal celebrations proved to be lonely affairs.

This is in contrast to the position of employees in most other entities where such strong legal contracts between employees and their employers do not exist. Indeed FRS 10 gives the example of a team of skilled staff employed by an entity to illustrate the operation of its definition of intangible assets. The skilled staff are certainly employed by the entity on a continuing basis for future economic benefit but the entity does not have the legal right to retain the staff if they hand in their notice. The entity therefore has insufficient control over the expected future benefits generated by the employees and cannot recognise them as assets. This is the current accounting recommendation in relation to accounting for employees. It is true that some high-tech companies try to prevent such employees from working for a rival firm, by getting them to sign 'garden leaf' contracts, so called because the contract stipulates that should the worker leave the firm, they cannot work for a rival firm – instead they have to stay at home watching the garden leaves. But even in this case, the firm is not thereby guaranteeing any future benefits to itself, merely denying such benefits to others.

However, since football players sign contracts which give football clubs legal rights to retain their services, players can be bought and sold separately from buying or selling the business as a whole and there is an active transfer market in football players, the conditions for football players to be classified as intangible fixed assets, as outlined in FRS 10, do seem to be fulfilled. The football industry is now considering the implications of FRS 10 in relation to capitalisation of players. (Indeed, the March 1999 budget introduced a measure to help football clubs adjust to the new accounting rules, to prevent these having adverse tax effects for the clubs).

So, if football players are accepted as intangible assets – or more precisely, if the services that they provide are accepted as intangible assets – the next question that needs to be addressed is how the football players should be accounted for.

What price Ryan Giggs?

There are three main issues that need to be addressed when deciding on the accounting treatment of football players. Firstly, should football players be capitalised in the balance sheet? Secondly, if football players are to be capitalised, at what value should they be capitalised? And thirdly, if football players are capitalised, should they be amortised and if so over what period?

Should football players be in the balance sheet?

To determine the accounting treatment of football players, two fundamental accounting concepts need to be taken into account, the concept of matching or accruals (linked with the accounting concept of realisation) and the concept of prudence.

Tangible fixed assets are generally capitalised on the balance sheet at their historic cost – that is, at the amount it cost the entity to acquire the asset – and are then depreciated over the asset's useful economic life. Intangible assets are also capitalised at historic cost and amortised over their useful economic lives, if they can be purchased or sold separately from buying or selling the business as a whole. This treatment arises from the operation of the accruals or matching concept linked to the concept of realisation.

The accruals or matching concept makes the distinction between the receipt and payment of cash on the one hand, and the right to receive cash or the generation of an obligation to pay cash on the other. Under the realisation concept, revenues are recognised as soon as they are capable of objective measurement – that is, when the revenue generating transaction is reasonably certain to be completed and not when cash is actually received. Under the accruals or matching concept, expenses are then matched against the revenues that are realised in order to obtain the profit of the entity. The expenses include that part of the fixed assets which is used up in the accounting period in order to generate the revenues. This is known as depreciation or amortisation.

Applying these concepts, football players should indeed be capitalised in the balance sheet and amortised over their useful economic life.

However, there is a caveat to this. According to another important accounting concept, namely prudence, assets – whether tangible or intangible – which are hard to measure and value are not capitalised in the balance sheet. The point is that accountants should always be prudent when deciding on the accounting treatment of any transaction. Generally speaking, revenues and profits should not be anticipated and should only be included in the financial statements when they are actually realised in the form of cash (or some other asset) – or at least are expected to be with reasonable certainty. Expenses and losses should, on the other hand, be provided as soon as they are known about even if the entity is not reasonably certain that the loss will occur. In addition, accountants should choose the lowest possible asset valuation whenever there is more than one possible valuation basis for the asset. Thus while the revenues or profits to be derived from the football player – whether through playing or being sold – cannot be known with certainty, the expense of having to pay for, say, another three years of the contract is known all too well. Hence for example the pay-off by Queens Park Rangers to Vinny Jones in early 1999, in effect to buy him out of his contract.

Thus, in common with other intangible assets, there are several uncertainties and problems in the measurement and valuation of football players. These include uncertainty over how much any particular footballer will actually contribute to the future economic benefit of the club. There are the unknowable issues of future injuries and loss of form, as well as uncertainty over exactly how long any player will actually stay at the club, and uncertainty over the timing of the benefits to be expected. Since the valuation of football players is difficult and the economic benefits generated from the service of players are uncertain and hard to measure, the concept of prudence would suggest that football players, in line with other employees, should not be capitalised after all.

Thus, the concepts of accruals and prudence indicate very different accounting treatments for intangible assets. Despite some merit in writing off intangible fixed assets due to the uncertainties involved in accounting for them, recent guidance from the accounting profession has focused on capitalising intangible assets where there is an active market for such assets and if they can be bought and sold separately from the business as a whole. Recent recommendations by the accounting profession have also stated that assets should not be excluded from the financial statements just because they are difficult to value. Indeed other uncertain intangible assets such as research and development are capitalised when appropriate criteria are fulfilled, despite the uncertainties involved in assessing the future economic benefits of such assets.

Since football players fulfil the requirements to be classed as intangible fixed assets, and in line with current thought on accounting for intangibles, the most appropriate accounting treatment for football players is indeed to be capitalised in the balance sheet.

At what value should football players be capitalised?

If football players are to be capitalised, the next problem is that of valuation. This issue is perhaps the most problematic, and is probably the main reason for employees in general being kept off balance sheets, and also the reason why, up until now, even football players have not always been included. Two broad approaches to valuing employees are cost based methods (for example historic cost, replacement cost, opportunity cost) and market value based methods (for example at the economic value of human resources). There is no single accepted way of valuing employees. Each method has some advantages and some problems. In all cases some subjective assessments will be necessary and it is this subjectivity, in part, that has caused employees to be left out of balance sheets to date, with the partial exception of football players.

However, the treatment of football players is a little less complex than for other employees. There is an active transfer market for football players who are regularly bought and sold by clubs. Thus, for players acquired by football clubs, the transfer fee paid by a club is a fairly independent value for a given player at a particular point in time. Thus football clubs can capitalise their acquired players at the cost of acquisition, which is the transfer fee paid, plus any 'signing on' fee. However, this 'signing on' component is different in that it would not be recouped by the club even if the player was transferred on straight-away, and also the distinction between what constitutes a signing-on fee as against wages is not clear either analytically or in practice. Firstly, clubs tend not to release details of wages and signing-on fees, and would presumably therefore be reluctant to produce such figures in their accounts for the purpose of capitalising an acquired player. And secondly, the signing-on fee can be a rather notional concept used for example to keep the wage at a lower rate than otherwise so as to avoid other players using a high wage for a new player in their own wage negotiations. Thus for example the current (May 1999) wage discussions between Manchester United and their captain Roy Keane are reported to include the idea of including a 'signing-on' fee to help bridge the gap between what he is demanding (reported to be around £2 million a year) and what the club's pay structure would allow (little more than half that figure).

This leaves the problem of how to deal with players who are not acquired but are, instead, developed internally by a club. (There is also the case of players who arrive on a free transfer which is not discussed here, but the same general approach, of capitalising such players at their estimated replacement cost, might be appropriate).

The problem with using the historic cost method, capitalising all the costs that relate to training and developing such players, is that these costs can be difficult to identify, and many young footballers who start training with a club are not successful. Even if the costs of developing a successful footballer are identified accurately, the costs will not reflect the value of the player once he becomes successful. One method of dealing with internally generated players might be to capitalise such players at their estimated replacement cost when they become successful – that is, the amount that it would cost to replace that player in the open market. Identifying a player's replacement cost does involve subjective assessment as the actual replacement cost can only be objectively determined when a player is actually replaced. However, this method is no more subjective than any other method of valuing players and provides useful information to different parties involved in football.

Whatever method is chosen for valuing players, a system for determining player valuations will have to be developed in agreement with the football industry. Such a system will need to be cost effective, yet also contain checks to ensure that player valuations are not misleading. Two suggestions are made here but more discussion on the most appropriate system for valuing players is still needed within the football industry.

One suggestion would be for each club to value their own players, maybe by the use of a specially appointed internal panel, as has been carried out by some clubs such as Manchester United in the past (even though in the case of Manchester United the resulting value was still not included in the balance sheet; it was just reported in the notes to the accounts). An alternative would be to have an external, independent panel of experts to value clubs' players, or at least to review valuations proposed by the football clubs themselves, to ensure that these are reasonable. Indeed an arbitration panel already exists to set transfer fees for players when clubs cannot reach agreement on this and it may be possible to extend the role of this arbitration panel to deal with player valuations on a regular basis.

Should football players be amortised?

With football players acquired by a club, there is a clear cost (the transfer fee and the signing on fee) in acquiring the players and, as for other fixed assets, football players could be capitalised at their cost to the football club and then amortised systematically over their useful economic life. Players that are not acquired could be valued at replacement cost or some other suitable value as suggested above and also amortised over their useful economic lives. The useful economic life of each player would have to be estimated but this would be no more difficult than estimating the useful economic life of other fixed assets. The transfer fee could be amortised over the life of the player's contract, over the expected remaining playing life of the player, or some other reasonably estimated useful economic life. With the Bosman ruling, players can leave clubs when their contract expires without clubs receiving any transfer fee, and hence amortisation over the life of a player's contract is the most appropriate amortisation basis. This is what will happen under the new accounting standard for intangible assets (the Financial Reporting Standard 10 referred to above), which applies for accounting periods ending after 22 December 1998. If players then choose to re-sign for a club, they could be revalued at the time of re-signing their contract. The revaluation could then be amortised over the new contract period.

Another and, perhaps, better treatment would be to capitalise acquired football players at their cost to the club – or estimated replacement cost to the club in the case of players that are not acquired. All players could then be revalued at their replacement cost at periodic intervals, making the basis of valuations of both acquired and internally developed players consistent with each other. Valuations could be carried out periodically, for example every one, two or three years, or some other suitable time interval as appropriate. Where circumstances change for a particular player, they could be revalued at the time of change of circumstance, even if it is not time for a periodic valuation. Increases and decreases in the value of players could be treated in a similar fashion to increases and decreases in the value of investment properties – that is, taken to a revaluation reserve (possibly called a player revaluation reserve) in the bottom half of the balance sheet. With this valuation method, no amortisation of football players would take place. To try and ensure that the periodic player valuations were reasonable, the arbitration panel or some other body developed by the football industry, as suggested above, could be introduced to set or review player valuations.

Further consideration of the above options will need to be undertaken before any consistent practice on valuation and amortisation is arrived at in practice. Current developments in the accounting profession – for example the move towards fair value and FRS 10 on goodwill and intangible assets – indicate that capitalising football players is an appropriate accounting treatment. However, there is as yet no consensus on how football players should best be actually accounted for in practice; there remain issues – such as the basis of capitalisation, how to ensure reasonable valuations of players and whether players should be amortised – to be satisfactorily resolved.

The capitalisation of football players by football clubs is a special case of employee valuation in general, and companies are increasingly recognising that their workers are valuable assets and hence that they ought to make balance sheets more reflective of this fact. However, the value and performance of companies is particularly important in take-over situations, and here football clubs may prove particularly vulnerable, particularly if clubs remain plcs and if the valuing of football remains obscure.

Take-overs

The problems associated with how to best account for and value football clubs becomes particularly acute when there is an actual or potential take-over bid. In such a situation, how should the value of a club be assessed? There are problems with the use of standard ratio analysis, with limited sets of accounts available and where the potential acquiring company may be in a very different industry to the football club. Ratio analysis – the calculation and analysis of key ratios from financial statements – is a valuable rule of thumb in helping to evaluate company performance. It highlights key relationships and draws attention to areas of either good or poor performance. However, calculating ratios for a company in isolation is meaningless. Some sort of comparison is needed – for example comparing the performance of one company over time, comparing the performance of a company against its budgeted results, comparing the performance of different companies at a given point in time, or comparing companies to industry averages.

When using ratio analysis there is always the problem of looking at accounts that are not representative of the business of the company. The available accounts may cover a period in which the company did particularly well or particularly badly. Incorrect conclusions might easily be reached if the accounts do not reflect the normal business of the companies being investigated. This situation is more likely if there is limited access to accounts, as is sometimes the case in take-overs. Indeed a particular problem with the football business is that financial results are very uncertain and change from year to year, especially post-transfer. (Overcoming this latter point is of course one of the purposes of the accounting reforms discussed in this chapter, above). Income and profits depend heavily on the club's performance each year, and this is much more variable than is the case in most businesses. The fact that the income will, thus, depend in part on expenditure on players does little to reduce this uncertainty; indeed, it adds additional elements of uncertainty, including over who the club might attract to play for it, and how such players might perform following a transfer.

Thus in the summer of 1998 it was generally recognised that to challenge in Europe, Manchester United needed to sign a top striker which would be likely to cost around £12 million, and various names were bandied about, some more serious than others. When Dwight Yorke was signed, it could be argued therefore that this did not actually reduce the uncertainty over the company's finances, since it had already been known that this sort of sum would be spent on a striker. The only question had been, who? Kluivert? Shearer? Or even Ronaldo? Once the signing was made, the fundamental uncertainty remained – who was Dwight Yorke? Was he any good? If so, why was he never the league's top scorer? More important, could he match up to Ronaldo in Europe? There is no doubt what the balance of opinion was at the time, as captured by the Manchester United fanzine *United We Stand* some time later in the season, with a full-page photo of Dwight Yorke captioned, 'The £12 million player no one wanted to sign', beneath which was the question, 'Humble pie, anyone?'.

With such uncertainty, it is hard to apply the usual concept of a 'representative' period in the football industry. As well as the problem of unrepresentative accounts, accounting policy choices by different companies can lead to even similar companies showing very different results, making meaningful ratio analysis a difficult task indeed.

Financial statements alone cannot give the whole picture. In most cases, information that cannot be quantified or information not available in the accounts, is the key issue. For example, information on the future plans of the acquiring company and the company being taken over, information about current values of assets including employees and information relating to the goodwill generated by the companies involved in the take-over is often more important than the financial information available. Indeed, one of the concerns expressed by many Manchester United shareholders during the 1998 take-over bid was the qualitative one of how the management of Manchester United might be affected by BSkyB, and more generally the concern that decisions would be taken that benefited BSkyB rather than Manchester United – let alone football in general. There was a significant number of shareholders who were against the bid – indeed, a majority in the sense that by the time the deadline to accept the offer arrived, only a minority of shareholders (whether measured by absolute number or percentage of share capital) had accepted. Yet little information was made available to them.

Corporate governance issues

The term corporate governance is sometimes used to refer to the separation of management and finance, and the resulting issues of how shareholders can maintain control. Needless to say, we are using the term in a rather broader sense, to refer to how the firm is governed by its management (which in the case of football clubs means the directors rather than the actual manager) and how in this process the interests not just of the financiers and shareholders are represented but also, most crucially in the context of this book, the fans of the club.

Many of the corporate governance issues relevant to football are discussed in chapter 10 by Branston et al. Here we discuss just two: firstly the stewardship role of directors, and secondly the representation of small shareholders on company boards. Since both these aspects take on a particular significance when the company is faced with a take-over bid, we would just add here the following. One of the points that has been well made in the academic literature – and recognised widely in policy discussion – is the idea that the onus should be on the acquiring firm to demonstrate that any proposed take-over would be in the public interest, rather than having the onus be on the public authorities to establish that it would act against the public interest. This applies with even greater force, we would argue, in the case of football clubs where the public interest aspects are so integrally involved in every aspect of the clubs' operation.

We note in passing the danger of asset stripping. The danger that a club might be bought because the land on which the ground stands could be a prime location for a supermarket or other commercial development is exacerbated by the nature, discussed above, of the other major assets – namely players' contracts – that could be sold.

Stewardship: 'the price is right'?

British company law on take-overs is notoriously lax, short-term and oriented to free market processes rather than the long-term good of the company, let alone the economy. This means that even if they wanted to, company directors are not allowed to consider what is in the interests of the company's customers – they have to accept, and recommend to other shareholders, any take-over bid that offers enough money. It also means that the Office of Fair Trading and the Monopolies and Mergers Commission (now the Competition Commission) may allow take-overs to go through even if these are against the public interest, provided free-market competition is preserved. In the case of BSkyB's attempted take-over of Manchester United, the MMC did in December 1998 take the unprecedented step of making public the letter in which they set out – to BSkyB and Manchester United – the various concerns they would want to consider during their deliberations.[1]

On the question of what discretion company directors have when faced with a bid to take over the company of which they are a director, there is a strong case for the Articles of Association of any company that owns a football club to include a specific duty on directors to give due weight to the long-term interests of that football club, and to the local community of which it is a part. There is indeed a case for including some stewardship requirement on all company directors, as discussed for example in chapter 10 below, and also by Kay and Silberston (1995).[2] But to make that case in the current context would risk diverting us from the key point at issue in this chapter, namely that football clubs play an important role in the sporting, cultural and social life of local communities, as well as nationally, and this should be given proper consideration when any club is faced with a take-over bid.

Were company law to be amended to include such stewardship functions as a normal part of good corporate governance then this might well serve the purpose required in the case of football clubs. But in the meantime, or alternatively, it would be a simple matter to introduce legislation – either by amending the Companies Act or through the remit of the office of the football regulator, if this is to be established, or else by a stand-alone bill – to require appropriate Articles of Association to be adopted by all companies that own football clubs. It would be vital that any such legislation clearly applied to all such companies so as to avoid it being circumvented through the use of holding companies that failed to adopt the relevant Articles of Association, as clubs have done to get round the Football Association's Rule 34. This rule required football clubs to adopt particular Articles of Association limiting the extent to which they could be exploited commercially. It was introduced by the Football Association, the industry's governing body, in recognition of the fact – and importance – of the broad public interest concerns around football and the danger that the commercialisation of the game would damage these public interests. However, Rule 34 has been circumvented to a large extent by the creation of plcs as holding companies of the football clubs, with only the latter being bound by the regulatory restrictions. (See chapter 10 for further discussion).

Representation of small shareholders

Several football clubs in Britain have wide share ownership. Thus, for example, 23 per cent of shares in Manchester United are held by small shareholders, most of whom are fans of the club, who bought shares primarily for this reason. The November 1998 Manchester United AGM was attended by more than 1,000 shareholders, mostly small shareholders. Yet there is no representation of this block of shareholders on the board, and there appears to have been no consideration by the board of how this might be best facilitated. At the 1998 AGM it was proposed by shareholders that one step towards this would be to create some sort of 'fans' forum' which might have some input, but the response to this by the chief executive Martin Edwards at the AGM was even more evasive than his response on other topics.

While the individual shareholding of each of these small shareholders taken separately is of course minute, it should be borne in mind that apart from Martin Edwards, who still owns 14 per cent of the shares (despite his continual efforts to offload them), the largest institutional shareholding is around 2–3 per cent and the largest of the other directors' shareholdings is also around only 2 per cent. The 23 per cent taken together is thus extremely significant.[3]

Indeed, one of the stated aims of the flotation of Manchester United in 1991 was 'to widen share ownership among the fans'. It is therefore surprising that there has been no attempt to secure any sort of representation of such shareholders on the board at Manchester United or indeed at almost any of the clubs. One exception is Northampton, where this was brought about through the action of the local council who were in a position to exert such influence because of the club's need to get local council support and funding for their ground development, on which, see chapter 11 by the elected director, Brian Lomax. For such schemes to become the norm, action at national level would most likely be required, whether from government, a regulator, the FA or the Football League and Premiership. It is certainly something that any regulator established following the report of the Football Task Force should actively consider and canvass opinion on at an early stage. In the meantime it might be pursued through the sort of changed ownership structures discussed in the chapters by Lomax (chapter 11) and Michie and Walsh (chapter 13), where even if only a small minority of shares were to take on a changed character, for example through Trust status, this could still be used as a vehicle for representation of this block on the board.

Regarding the situation when a take-over bid is made, the fact that football clubs have this rather unique shareholding composition, with a mass of small shareholders who are fans of the club and have a great emotional attachment to their ownership of the club, gives a particular significance to an aspect of British take-over law that does not normally attract much comment, namely that once an acquirer has 90 per cent of a company's shares, the remaining shares can be compulsorily purchased. In the case of, for example, BSkyB's bid for Manchester United, this would have involved literally thousands of shareholders being forced to part with their shares against their will. Whatever the logic of this piece of take-over law, it clearly has rather particular implications when applied to football clubs, and should certainly not be applied unless Parliament decides explicitly that this really is an intended outcome of the current legislation.

Conclusion

A study of clubs' accounting practices by Arthur Andersen & Co. (1982) found that these were chaotic, with different accounting presentations used by each club, a lack of disclosure of sources of finance and valuation of players, and different accounting years used. The Chester Committee of Enquiry did recommend standardised accounting practices for clubs, and also that, 'The League should take a greater interest in the accounting practices of clubs and improve its access to information on the financial state of clubs' (Football League,

1983). However, little was done along these lines and in the meantime many clubs have floated on the Stock Exchange. The football industry thus raises a number of interesting issues for accounting and legal academics and practitioners. These are outlined above and here we conclude by stressing the key policy implications of some of this discussion, particularly as it relates to instances when a club is faced with a take-over bid. We argue that the valuation of football players and employees in general is an important issue which needs to be addressed. The fact that many football clubs are now plcs and hence vulnerable to asset-stripping take-overs makes it particularly worrying that what may well be the major assets of the club are not reported in the financial accounts. This is changing as a result of the new accounting rules issued by the Accounting Standards Board (Financial Reporting Standard 10), and it will be interesting to see the consistency of approach between clubs in applying these new practices.

We would also recommend changes to the Companies Act and competition policy more generally. As indicated above, the problems associated with the high rates of take-over activity in Britain, engendering as it does short-term attitudes and behaviour by companies, poses especial dangers to the football industry. The advent of digital and pay-per-view TV threatens to unleash these dangers in Britain as media companies seek to divide up the football broadcast content providers. This is just one instance – although we would argue a key one – of why it is that if this country is really to be modernised, the government should amend the Companies Act. When faced with a take-over bid, directors should have regard to the long-term interests of the company itself and its customers, not just the bid price. Competition law more generally should be amended so that those making a take-over bid should be required to demonstrate that it is in the public interest. And finally, shareholders should not be forced to sell, against their will, as happens when 90 per cent of the shares in a company are acquired.

These proposals are particularly important and urgent in the case of the football industry. We have also argued above that particular attention should be paid to representation of small shareholders on company boards. While the need for national action should be impressed on the relevant authorities, this aspect should also be borne in mind when considering alternative ownership structures, one benefit of which might be to introduce such representational structures.

Notes

[1] In the event, public-interest concerns featured prominently in the government's April 1999 blocking of BSkyB's bid for Manchester United, on which see chapter 5.

[2] 'Corporate managers are not the agents of the shareholders, but the trustees of the assets of the corporation, which include its reputation, its distinctive capabilities and the skills of the employees and the suppliers. Their objective should not be to maximise shareholder value but to further the interests of the business.'(Kay and Silberston, 1995, p. 84).

[3] In May 1999 a new organisation, 'Shareholders United', was launched to represent the interests of supporter-shareholders in Manchester United.

References

Accounting Standards Board (1995). *Statement of Principles for Financial Reporting.* Exposure Draft, ASB Publications.

Alexander, M.O. (1971). 'Investments in People'. *Canadian Chartered Accountant*, July, pp. 38–45.

Arthur Andersen & Co. (1982). *The Finance and Taxation of Football Clubs*, Football Association and Football League, London.

Brummet, R.L., Flamholtz E.G. and Pyle W.C. (1968). 'Human Resource Measurement: A Challenge for Accountants'. *The Accounting Review*, April, pp. 217–24.

Cannon, J.A. (1976). 'Applying the Human Resource Account Framework in an International Airline'. *Accounting, Organisations and Society*, pp. 253–63.

Deloitte & Touche (1998). *Annual Review of Football Finance*, Manchester: Deloitte & Touche.

Financial Reporting Standard 10 (1998). 'Goodwill and intangible assets', *Accountancy*, February, pp. 121–134.

Financial Reporting Standard Exposure Draft 17 (1997). 'Measurement of Tangible fixed assets'. *Accountancy*, December, pp. 108–127.

Flamholtz, E.G. (1976). 'The Impact of Human Resource Valuation on Management Decisions: A Laboratory Experiment', *Accounting, Organisations and Society*, February, pp. 153–66.

Flamholtz, E.G. (1985). *Human Resource Accounting*. Jossey-Bass Publishers, 2nd edition.

Football League (1983). *Report of the Committee of Enquiry into Structure and Finance* (Chairman Sir N. Chester), Lytham St Annes.

Grojer, J.E. and Johanson, U. (1998). 'Current development in Human Resource Costing and Accounting, Reality Present, Researchers Absent', *Accounting, Auditing and Accountability Journal*, Vol. 11, No. 4, pp. 495–505.

Harverson, Patrick (1998). 'Fair share ruled out for football fans', *Financial Times*. 12 December.

Jaggi, B. and Lau, H. (1974). 'Toward a Model for Human Resource Valuation', *The Accounting Review*, April, pp. 321–29.

Jennett, N. and Sloane, P.J. (1985). 'The future of League football: a critique of the report of the Chester Committee of Enquiry'. *Leisure Studies*, Vol. 4, pp. 39–56.

Kay, J. and Silberston, A. (1995). 'Corporate Governance'. *National Institute Economic Review*, August 3/95, No. 153, pp. 84–97.

Lev, B. and Schwartz, A. (1971). 'On the Use of the Economic Concept of Human Capital in Financial Statements'. *The Accounting Review*, January, pp. 103–112.

Morrow, S. (1997). 'Accounting for Football Players. Financial and Accounting Implications of "Royal Club Liègois and Others v Bosman" for Football in the United Kingdom'. *Journal of Human Resource Costing and Accounting*, Spring, Vol. 2, No. 1, pp. 55–71.

Pfeffer, J. (1998). *The Human Equation: Building Profits by Putting People First*. Harvard Business School Press.

Shleifer, A. and Vishny, R.W. (1997). 'A Survey of Corporate Governance'. *The Journal of Finance*, June, Vol. LII, No. 2, pp. 737–83.

8. Whose Game is it Anyway?

Stakeholders, Mutuals and Trusts

Jonathan Michie and Shay Ramalingam[1]

Examples of local and fan ownership and control of football clubs are described in detail in other chapters in this book, namely Barcelona FC's fan-ownership structure (see chapter 12 by L'Elefant Blau)[2] and Northampton Town FC's Trust set-up (see chapter 11 by Brian Lomax). There are many other examples of either local ownership or fan involvement which bind sporting clubs to the local community.

In the UK, Barnsley Football Club is a small but financially sound company, and recently enjoyed a season in the Premiership (1997–98) before relegation. Profits have been generated in many years and, more importantly, significant losses have been avoided. The club has strong links with the local community and the shareholding is widely spread, mostly amongst local people, with no controlling interest held by the directors. Support is received from the local authority and central government, including from funds dedicated to the regeneration of industrial towns. The club is planning developments that will yield positive externalities to the local environment, such as for a centre of footballing excellence.

In the US, the Green Bay Packers have maintained local fan and community ownership whilst becoming one of the most successful teams in American football history. The three-time winners of the Superbowl (and runners-up in 1998) represent a small Wisconsin city of a mere 100,000 inhabitants, in competition with the country's population giants. This has endeared them to the nation's football fans, many of whom are intrigued by the David v Goliath concept and the Packers' unique status as a publicly owned not-for-profit corporation. First established in 1919, the not-for-profit organisation has uniquely evolved through time to become a formidable force in American football. In 1935 a fan fell from the stands, sued and won a $5,000 verdict and the insurance company went out of business. The Packers went into receivership and were just about to declare bankruptcy when Green Bay businessmen came to the rescue, raised $15,000 in new capital and reorganised the club. In 1949 a further $125,000 was raised in a giant stock sale all over the state. The team's 4,634 shares are fixed in value at $25 and are subject to strict transfer rules. They can be left to relatives but cannot be sold to outsiders without first offering them to the team. Any one person can hold a maximum of 200 shares. If the team is sold, the proceeds must go toward a local war memorial:

> In an era when the 'home-town team' routinely relocates based on the profit-maximising whims of the wealthy owners, several major cities – particularly those with substantial public investments in sports arenas – now wish they had embraced Green Bay's foresighted ownership solution as a way to anchor these quasi-community assets.[3]

The aim of this chapter is to consider possible mechanisms for getting from where we are now – with over-commercialisation threatening the future of the game – to where we want to be, with clubs being run in the interests of supporters. In the following section we describe the current problems in terms of conflicting 'stakeholding' interests. We then discuss a form of company structure that has been used in the past – and continues to be used – to overcome such problems, namely 'mutualisation'. An alternative option, of holding shares in Trust, is then considered.

Some are more equal than others

The term 'stakeholder' refers to individuals or companies with a legitimate stake in an organisation, where the term 'stake' is used in a rather broad sense. UK company law does acknowledge that the limited liability company does not simply represent the interests of the shareholders alone. However, at present this wider remit extends only to creditors and employees. In reality the firm represents an arena in which there is a potential clash of many interests. Stakeholders include investors, creditors, employees, consumers and the general public, each having their own interests. Under the law as it stands, the directors of a company primarily owe their duties to the company as an abstract entity. Since this abstract entity potentially covers all of the interests mentioned above, the directors of a company have to weigh them up in practice and resolve any conflicts between them.

The law is presently unsatisfactory, however, in that if directors act in the interests of the consumer and/or the wider public interest at the expense of, for example, shareholders, they may be held to have committed a breach of duty. Indeed this is also true if the directors concerned have merely yielded to government or other legitimate external agency pressure. Thus some stakeholders are certainly more equal than others.

Until the Companies Act of 1980, directors would have been in breach of duty by considering employees' interests at the expense of investors. Social responsibility and employee participation are only now, really, part of respectable parlance in modern industrial relations. The enfranchisement of other stakeholder groups in the name of social responsibility has not been widely accepted as yet. The slow development of the law is echoed in the findings of the Hampel Committee on Corporate Governance[+] which in chapter 24 of its findings states that:

> To redefine the directors' responsibilities in terms of the stakeholders would mean identifying all the various stakeholder groups; and deciding the nature and extent of the directors' responsibility to each. The result would be that the directors were not effectively accountable to anyone since there would be no clear yardstick for judging their performance. This is a recipe neither for good governance nor for corporate success.

The logical implication of this is that if the interests of football supporters, a loyal and some might argue, the central stakeholder group, are considered by a board of directors to be in conflict with investors, the directors would be liable for breach of fiduciary duty were they to act in the interests of fans. That this is the current reality is, of course, demonstrated with sickening regularity, most dramatically in the recent past with the taped conversations of the Newcastle United directors deriding the fans and gloating over the ease with which the club was able to exploit them. We would argue that directors are – or at least should be – *de facto* in a fiduciary role with respect to supporters of a club, and that this should be recognised in law.

Stakeholders must be made stakeowners

Whilst we would, therefore, advocate a change to the law in this respect, we have written this chapter in the context of the current legal context. Thus, in order to enfranchise supporters as stakeholders one must first make them joint owners as well.

Football clubs were originally organised to service a local supporter base. In this sense there has been spatial competition for support and these clubs can be viewed as being local monopolists especially given the few imperfect substitutes available for leisure consumption. Increasingly, cash-rich but time-poor consumers have been offered other leisure options but few directly rival the characteristics of the consumption bundle that football offers in terms of branding. The role of the brand is to create institutional stability in terms of loyalty amongst supporters. This gives particular power to the clubs vis-à-vis the supporters once a particular fan base of support has been won.

Supporters also have to deal with the co-ordination problem involved in marshalling a large body of actors. Most fundamental, though, is the absence in British company law of any legal legitimacy for fans in matters of key strategic interest. (This is discussed in detail in chapter 7 above and chapter 10 below).

Clearly agents that have a financial interest in the firm wish to maximise financial returns. Fans do not especially care about the size of net profits at a club – only that their club can carry on as a going concern and can thereby enjoy club success into the future. Indeed, success is likely to be maximised by increasing spending on players (transfer fees and wages, and youth development) beyond the point of profit maximisation. There is a parallel here with the conflict discussed in the economics and management literature, between the interests of the owners of a firm in maximising profits, and the interests of the managers in maximising other variables such as sales growth.

Given this misalignment of objectives there exists a natural tension between different stakeholders in the organisation. Given the relative power of club owners vis-à-vis supporters it could be argued that there would be negative welfare consequences from allowing this conflict to continue unchecked. It is our contention that this misalignment of objectives could be lessened if the conflict between capital and consumers could be channelled more constructively. One way to overcome such a conflict of interest would be for clubs to be owned not by shareholders but by the 'customers' – that is, the fans. This idea has a long history in theory and practice, including through the development of 'mutuals', to which we now turn.

The 'Mutual Form' defined

There are many ways in which firms can be structured and the mutual form is just one. The mutual form has immediate resonance in football given the economic definition of a club as per Cornes and Sandler:[5]

> . . . a voluntary group of individuals who derive mutual benefit

161

from sharing one or more of the following: production costs, the members' characteristics or a good characterised by excludable benefits.

Although each different type of firm performs the same economic role in the system, there are several differences between them:

- In ownership structure: who owns the firm?
- The nature of ownership stakes (as between, for instance, tradeable shares or liquid deposits).
- Who takes the residual risk?
- How are 'principal agent' relationships handled when, inevitably in large firms, there is a split between owners and managers?
- To whom managers are accountable?
- How may ownership change (for example, through mergers, take-overs and so on)?

Typically a mutual form is one where the customers own the business through their participation in the business. As such, voting rights and ownership stakes are assigned to members as per shareholders but no financial ownership instrument can be traded with third parties. Ownership can only come through active participation in the business or enterprise. Thus a mutually owned football club would be one owned by active supporters. Shares would not exist; a notional ownership would be conferred on all actively participating stakeholders in the business.

Ownership may only change in a notional sense when participants leave the business and new participants join. Ownership may only change substantively when a vote is carried for demutualisation. In this case shares are allocated to members and subsequently sold on.

The removal of the tension between stakeholders has yielded financial efficiency gains in mutual forms of organisation in the financial services sector. Miles[6] (1991) argued that the absence of a tension between shareholders and customers at building society mutuals resulted in the spread between borrowing and lending rates being 0.42 percentage points lower than at traditional banks. Indeed, even the Hampel Committee conceded that directors can meet their legal duties to shareholders, and can pursue the objective of long-term shareholder value successfully, only by developing and sustaining effective stakeholder relationships in an organisation.

In addition to the problem of tension between stakeholders, the mutual form of organisation can be more efficient in dealing with 'agency' problems in joint stock firms. Mutuals typically have unique 'residual claims' allocation:

The decision of a claim holder to withdraw resources is a form of partial take-over or liquidation which deprives management of control over assets. This control right can be exercised independently by each claim holder. It does not require a proxy fight, a tender offer or any other concerted take-over bid. In contrast, customer decisions in open non-financial corporations and the repricing of the corporation's securities in the capital market provide signals about the performance of its decision agents. Without further action, however, either internal or from the market for take-overs, the judgement of customers and of the capital market leave the assets of the open non-financial corporation under the control of the managers (Fama and Jensen, 1983, p. 318).[7]

Thus mutual 'members' can vote with their feet and take their capital elsewhere. The directors no longer have access to these assets. In a joint stock corporation, however, when investors sell their shares and take their capital elsewhere, the assets are typically still under the control of the managers concerned.

Loyalty amongst fans for football clubs means that fans are unlikely to vote with their feet. Supporters as owners are therefore unlikely to exercise 'Exit' discipline on managers. There are significant sunk costs in club support which are translated into loyalty. Whilst the mutual model would thus appear redundant we would argue that instead of 'Exit', mutual ownership would provide equally rigorous discipline on management through the power of 'Voice'. Of all the stakeholders in the UK economy, we would expect football supporters to be excellent proponents of 'Voice' discipline at general and extraordinary meetings, given the opportunity.

In addition to providing sources of efficiency gains, mutual forms of ownership have particular advantage when social relationships in markets are important. The relative dominance of mutual forms of ownership in the mortgage market could thus be explained in terms of this ability to sustain long-term relationships with consumers. This form of ownership would also be suited to football clubs given the long-term nature of the relationship between club and supporter.

However, in the financial services sector, consumers stand at both ends of the 'value process'. They demand cash from building societies in the form of loans, but also provide cash in the form of savings. Thus, there is no particular need for a third party supplier of capital – such as shareholders – to step in to supply funds.

In the football industry there is a rather different value process, relative to that involved in financial services provision. The consumers (fans) do stand at both ends of the value process in one sense, since by creating the atmosphere at grounds they contribute to the collective production of what is being 'consumed' both by those at the ground and by those watching on television (either simultaneously or at some other time) and on radio. Indeed, one of the problems with the over-commercialisation of the game is that the fans who do most to create this atmosphere are precisely those being squeezed out, being replaced by a different set of fans – for whom the term customer or consumer might be more appropriate – who do not so contribute.

Many fans do also contribute capital, at least in the sense of being creditors, both through buying their season tickets in advance, and also in some cases by paying to be 'members' of the club. However, in the case of football clubs there has been a need for additional capital. It may be that if clubs had been organised as mutuals then ways would have been found to have raised the necessary revenues with that corporate structure. But as it is, there have historically been third party suppliers of capital to fund club development – be it a local businessman, local authority, government grants or, increasingly, the stock-market.

Is the mutual concept feasible?

In the context of the huge increase in commercialism within football in Britain, with increasing numbers of clubs going to the Stock Exchange to raise large amounts of capital, would it be feasible to establish a mutual, given that there would then be no shareholders? In other words, how could the existing shareholders be bought out? Mutualisation would require the acquisition of all shares in the football club, the cancellation of these shares and the rewriting of the club constitution to reflect mutuality. In the modern joint stock company this would entail potentially redrafting memoranda of association and the articles of association but, more importantly, would require finding the resources to buy up the existing share capital. The central issue in this mutualisation process is thus the acquisition of shares.

Given that the share capitalisation of clubs ranges from several hundred thousand pounds-worth of shares to as much as £600–£700 million, the financial undertaking involved in a complete buyout of shares could prove too difficult for the largest clubs even with a willing sponsor. Government support for such schemes could only be regarded as realistic for the smaller community clubs.

A possible mechanism would be via the Football Trust which has already made large grants to clubs. Indeed the previous awards made by the Football Trust could be seen as a chance missed to secure ownership rights for supporters in return for this financial support.

Existing supporter-shareholders might be wary of supporting mutualisation given the implied loss of private benefits in the form of dividends, particularly if the equity held represented a significant proportion of their private savings. Mutuality would mean that private residual rights would instead accrue to the wider mutual membership.

At some clubs, a debt issue could be used as part of a capital maintenance plan to buy back shares and cancel them with the shareholders' approval. This would have the benefit of providing current shareholders with a fair price for their shares whilst capturing the voting power and benefits of ownership for all supporters. A clear disadvantage here is that a debt issue, even if on favourable repayment terms, brings with it the financial risks associated with a highly geared financial structure. When one considers that football is a particularly risky business with the majority of clubs struggling to break even, such a debt structure may be inappropriate. The majority of teams are not financially strong.

Supporter trusts as a practical alternative

An alternative to full mutualisation would be to establish a supporter trust. The essence of a trust is that the owner of specific property is subject to personal obligations governing how it should be used and applied.[8] Three generic types of trusts can exist and the nature of their existence stems from the way in which obligations governing the trust are created:

- *Express intention to impose trust obligations* – 'Express Trust': this is applied where an owner places assets into trust for the benefit of beneficiaries.
- *Implied intention to impose trust obligations* – 'Implied Trust': this is applied to property in relation to voluntary transactions (not under contract). There is a presumption that in the transaction the purchaser is not making a gift of money to the vendor and so the goods are held in an implied trust.
- *Imposed trust obligations* – 'Constructive Trust': this is where the unconscionable behaviour of the owner of property demands that the law imposes a constructive trust where the owner is required to hold the property for the benefit of others.

Given the past behaviour of most club directors, it might be argued that there would be a case for the third category of trust to be imposed on them. Realistically, though, we are looking at the first. Such a supporter trust would act as a co-ordinating mechanism. With a supporter trust it is envisaged that voting rights associated with shares can be expressly allocated by proxy to the board of trustees but the financial return from the shares owned could still be received by the owners. The board of trustees would then act on behalf of the supporter collective.

A trust is an ideal vehicle for supporter-ownership because it provides for the sharing of ownership of property. It is a truly mutual instrument. Co-ownership can be effected by means of either joint-tenancy or tenancy-in-common. Under joint-tenancy, all supporters would be jointly entitled to the whole of the co-owned property, so that they do not have specific shares. In the event of the death of one joint tenant, his or her interest passes automatically to the other remaining joint tenants under the principle of survivorship.

Under tenancy-in-common, co-owners enjoy undivided shares in the co-owned property, which may be equal or unequal, and survivorship has no application. However, all the co-owners enjoy the right to use and enjoy the property, and no co-owner can regard part of it as representing his or her 'share' alone. We would suggest that tenancy-in-common could exist amongst all supporters, and employees, whilst the owners of the trust property could still retain dividend earning rights. This framework could be established clearly in the objects of the trust, which could also define trustee roles and responsibilities.

As trusts can separate ownership and control, and can sustain joint ownership, they are an ideal vehicle for collective investment. The fiduciary duty of management trustees is no less than that of directors and in both cases the law provides that breach of obligations can lead to prosecution and compensation. The trustees' job would be made that much easier by virtue of the fact that they only had to maximise the welfare of the employees and supporters.

Conclusion

We have argued that mutual organisations are highly effective in removing stakeholder conflict, as seen in the financial services industry in the form of mutual assurance firms and building societies. We argue that this form of organisation would suit the culture, ethos and objectives of football clubs and should be encouraged to promote a diverse and modern economic system. However, given the size of the task to achieve mutualisation, the establishment of supporter trusts would be a significant intermediate step. This is discussed further in chapters 11 and 13.

Notes

[1] The views represented here are the independent views of the authors and do not represent the views of Arthur Andersen or any other third party. We would like to thank Simon Deakin, Dan McGolphin and Paul Keen for their comments. Any remaining errors are our own.

[2] For an unofficial translation of Barcelona Football Club's Statutes see http://www.imusa.org/libraryd/barça.htm.

[3] Gates (1998, p. 69). For an excellent discussion on the abuse of fan loyalty by club owners in the States, see Michael Moore's book, *Downsize This – Random Threats From an Unarmed American*. London: Boxtree, 1997.

[4] Hampel Committee Report (1998). *Committee on Corporate Governance: Final Report*. London HMSO.

[5] Cornes, R., and Sandler, T. *The Theory of Externalities, Public Goods and Club Goods*. Cambridge University Press, 1996.

[6] Miles, D.K., *Economic Issues in the Reform of Building Societies Legislation*. Birkbeck College: London, Mimeo, 1991.

[7] Fama, E. and Jensen, M., 'Separation of Ownership and Control'. *Journal of Law and Economics*, 28, 2, 1983, pp. 301–26.

[8] For an analysis of the law of trusts and equitable obligations, see R. Pearce and J. Stevens, *The Law of Trusts and Equitable Obligations*. Butterworths, 1998.

9. The Evolution of Irish Plc Co-operatives:

Lessons for English Football Clubs

Anne Bourke

Introduction

This chapter starts by briefly considering the factors which have contributed to recent changes in football in England. While many developments are positive (for example better spectator facilities), there are indications that business imperatives in the game are now determining the sporting aspects and not vice-versa. The more overt signs of corporate involvement in football are reflected by the ownership structures recently adopted by many clubs, most notably quoted public limited company (plc) status. Individuals associated with certain leading football clubs recognised some years ago the potential to reap financial gains. For them there has been much financial success – but are current ownership structures adequate to protect the fundamental role of the game as an important cultural asset?

There are several possible ownership arrangements for football clubs (as discussed in other chapters in this book); the option proposed in this chapter is the plc co-operative. Dairy co-operatives are common in Ireland, and although four of the leading co-operatives adopted plc status in the late 1980s, the essence of co-operative ownership has been maintained. The new organisational structure which evolved is not replicated in any other country, and is unique in that it caters for the long-term interests of the farmer-owners who supply their produce to the co-ops. Parallels between developments in the Irish dairy sector and English football exist, especially in relation to their financial requirements during the mid-1980s. Both sectors were under-capitalised but needed to raise significant funds to modernise their plant and equipment. It is acknowledged that while there are fundamental differences in relation to operational issues in both sectors, from an ownership perspective the Irish co-operatives incorporate the interests of a broad sector of the population. This is important in the way co-operatives contribute to the maintenance of social cohesion in rural areas. There is no reason why such an arrangement cannot be put in place at football clubs, as it would broaden the ownership base and attend to some of the concerns of football fans.

Setting the scene . . .

Conn (1997) asserts that had the English Football Association (FA) been more in tune with the needs of soccer during the 1980s, many of the changes which have occurred since then might not have happened, or might have taken a different format. Drawing on the FA publication *Blueprint for the Future of Football* published in 1991, he suggests that this document, with its emphasis on pursuing the middle-class consumer, struck the wrong strategic note. According to Conn the first requirement needed to bring the game into the modern era was unity in its administrative structures and the pursuit of a clear vision for the good of the whole game. The fact that the idea floundered on the steps of FA headquarters at Lancaster Gate has possibly, more than any other factor, contributed to the fragmentation of the game. In 1992, 22 clubs managed (and were supported by football's governing body, the FA) to break away from the English League and form their own league.

The necessity for clubs to upgrade their facilities had been recognised in the wake of the Hillsborough Disaster. The *Taylor Report* recommended investment in all-seater stadia, which clubs in the top two divisions were compelled to complete (with some government aid), but at a considerable cost. As a result of the investment required it was imperative for clubs to adopt a more professional approach to financial management and organisational structure. Every single top football club, in order to pay for the costs of stadium modernisation demanded by the *Taylor Report*, has undergone either a take-over, a flotation or a financial reorganisation of some sort (Conn, 1997). These pacts were not like the old deals, when the shares were hawked around pubs or money invested in return for a seat in the directors' box and a name in the programme. Football clubs had become investment vehicles and this new investment represented conventional corporate dealing. But it could have been otherwise as the evolution of the Irish plc co-operative detailed in this chapter illustrates.

Football – a business or sport?

The peculiar economic nature of sport has long been recognised by football analysts and economists. Rothenberg (cited by Dempsey and Reilly (1998, pp. 20-21)) wrote the following about American baseball over 40 years ago in a classic analysis of the sports business that still applies to football today:

> Two teams opposed to each other in play are like two firms producing a single product. The product is the game, weighted by the revenues derived from its play. With game admission prices given, the product is the game weighted by the number of paying customers who attend. When 30,000 attend, the output is twice as large as when 15,000 attend. In one sense the teams compete; in another they combine in a single firm in which the success of each branch requires that it be not 'too much' more efficient than the other. If it is, output falls.

Rothenberg stresses the fact that football, like business in general, is characterised by uncertainty of outcome, but this case is unique by virtue of the fact that two firms (teams) must engage in the production of a single product (the game). Should the pattern of results of games become too predictable, there is a loss in entertainment value, expressed in economic terms as a downturn in output. While, in general, competition is dependent on firms competing in the same industry, the essence of football is different – two teams must co-produce, so that there is a 'match' and a joint product.

A further distinguishing feature of football is that the customers (fans) are an integral part of the product. Many clubs have adopted a 'business' approach to their activities, but at the risk of alienating their fans (see chapters 1 and 2). It is widely acknowledged that soccer for many people is a religion, gives rise to passion and can be a source of unity or disunity. It has been asserted that (real) fans are an 'endangered species' given the new forms of ownership, but it is possible to accommodate important sociological dimensions, by adopting a co-operative style of ownership in football clubs. In the following paragraphs the essence of the co-operative arrangement is detailed and background information provided in relation to the conversion to plc status by four Irish dairy co-operatives during the late 1980s.

Co-operatives – what are they?

Co-operatives developed as a means of organising large-scale operations (Smith, 1983). Most co-operatives date from the Industrial Revolution, though some, such as those making Gruyère or Emmenthal cheese in France and Switzerland were formed before the thirteenth century. There is no clear-cut commonly accepted understanding as to what a co-operative is (Hind, 1997). The author contends that many authors have attempted to provide a workable definition and conceded defeat. According to the Registrar of Friendly Societies the features distinguishing co-operatives from non-co-operatives are as follows:

(a) Conduct of the business must be for the mutual benefit of the members, with the benefits they receive deriving mainly from their participation in the business.
(b) Control of the co-operative must be vested in the members equally e.g. the principle of one member, one vote is fundamental.
(c) Interest on capital will not exceed a rate necessary to obtain and retain sufficient capital to carry out the co-operative's objectives.
(d) Profits, if distributable, will be distributed in relation to the extent members have either traded with the co-operative or taken part in the co-op's business.
(e) Membership must not be artificially restricted with the aim of increasing the value of any proprietary rights and interests.

Co-operatives are constituted to ensure a genuine community interest among members, based on something other than the amount of capital they have placed in the organisation. The purpose of the co-operative dictates its way of working, but is often ill-defined. The objectives may be categorised as economic and non-economic. According to Smith (1983) the co-operative follows its own interest, seeking for the members the best possible return on milk supply, labour or grocery purchases as the case may be. Co-operatives have become composites: it is a co-operative as far as members' own trade is concerned but capitalist in relation to outsiders. *A co-operative is an association of people rather than capital; capital subscription does not form the basis of voting power.* In most co-operatives each member has one vote irrespective of the amount of equity he has contributed.

The Irish dairy industry has traditionally been dominated by co-operative organisations which are owned by the suppliers of the co-operatives. Co-operative rules ordain that the shareholdings in these co-operatives can only be traded at par value while the level of return in terms of share interest is also limited by co-operative rules. Some amalgamations occurred in the 1970s which reduced the number of co-operatives and increased the membership of individual co-operatives, but the core ethos of co-operatives remained. At that time in the US, two forms of reorganisation of co-operatives emerged: (a) conversion to corporate status and (b) refinement of traditional co-operative principles and practices. In the Irish dairy sector the new form of organisational structure which evolved was a combination of corporate and co-operative, which importantly for the farmers, retained the co-operative dimension.

Shift to plc status

There is little doubt about the success of the co-operative movement in Ireland, especially in the dairy sector where co-operatives or co-operative-controlled firms account for virtually all the milk purchases from farmers (Harte, 1997). In 1992, the dairy co-operative sector in the Republic of Ireland employed 19,462 people and generated a turnover of £4,954 million. The conversion by some Irish dairy co-ops to plcs has been referred to as an 'entrepreneurial event' (Mahon, 1998). According to Harte, the two primary reasons for the change to plc co-ops were: (a) the need to gain additional capital for growth and (b) the need to provide shareholders with a current market value for their shares. A third reason was the need to provide a mechanism to reward and promote executive staff.

The general method by which traditional co-operatives were converted to plc co-ops was as follows. A new public company was formed with two types of share capital, 'A' and 'B' shares, having equal ranking. The 'B' shares were issued to the original co-operative in exchange for its assets and subsidiary companies. Some of the 'A' shares were then offered to farmers and employees at a discount on the expected market price of the shares. Further 'A' shares were then placed in public flotation. As currently constituted, the shareholding of the co-operative in the public company must be maintained above 50 per cent, giving the co-operative majority control. This control structure is copper-fastened by requiring agreement by 75 per cent of farmer members in two consecutive extraordinary general meetings to permit the co-operative shareholding to fall below 50 per cent.

Four Irish dairy co-operatives opted for the conversion in the late 1980s: (a) Kerry (b) Avonmore (c) Waterford and (d) Golden Vale and details of the changeover are provided in Appendix A. However, it must be noted that there are slight variations in the approach adopted by the organisations and some changes have occurred more recently. For instance, the co-operative shareholding in the Kerry Group was reduced recently, but only following the agreement of 75 per cent of farmer-shareholders as specified above.

Effects of the ownership change

Farmers have had a long tradition of involvement in the co-operative movement and are by nature conservative. Many were reluctant to convert the co-operative society to a plc. But an important element of the new structure is that farmers were allowed to retain some 'control' in the running of the co-operative. As a result of the introduction of the new structure, each farmer has in effect a two-stock portfolio, as three of the co-operatives (Avonmore, Waterford and Kerry) have retained in some degree a substantial interest of the co-operative predecessor. Farmers' portfolio management is unique in that it is two tiered – they hold tradeable plc shares, which also entails involvement in non-marketable assets. This involvement is due to their holding non-tradeable 'B' shares in the vestigial society co-operative of their plcs.

According to Hogan (1989) the introduction of co-operatives to the Stock Exchange represents the single most important advance in broader share ownership in Ireland during the past two decades. Between them, the co-operatives have 22,500 shareholders from diverse rural areas, the vast majority of whom are unlikely to have had any previous direct share ownership. From the farmers' perspective, one further positive aspect worth noting in relation to the restrictive share structure is that it was designed to prevent a take-over of the business.

The plc co-op structure provided a new funding mechanism for these organisations, but it also had more far-reaching effects. Along with solving the funding problem, it provided a means by which many of the problems associated with vertical ownership by farmers, and with the co-operative structure, could be overcome. Incentives to managers were enhanced through the use of staff equity participation and the use of stock options. It provided a mechanism by which the 'strait-jacket' aspects of the co-operative form could be shed and the growth potential of the enterprise realised (Harte, 1997).

Despite the common perception that a co-operative structure may retard organisational development and limit the organisation's potential for raising finance and adopting a market focus, evidence exists to suggest that the plc co-ops have experienced major growth since the new structure was adopted. For example, the Kerry Group plc turnover has risen from £265.2 million in 1986 to £1,344.1 million in 1997; and its operating profit has increased from £11.2 million in 1986 to £104.9 million in 1997. This group has internationalised it activities mainly by acquisitions and now has many wholly owned subsidiaries outside Ireland – in Europe, North America, Australia and New Zealand. Similar patterns of growth and expansion have been recorded by the other three plc co-ops referred to in this chapter.

Parallels for football clubs

Some football analysts and indeed supporters will argue that television and television money has made a major contribution to the new-found popularity of soccer. According to John Williams (Dempsey and Reilly, 1998, p. 230), people now want to be identified with a football club, not because it is a gritty and working-class tradition, but because it is fashionable in a consumerist way which offers a connection to the authentic. Showing an interest in the game is like saying, 'I am aware of what is happening'. It is becoming a fashion accessory. Fans are no longer simply the people that come and watch and offer their allegiance to a single club. New fans are becoming, in the truest sense of the word, *consumers*.

But this was not always the case. Football clubs during the 1980s lacked organisational skills and focus, which became evident with such catastrophes as the Heysel and Hillsborough stadium disasters. By 1990, clubs were being compelled to invest in their facilities and as Conn (1997) has charted, short-termism ruled. Consequently the funding strategies employed allowed individuals with money, who professed to having an interest in the game, to gain control of many clubs as the clubs scrambled to find benefactors with the necessary finance or the connections to raise it. The ownership structures of football clubs were rarely discussed, and there were inadequate regulations in place to protect the unique characteristics of the sport (see chapters by Conn, and Michie and Walsh). Had a more long-term approach been taken, and the core support of the game been better informed and organised, the game might be in better shape today.

The plight of the dairy industry in Ireland during the mid-to-late 1980s was slightly different in some respects from that of football in England. There was plenty of interest in its fortunes, but its income streams in dairy produce were heavily regulated. The introduction of milk quotas forced dairy co-operatives to consider diversification strategies. To extend their business activities beyond the milk business, it was essential to change the organisational ethos and introduce a more professional style of management and gain access to large-scale capital funds. The management style of co-operatives was very conservative and bereft of a visionary perspective. The notion of conversion to plc status was not greeted warmly by a large proportion of members of the co-operatives, but the arrangements put in place guaranteeing these members 'control' of the new business structure (as outlined earlier) went a long way in allaying members' fears.

By way of comparison, Manchester United changed its organisational structure becoming a plc in 1991. It currently has 27,737 small shareholders controlling 23.4 per cent of the issued capital (*Annual Report*, 1998). It has been documented (Conn, 1997, chapter 2) that many years ago people who had shares in the club were relieved of them by individuals who possessed business acumen and an appreciation of the real value of shares in a private company. Had there been a broader and more informed shareholder base in the club prior to the conversion to a plc, plus the recognition of the need to maintain this in order to protect the sporting ethos of the club, then the plc co-operative would have offered a neat alternative club structure to the straight plc structure ultimately adopted. The adoption of co-operative principles (giving one person one vote) would not have restricted the growth and development of the club, as the Irish dairy co-operative experience illustrates.

It is interesting to note that reports on the financial state of the game in England constantly refer to the divide between the rich and poorer clubs, the scarcity and high cost of players, and poor financial results achieved by the majority of clubs. Ownership structures are examined especially when times are tough, and it is heartening to note that Trevor Watkins (in order to save Bournemouth from financial ruin in 1996), has put in place a supporters' and community trust. This arrangement, in Watkins' view, puts the club in the hands of people whose loyalty will last much longer than that of any potential white-knight businessman chairman, coming in on an agenda of his own to put money into the club (Dempsey and Reilly, 1998, pp. 207–12).

Concluding comments

Farmers and football fans have much in common in that they are both the 'life line' of the co-operative or club. Andy Mitten (1998) asserts that a football club isn't just like any other business and football fans aren't just like any other customers. A fan supports a club because in his view it is in the blood, usually passed down from generations before, and with that support comes an emotional investment that exceeds any share, dividend or equity option. Without supporters (fans) football clubs will cease to exist. They are as important for the long-term fortunes of the club as farmers have been for the continued existence of dairy co-operatives. Changing demands of the dairy sector in Ireland led to the reorganisation of co-operatives, and it is interesting to observe that the important role of farmers (as suppliers) has been, and continues to be, acknowledged. The adoption of plc status by several clubs has created new masters for the enterprise – the city and shareholders. Perhaps, this might not be such a negative thing had the clubs concerned fostered communication with the (shareholder) fans and put in place a communication channel similar to the arrangement for institutional shareholders. It appears that senior executives, consultants, analysts and their advisors believe that the fan base is stable and secure. It remains to be seen whether their further alienation and exploitation may prove in the long term 'to be a bridge too far'.

It is clear that current corporate governance arrangements in many clubs (whether private or public companies) concentrate ownership amongst a few, and ensure that fans have little or no involvement. A list of the wealthiest soccer clubs in the world now includes several English ones and while investors and shareholders are impressed by these facts, it should be noted that there are clubs in the lower divisions of the league which are struggling for survival – Leyton Orient, Cardiff and Scunthorpe (Nichols, 1999). In fact, the *incomplete* implementation of the recommendations of the *Taylor Report*, together with the increasing money flowing into the game from TV revenues have contributed to the circumvention of the Football Association's Rule 34 (see chapters by Conn, and Michie and Walsh) which was meant to protect clubs from financial exploitation. The transition to plcs by many clubs was smooth, with the FA paying little heed to the flouting of the sentiments of that rule by the creation of holding companies. The main consequence of the new structures adopted by clubs (aside from the profits gained by directors) has been the distancing of the fans from their clubs (see the discussion in the chapter by Hamil on the 'fan equity' concept). It was not essential to pursue such a course of action. There are other options for ownership as has been demonstrated by the case of the Irish plc co-operatives.

Appendix

(a) Kerry Co-operative Creamery was the first co-operative to turn all of its assets into shares in a Public Limited Liability Company – Kerry Group plc. It swapped all of its assets into 90 million 'B' shares in the newly founded plc. The co-op had authority to increase this number to a statutory maximum of 102 million 'B' shares. Kerry Group plc could also place 98 million 'A' shares on the Stock Exchange. The 90 million 'B' shares owned by Kerry Co-operative Creameries Ltd were non-marketable and were indirectly owned by the 6,000 shareholders in the co-operative. This would ensure that effective control of the organisation remained in the hands of the co-operative members. Subsequently, Kerry has converted all of the 'B' shares into 'A' shares, thus they are tradeable on the Stock Exchange, allowing the co-operative to reduce its shareholding in the plc if the co-operative members wished. As at the year-end 1997, Kerry Co-operative Creameries Ltd owns 38 per cent in the Kerry Group plc. (See *Annual Report*, 1997).[2]

(b) Avonmore and Waterford had structures similar to Kerry Group plc whereby the co-operative retained majority control of the plc by owning the non-marketable 'B' shares, which accounted for more than 50 per cent of the total shares issued. Avonmore co-operative in 1988 placed all its assets in Avonmore Foods plc[3] in exchange for 100 million 'B' shares in the plc. They subsequently issued 39.1 million marketable 'A' shares. The issue of shares by Avonmore Foods plc was bound by a statutory maximum of 196 million.

(c) Waterford Co-operative Society in 1988 was turned into a holding company, owning the majority of shares in the new Waterford Foods plc. Statutory authorised share levels were determined to be 115 million 'A' shares and 120 million 'B' shares.

(d) In the case of Golden Vale the arrangement is slightly different, as the co-operative does not control the plc by owning the majority stake. Instead the plc owns 2 million of the 2,004,243 shares in the co-operative Golden Vale Food Products Limited. The less than 1 per cent co-operative ownership not held by the plc is accounted for by the 4,243 co-operative shares held by the milk suppliers. The co-operative Golden Vale Food Products Limited is a pure co-operative, as each member has only one vote in the running of the co-operative regardless of the number of shares held. Thus the plc has only one vote, the same as any other supplier. So while the co-operative does not control the plc, it does control the milk pool and is also responsible for primary processing.

Notes

1. Rules for co-operatives are approved by the Irish Co-operative Organisation Society Limited (ICOS).
2. In order to allow the co-operative stake in Kerry Group plc to be reduced to a level below 50 per cent, two extraordinary general meetings (EGMs) were held and the change was supported by 75 per cent of the membership.
3. Avonmore announced a name change for the Avonmore Foods plc on 19 January 1999. It will be known as Glanbia.

References

Conn, D., 1997. *The Football Business*. Edinburgh: Mainstream Publishing.

Dempsey, P. and Reilly, K., 1998. *Big Money Beautiful Game*. London: Nicholas Brealey Publishing.

Dunning, E., 1997. 'The Social Significance of Soccer'. CRSS Leicester University.

Football Association (1991). *The Blueprint for the Future of Football*. London: The Football Association.

Harte, L., 1997. 'Creeping Privatisation of Irish Co-operatives: A Transaction Cost Explanation', in Nilsson, J. and van Dijk, G. (eds.), *Strategies and Structures in the Agro-food Industries*. Van Gorcum.

Hogan, J., 1989. Privatisation in Ireland – the example of Dairy Co-operatives, *Working Paper No. 3*. Centre for Study of Financial Markets, Michael Smurfit Graduate School of Business, University College, Dublin.

Hind, A., 1997. The Changing Values of the Co-operative and its Business Focus. *American Journal of Agricultural Economics*. Vol. 79, No. 4, pp. 1077–82.

Horsman, M., 1997. *Sky High – the Inside Story of BSkyB*. London: Orion Books.

Mahon, B., 1998. *The Irish Dairy Industry: a Study of Farmer Members' Equity Shares in the Co-ops and Co-op plcs*. Unpublished Masters Dissertation, Faculty of Agriculture,

University College, Dublin.

McDonnell, N., 1998. *Issues in Portfolio Management for Farmers with Equity in Co-operative Plcs*. Unpublished MBS Dissertation, Smurfit Graduate School of Business, University College Dublin.

Mitten, A., 1998. 'Northern Soul', *Manchester United*. Vol. 6, No. 11, p. 11.

Nichols, P., 1999. In Serious Need of Promotion. *The Guardian*. 20 February.

Nilsson, J. and van Dijk, G., 1997. *Strategies and Structures in the Agro-food Industries*. Van Gorcum.

Smith, L., 1983. 'Economists, Economic Theory and Co-operatives' in Kennedy, L. (ed.), *Economic Theory of Co-operative Enterprises*. The Plunkett Foundation for Co-operative Studies.

Inquiry by the Rt Hon Lord Justice Taylor (1990). *The Hillsborough Stadium Disaster: Final Report*. Cm962. London: HMSO.

10. Modern Corporations and the Public Interest

Rob Branston, Keith Cowling, Nestor Duch Brown,
Jonathan Michie and Roger Sugden

Controversial issues of corporate governance are not new. It is over fifty years since Berle and Means (1932) raised the possibility of the managers rather than the owners controlling US corporations. Since then much attention has focused on how corporations are governed, and by whom. Controversy continues. The issue of who has control, and in whose interest that control is wielded, remains of relevance to all sorts of everyday issues. In Britain these issues resurfaced around the attempted take-over of Manchester United plc by BSkyB, itself 40 per cent owned by News International, the parent of which is News Corporation.

Manchester United attracts considerable attention. Internationally, 'soccer' is widely seen to impact significantly on people's everyday lives. News Corporation controls interests in 49 countries[1] and is itself high-profile, not least because in Rupert Murdoch it has a chief executive and chairman who has captured international headlines. This take-over bid therefore raised questions about how soccer clubs should be governed, and in whose interests.

The urgency of asking – and answering – these questions is demonstrated by the emergence of other media groups showing interest in English soccer clubs. Carlton have had talks with Arsenal. Granada have been rumoured to be interested in Liverpool (amongst other clubs). NTL took a shareholding in Newcastle United with an option for an additional share purchase, to take a majority stake, provided BSkyB's bid was not halted by the Monopolies and Mergers Commission. When the government, in April 1999, did block the BSkyB bid, they also referred the NTL move to the Competition Commission (as the MMC had become), upon which NTL withdrew.

Many of the other chapters in this book argue that soccer is unique because of the way it touches people's everyday lives, and hence the governance of soccer should be treated differently to the governance of other production activities. In this chapter we argue that the importance of taking a wider, more democratic approach to decision-making should be pursued not only in the case of football clubs, but more generally. There is a widespread problem with modern corporations being hierarchies where strategic decisions are taken by an élite few in pursuit of their own interest. If corporations were to be governed in the 'public interest' the governance process would need to be characterised by more participation.

The firm as a decision-maker

A starting point for most analysis of the firm is Coase (1937) who sees 'markets' and 'firms' as alternative means of co-ordinating production. He defines a firm as the means of co-ordinating production without using market exchange, and sets about exploring why markets are sometimes 'superseded'. However, Coase's ideas are rooted in planning, not in the macroeconomic sense of central planning, but microeconomic planning. This is a point that subsequent readers of Coase have either ignored or lost, certainly over recent years. Yet his fundamental concern with planning is clear. Whilst Coase observes that co-ordination by markets entails 'planning by individuals' who 'experience foresight and choose between alternatives', he is especially interested in the 'planning within our economic system which is quite different from . . . individual planning . . . and which is akin to what is normally called economic planning'. He in fact sees firms as islands of economic planning.

This concern with planning points to the relevance of a recent and extensive literature on strategic decision-making in modern corporations, and hence to an economic analysis centred on strategic decisions rather than markets. The significance of strategy is suggested by Zeitlin (1974) who argues that the power to control a corporation implies the ability to determine broad corporate objectives. Essentially, to make strategic decisions is to plan the overall direction of production and hence govern the corporation. This includes the ability to determine in a broad sense a corporation's geographical orientation, its relationship with rivals and its relationship with the labour force. For example, in the case of Manchester United a decision has been made to sign a 'memorandum of co-operation' with the Belgian soccer club Royal Antwerp; this is an issue of geographical orientation, since the agreement allows the clubs to exchange players and thus by-pass Britain's relatively strict labour laws whereby work permits are only granted to non-European Union

soccer players if they can show that they are established inter-
nationals.

Strategic decisions on Manchester United's relationship with its
rivals include key decisions on the ways in which it allies itself with
other clubs in pursuing the prospect of a 'European Super League'.
This includes its decision on membership of the so-called 'G-14',
which has been conceived as a permanent body representing the
interests of 14 of Europe's 'biggest' soccer clubs. Strategic decisions on
its relationship with the labour force include decisions about the form
of the pay structure for players. See, for example, the 1998 *Annual
Report*: 'The growth in player wage levels remains the most demanding
component of our total wage cost structure . . . Your board has taken
a firm and fair view of the wage levels appropriate for our players and
we have not violated these levels in current players' contract and
transfer negotiations.'[2]

The impact of corporations turns crucially on who governs and on
what basis they make their decisions. Decisions are generally made in
the interests of the decision-makers. The impact of corporations is
therefore very much dependent upon who makes such decisions.

Who governs?

The recent literature on corporate governance considers the nature of
this controlling élite by analysing the relationship between
shareholders and managers: can the shareholders exert sufficient
control over the managers to ensure that it is their (and not the
managers') agenda that the company follows?

Many authors highlight the differences between the Anglo–US type
of corporate governance with that observed in continental Europe. In
reality these different structures have only superficial effects on the
controlling élite and the overall conclusions reached are broadly the
same; *de facto* control of the corporation rests between an élite group
of (large) shareholders and the company board.

It is said that the two main differences that separate the Anglo–US
economies from that of other countries are, first, their firm ownership
structure and, second, their prevalence for take-overs. In many
continental countries corporate ownership is concentrated in the
hands of a small number of other firms, banks, families or individuals.
For example, of the 200 largest companies in Germany, nearly 90 per
cent have at least one shareholder with at least 25 per cent of the
equity. This can be compared with the top 200 British companies
where two-thirds have no shareholder with more than 10 per cent of
the equity. This concentrated ownership in the continental system

(together with other factors) means the shareowners are more directly involved in the management of these corporations and so can exert a degree of direct control over them.

However, this does not mean to say that shareholders in Anglo–US companies have no real means of influence when looking at the control of the corporation. When discussing the British system, Holland (1995) highlights the fact that 'institutional influence and intervention is normally conducted through co-operative relationships with investee companies. Much of this process of influence and intervention . . . was conducted away from the public gaze'. Therefore, although unseen, the system does actually function along similar lines to the continental model, where large shareholders can, and do, have contact with and influence over the boards of the modern corporation. In the case of Manchester United, this is explicitly recognised in the *Annual Report*: 'Communications with shareholders are given a high priority. *There is a regular dialogue with individual institutional shareholders* as well as general presentations after the interim and full year results are announced. There is also opportunity for individual shareholders to question the chairman at the annual general meeting.'[3]

It is only the larger shareholders that have direct access to and influence over the board. The smaller shareholders are excluded from these links, which concentrate shareholder power in the hands of the 'privileged élite' with access. In the case of Manchester United this was illustrated rather graphically by the ejection from the premises of shareholders who were distributing leaflets at their own 1998 AGM – the owners of the company being ejected from company premises by paid company staff. On the rather peculiar treatment of shareholders who happen to be fans, see the article by Patrick Harverson in the *Financial Times*, 12 December 1998, in which he reports that some clubs go to extreme lengths to avoid questions from such shareholders: 'Sunderland, for example, held its first annual meeting as a public company in London on the day of a match that many of its shareholder-fans would have attended in Bradford.'

The process of concentrating shareholder power within an élite group is further increased by the preference in many continental countries for dual-class shares, where the different classes carry different voting rights. For example, in Denmark class 'B' shares cannot have less than one-tenth of the voting rights of class 'A' shares and in Italy only 50 per cent of equity need have any voting rights. Indeed, this habit in many countries has become the norm, with 75 per cent of quoted firms in Denmark and Sweden having dual-class shares, and with Switzerland (among others) only slightly lower at 68 per cent. This means a subset of shareholders control the voting rights of the company and so this élite group may be especially influential.

In other countries, such as the UK or Japan, not more than 1 per cent of listed companies have dual-class shares, with these countries instead preferring the one share/one vote system. However, equal voting rights per share is still not enough to ensure that influence becomes widely spread among the shareholders. It is argued by Tricker (1997) that 'information has always been central to the exercise of power, and so it is with governance power', yet Russell Reynolds Associates (1998) reports that 'investors say they do not have enough information'. Without the general availability of genuine information, the majority of shareholders cannot effectively monitor management and so they have little corporate control. That some shareholders are somewhat more equal than others when it comes to being provided with information was illustrated in the case of Manchester United at their 1998 AGM. The finance director claimed that the reason that the majority of shareholders present were opposed to the actions of the board was that the board had more information than the shareholders did, hence the board knew better. The shareholders (that is, the owners) had not been provided with sufficient information. Quite.

The large institutional shareowners who regularly meet management are the only groups with the incentive and opportunity to access the information needed to monitor management. Consequently the AGM fails to provide an appropriate forum for achieving real democratic shareholder control as a group of élite shareholders hold all the information and sufficient incentives.

However, there is a widespread and growing demand for disclosure, transparency and access to corporate information. Recent events (at least in Britain) have meant an increased role for non-executive directors who are expected to critically evaluate the policies and strategies of their executive colleagues. However, this does not appear to have resulted in any significant change to the information that is provided to the general shareholders and so the status quo has yet to be significantly changed.

It cannot be denied that take-overs are a significant influence on the corporate governance of Anglo–American economies. In the UK there are approximately double the number of take-overs than in France or Germany. Hostile bids are common in the UK, while there have only been four successful hostile bids in Germany in the post-war period. The take-over market is not so vigorous in continental markets partly because it is not needed; by their direct and official involvement, large shareholders in continental firms have sufficient control of the company.

This means in both the continental and Anglo–US system the end result is the same; shareholder power rests with an élite group of the shareholders, through concentrated ownership, restricted voting practices, restriction of corporate information and active take-over markets.

Does this élite group of powerful shareholders control the firm? In some respects the answer must be yes and in some respects no; the modern corporation is a complicated entity and makes many strategic decisions. It is unrealistic to expect that all these can be made with the understanding of the 'controlling' shareholders. It is only the major and most important with which they involve themselves (either directly or indirectly), leaving senior managers with a high degree of autonomy. In the case of football clubs, it should be noted, the senior managers are in fact the directors. The position of manager at a football club is a far more precarious one than in most companies, and the remit and level of responsibility rather lower. In general at football clubs, the only 'managers' able to make decisions concerning the company are the directors. When the term 'senior manager' is used in this chapter it is used to refer to those who have this sort of degree of decision-making power – and should thus be taken to refer to the directors.

Only when these 'senior managers' deviate significantly from the wishes of the 'élite shareholders' will the shareholders exercise their actual control. Therefore it is likely that *de facto* control of the modern corporation rests somewhere between a subset of shareholders and the top managers, while the theoretical control rests alone with the subset of shareholders.

Implications

Identifying who governs corporations has significance because interests vary across those concerned about, and affected by, a corporation's activities. This variation would be reflected in different strategic decisions and hence differences in the impact of corporations on society.

BSkyB's attempted take-over of Manchester United demonstrated major differences of opinion amongst its existing shareholders,[4] one of which is BSkyB itself.[5] In early September 1998, following the announcement of the bid, over 200 shareholders in the soccer club formed an informal group, Shareholders United Against Murdoch (SUAM). This group issued a report arguing that BSkyB's bid under-valued Manchester United, being founded on BSkyB's interest in selling entertainment and not on a specific interest in soccer:

> The potential take-over . . . and similar transactions involving
> other football clubs and media companies across the UK and

Europe may trigger a change in the structure of football as a commercial entertainment activity and as a professional sport. It is difficult to see how these changes could enhance the underlying value of clubs like Manchester United. The attraction of football as a spectator sport lies deep in the culture and traditions of sport. It involves the level of engagement of the individual (far more so than a film for example), and the essential competitiveness and unpredictability of on-field results. The excitement and engagement generates demand, and that generates revenues. Large-scale consolidation or domination of football clubs could reduce competition and erode local rivalries threatening the popularity of football as mass entertainment. BSkyB is willing to accept this potential diminution in value of football programming over the longer term because the value may well migrate to their other channels (films or some other content). They are therefore discounting this possibility in their bid for United.[6]

The argument is essentially that BSkyB's interest in selling entertainment would take Manchester United down a strategic route which other shareholders with a different interest focused more narrowly on soccer would resist. It can be argued that BSkyB's interest is not just selling entertainment; the News Corporation has an interest in media outputs more generally, with operating earnings in 1998 being derived from television (35 per cent), newspapers (25 per cent), magazines and inserts (22 per cent), filmed entertainment (15 per cent) and books (2 per cent).[7] Such an interest in media outputs is even further removed from a specific concern with soccer than is an interest in entertainment.

There is also a clear inference in the SUAM report that, amongst shareholders, those who are senior managers (that is, the directors) may have a different interest to others; most of the directors of Manchester United were offered lucrative employment contracts for the future, conditional on the success of the take-over bid.[8] In short, it seems clear that amongst current shareholders in Manchester United, there are differences of opinion about the most desirable strategy.

Moreover, subsets of shareholders are not the only groups with an interest in the activities of the soccer club. There are also, for example: employees (in 1998 Manchester United plc employed 46 players and 417 others, as well as a further 1,170 temporary staff on match days);[9] supporters of Manchester United in Manchester and in other localities in various parts of the world;[10] and indeed followers of soccer more generally. The firm's Old Trafford stadium currently accommodates 55,300 and there are plans to increase capacity to 67,400. It is likely that those people attending the live games have a specific interest in soccer that overlaps with that highlighted in the SUAM report. As for the interests of soccer supporters more widely, that these might diverge from the interests of others is explicitly recognised by the English Football Association.[11] Fears over the commercialisation of soccer led the Association to introduce Rule 34, which requires soccer clubs to adopt Articles of Association constraining the extent to which the clubs can be commercially exploited. To some degree the Rule has been circumvented by the use of plcs as holding companies for soccer clubs, with only the latter being bound by the Association's regulations. In the case of Manchester United, the plc's position is unambiguous, as an extract from its prospectus reveals:

> ARTICLES OF ASSOCIATION OF MEMBER CLUBS: Under the rules of the Football Association, member club companies are required to have provisions in their Articles of Association, *inter alia*, restricting the dividends payable on their shares to the maximum from time to time allowed by the Football Association (presently 15 per cent per annum of the amount credited as paid up on the shares) and providing that, on a return of assets on a winding up, shareholders are only entitled to a return, equivalent to the amount paid up on their shares, the remaining assets being distributed to the Football Association Benevolent Fund or to some local club, institution or charity approved by the shareholders. These rules do not apply to the Company. As a result of the agreement referred to in paragraph 8(b) of Part VII whereby the fixed assets and non-footballing business of the Club will on 31 July 1991 be transferred to the Company, a substantial part of future advertising, sponsorship and promotion income will accrue to the Company, rather than the Club, and the Company will, in future, receive rental income from the Club in respect of the use of Old Trafford. The terms of appointment of any paid executive director of a member club must be approved by the Football Association and by the Football League and any such paid executive director must be full time; *these restrictions apply to the Club but do not apply to the Company.*[12]

Both the existence of Rule 34 and its deliberate circumvention illustrate significantly divergent interests; if the divergence was not significant there would presumably be no need for circumvention.

Recognising such variation in interest in a corporation's activities, we suggest that corporate governance is a central issue for public policy. The impact of modern corporations is very much dependent upon who makes the strategic decisions. Strategic decisions are typically made by a subset of those having an interest in a corporation's activities. In making those decisions this élite pursues its own interest. This raises a serious problem if, as a matter of public policy, it is seen as desirable that corporations' activities should serve the public interest. The problem is one of strategic failure: concentration of strategic-decision-making power in the hands of an élite implies a failure to determine the strategic direction of production in the interest of the community at large. To avoid such failure, more people affected by strategic decisions should be involved in the process of making those decisions. Ways should be found of democratising strategic decision-making.

For market-centred approaches to economic welfare, even if a corporation is governed by sectional interests, those with other interests can make take-over bids in a competitive capital market or can establish new, competing corporations.

But it is not possible for those with an interest in a particular soccer club to establish a new, competing club because clubs are unique, attracting a support that cannot transfer its allegiance elsewhere. Soccer fans almost invariably support only one team and this support is translated commercially through attending matches, watching or listening to them through television or radio, and through purchasing associated products. Such consumers cannot easily, or indeed at all, switch their consumption to another club. Support and loyalty creates a lock-in to one club, and indeed this is part of the allegiance and rivalry that is at the heart of soccer's culture.[13] For example, those fans with a significant interest in Manchester United but not involved in making its strategic decisions are not in a position to establish a second Manchester United; they are necessarily fans of the original club. Hence, representation of their interest in governance of the firm necessitates instruments that would bring them into the firm's decision-making process. The challenge of public policy is to design and implement such instruments.

Increased participation

One possibility is to consider the provisions of company law to introduce changes which would widen involvement in strategic decision-making. To pursue this we examine English experience.

We have argued that the existing economics literature places *de facto* control of the typical large, modern corporation between an élite group of (large) shareholders and the company board. In English company law, for example, this is reflected in the notion of shareholders being a company's 'members', who elect, and in theory, monitor the board of directors:

> the two organs of the company recognised by company law are the general meeting of shareholders (which may not necessarily include all the shareholders, since some shares may not carry votes and preference shareholders may have limited voting rights) and the board of directors. The board of directors manages the company and makes business policy decisions and the general meeting of the shareholders as a body elects the board and decides an organic change.[14]

The prime duty of directors is to act in the interests of the company – seen explicitly in the case of soccer by the Court of Appeal's decision in *Fulham Football Club Ltd v Cabra Estates plc*[15] – but this is essentially equated with the shareholders' interests:

> traditionally, this obligation to act *bona fide* in the interests of the company has been defined as an obligation to act in the interests of the shareholders and it is the directors' subjective opinion as to the interests of the corporators as a general body, balancing the short-term interests of the present members against the long-term interests of future members, which counts.[16]

One possibility is to increase participation in a corporation's strategic decision-making by building on the concept of membership of a company and on the idea that senior management must act in the interests of members; to widen membership beyond shareholder investors, including *as members* others with an interest in the corporation's activities.

The prospect of senior management having a duty towards all of those interest groups with a stake in a company has recently been rejected by the Hampel Committee on Corporate Governance, which concluded:

> to redefine the directors' responsibilities in terms of the shareholders would mean identifying all the various stakeholder groups; and deciding the nature and extent of the directors' responsibility to each. The result would be that the directors were not effectively accountable to anyone since there would be no clear yardstick for judging their performance. This is a recipe neither for good governance nor for corporate success.[17]

However, it would seem to us that this issue is far from closed. It is curious, moreover, that whilst some consider it appropriate for a corporation to be governed in the interests of only one amongst a set of stakeholders, the same is not considered appropriate for a nation. According to the Hampel Committee, the directors of Manchester United would not be accountable to anyone if they owed significant duties to shareholders and to others. Yet it is commonly argued that the government, for instance, should be accountable to the electorate, made up of many varied and diverse interests.

The precise way in which membership might be widened and directors vested with duties towards all those members is something that would need to be developed. Given the nature of soccer, its role in the culture of localities and its essence as a spectator sport, the focus should be on supporters. Within this there could be further focusing, perhaps on supporters who are match season-ticket holders, this being seen to imply a level of commitment and corresponding interest that stands such people apart from others. It is also interesting that Manchester United identifies a category of supporters as 'members', who on payment of an annual fee receive certain 'privileges' regarding ticket applications etc., and who therefore might also be seen as a suitable group of supporters to concentrate upon in considering company membership.

One option might be to introduce a company law which would enable Manchester United supporters who are members of the soccer club to be members of the company as well. This would entail problems in ensuring effective corporate governance, such as identifying the distribution of votes for electing the board in a way that ensures effective power sharing. For example, to have one member one vote would yield a different electoral process (and one in which either supporters or shareholders were in danger of swamping the other, depending on the numbers involved) compared to having one vote for each supporter and one for each share; in existing company law, buying shares means buying votes – it is a case of one (certain type of) share one vote and not one shareholder one vote. The current position is again curiously different to what is often considered an appropriate voting process for the governance of nations; the buying of votes in British parliamentary elections was eradicated in the nineteenth century, before company law enshrined the practice into the governance of public, limited liability corporations.[18]

It should be emphasised that introducing new interest groups into the membership of companies would only have the effect of increasing participation in decision-making if those interest groups have real power to elect and monitor the board of directors. This raises the crucial issue of information and, as noted above, existing members lack sufficient information. This is a well-known problem that would need to be addressed. Moreover, the role of directors would need to be given fresh thought. Whilst it might be reasonable to maintain the directors' prime duty as acting in the interests of members, if members are to encompass explicitly more wide-ranging interests, it might be appropriate to see directors as having a mediating role, very different to the current situation. In theory, directors in existing company law might be said to have one master, although in practice we have seen in the case of Manchester United how there are significant differences of opinion across groups of shareholders. But if directors owe a duty to act in the interests of all members and these members have apparently differing views about a company's strategic direction, perhaps a director's explicit role and duty should be to draw out such conflicts, to provide arenas for discussion and resolution, for elucidating compromise among interested parties and to mediate across different interests in the strategic-decision-making process.

Going forward

We have indicated some of the issues in company law that must be addressed if there is to be effective economic democracy. One immediate way forward would be to ensure that democratically controlled public agencies monitor firms' activity and secure effective representation of the public interest when corporations make strategic decisions. Even where a soccer club is otherwise under the control of an élite few in pursuit of their own interest, the interests of others can be brought into account by appropriate public agencies acting on their behalf. Cost considerations alone would mean that such a process would have limited effect; public agencies could not costlessly monitor all strategic decisions of all companies at all times, and could not on all occasions effectively represent the interests of those otherwise excluded from the strategic-decision-making process. But some degree of increased participation in strategic decision-making can be provided.

Indeed public agencies are already given roles to some extent in line with this suggestion. For example, BSkyB's attempted take-over of Manchester United was referred to the Monopolies and Mergers Commission (MMC) by the Secretary of State for Trade and Industry, following a recommendation by the Office of Fair Trading (OFT) that there were 'concerns for the wider public interest'. The Commission, in investigating:

> must take into account all matters that appear to be relevant in

considering the public interest but in particular it must have regard to the desirability of maintaining and promoting competition in the UK, of promoting the interests of consumers, purchasers and other users of goods and services in the UK in respect of prices, quality and variety of goods and services; efficiency and innovation, the balanced distribution of industry and employment, and exports.[19]

Once the MMC (now the Competition Commission) reports to the Secretary of State, if it concludes:

> that the merger may not be expected to operate against the public interest then there is no statutory power vested in the Secretary of State to stop it. Where there is an adverse finding by the MMC, in practice, the Secretary of State tries a voluntary approach first and there is provision for the Secretary of State to ask the Director General [of Fair Trading] to seek undertakings from the various parties as to their future conduct. The Secretary of State can refuse to allow the merger to proceed even though the Commission has indicated that conditions to remedy the adverse effects would suffice. Equally, the Secretary of State may allow the merger to proceed even though the MMC recommended that it should be halted.[20]

A policy to complement effective merger control would be regulatory offices for particularly important sectors in an economy. These could be charged with safeguarding the public interest in strategic decision-making. The government-appointed Football Task Force has been considering the need for a regulator to oversee the sector. We would support the idea of a regulator with the responsibility and ability to monitor the strategic activity of clubs and their controllers, and to act to secure effective representation of the public interest when strategic decisions are made.

Notes

[1] *News Corporation Financial Report.*

[2] *Manchester United plc Annual Report 1998.* p. 4.

[3] *Manchester United plc Annual Report 1998.* p. 20, emphasis added.

[4] According to the *Manchester United plc Annual Report 1998,* as at 31 July 1998 there were 27,864 shareholders in the company; 122 of these were institutions (holding 59.6 per cent of all shares), 5 were directors (holding 17 per cent of all shares) and 27,737 were small shareholdings (amounting to 23.4 per cent of all shares)

[5] As at 9 October 1998, British Sky Broadcasting Group plc had 9.1 per cent of issued share capital, *Manchester United plc Annual Report 1998.*

[6] *SUAM*, 'BSkyB and Manchester United plc. An Analysis of the Offer', distributed as part of a press release on 20 October 1998, and available from their website, www.stopmurdoch.com.

[7] *News Corporation Annual Report 1998.* In addition, 1 per cent of operating earnings were derived from other activities.

[8] These were detailed in the 1998 Offer Document.

[9] *Manchester United plc Annual Report 1998.*

[10] For example, Greg Dyke, currently a non-executive director of Manchester United plc, has observed that 'people who support United . . . feel that it is theirs'. (BBC Radio interview, 14 December 1998).

[11] See Michie *et al* (1998), and also chapter 2 by David Conn.

[12] *Manchester United plc Prospectus.* 1991.

[13] See Michie *et al* (1998).

[14] Farrar and Hannigan (1998). p. 303.

[15] [1994] 1BCLC363.

[16] Farrar and Hannigan (1998). p. 381.

[17] Hampel Committee Report (1998). para. 1.17.

[18] In practice, the buying of votes in national elections continues, in a sense, through the use of lobbyists and advertising.

[19] Farrar and Hannigan (1998). p. 615.

[20] Farrar and Hannigan (1998). p. 616.

References

Berle, A.J. and G.C. Means (1932). *The Modern Corporation and Private Property*. New York: Macmillan.

Coase, Ronald H. (1937). 'The Nature of the Firm'. *Economica*, IV, pp. 386–405.

Farrar, J.H. and B.M. Hannigan (1998). *Farrar's Company Law*. London: Butterworths.

Hampel Committee Report (1998). *Committee on Corporate Governance: Final Report*. London HMSO.

Holland, J.B. (1995). 'The Role of UK Financial Institutions in Corporate Governance'. *Certified Accountant*, October, pp. 28–29.

Michie, J. *et al* (1998). 'Evidence for the Monopolies and Mergers Commission on the Proposed Acquisition of Manchester United plc by British Sky Broadcasting Group PLC'. Mimeo, Birkbeck College, London. (Summary published in MMC Report, 1999.)

Russell Reynolds Associates (1998). 'Setting New Standards for Corporate Governance: 1997 US Survey on Industrial Investors'. *Corporate Governance*, 6(1), pp. 67–68.

Tricker, B. (1997). 'Information and Power – The Influence of IT on Corporate Governance'. *Corporate Governance*, 5(2), pp. 49–51.

Zeitlin, M. (1974). 'Corporate Ownership and Control: The Large Corporation and the Capitalist Class'. *American Journal of Sociology*, 79(5), pp. 1073–1119.

11. Supporter Representation on the Board:

The Case of Northampton Town FC

Brian Lomax

Football supporters as customers and investors

At the heart of this chapter is the contention that football supporters are not only customers but also investors. They invest not only their money but their loyalty and commitment in their club. If I visited the fishmonger each week and was sold mouldy fish, I would cease to shop there. That is the customer relationship. But football supporters continue to invest however substandard the product may be. (See chapter 1 by Sean Hamil for related discussion on the concept of 'fan equity').

From our experience over the last seven years, the Northampton Town Supporters Trust would strongly recommend that every football club should have elected supporter representation on the board of directors. Not only is it right, but it also works. But in order to be effective, it must have certain characteristics, which I shall discuss at the end of this chapter.

I wish specifically to address the first three items of the Football Task Force's terms of reference: anti-racism, disabled access and greater supporter involvement in the running of clubs. (For further discussion of the remit of the Football Task Force see chapter 3). I seek to express the view that, at least in the case of Northampton Town, these three issues are organically linked and interconnected. In order to establish this case, a brief introductory explanation of the origins and role of the Northampton Town Supporters Trust is necessary.

Northampton Town Supporters Trust

The Trust was formed in January 1992, as a result of a large public meeting attended by over 600 supporters. This meeting was called by a group of ordinary supporters, including the Fanzine editor and myself, in response to a financial crisis at the club and a series of misleading statements issued by the then chairman. The club were reluctant to send representatives to the meeting, but relented at the last minute, and the situation disclosed was a debt approaching £1.6 million. At the time, this represented more than two years' turnover for the club.

The Trust was set up with two objectives: firstly, to raise money to save the club (but not for the then current regime), and to be accountable to the supporters for the expenditure of that money; and secondly, to seek effective involvement and representation for supporters in the running of the club in order to ensure that such a situation would never occur again. In this second respect, the Trust marked itself out as distinct from the normal run of supporters clubs, in that from its inception it had an inescapably political dimension. In this we were forerunners of a variety of Independent Supporters Associations and other similar bodies, who have sought not just to support their club but to change the way it was run and how it related to its supporters.

We have also since advised or assisted in the formation of several Trusts at other clubs, with similar objectives at Kettering Town, Middlesbrough, Plymouth Argyle and AFC Bournemouth. These Trusts have enjoyed varying degrees of success, the most notable being AFC Bournemouth, to which I will refer later. We are also advising groups who wish to form similar Trusts at Dundee United, Manchester City, Partick Thistle, Lincoln City and Chester City among others.

In financial terms, the Trust has fundraised and paid over £90,000 into Northampton Town FC in the subsequent five years, with funds still in hand, and we own 26,552 shares in the club, over 7 per cent of the total issued. The sum invested bears good comparison with that of any individual director over the period. In terms of representation, the club went into administration in April 1992, and the administrator, Barry Ward, invited the Trust to elect two full board members. This has now been reduced to one, but that place is guaranteed by Northampton Borough Council until at least the year 2019 as a condition of our lease and licence to occupy our new stadium at Sixfields.

This stadium, built and owned by Northampton Borough Council with the aid of a £1 million grant from the Football Trust, is a perfect symbol of the partnership between the local authority, the football club and the Trust. It is truly a community stadium. The leader of the council has recently said that he regards the Trust representative on the board as representing not only the supporters, but the community as a whole.

I now turn to the Task Force terms of reference, with the assertion that certain key developments at the football club have stemmed entirely from the Trust being represented on the board, and the three-way partnership with the council described above.

The elimination of racism

In November 1995 a Working Party was set up to organise the relaunch of the 'Let's Kick Racism Out Of Football' campaign. I was asked to chair this Working Party. After successfully achieving the initial objective, at our home match against Darlington in February 1996, we decided that this one-off gesture was insufficient, and we set ourselves the task of drafting an equal opportunities policy for the football club.

We examined various examples, and chose to base it upon the policy of the charity of which I am chief executive, but adapted to meet the particular needs and circumstances of a football club. It was adopted unanimously by the board of directors in October 1996, and again in public on the pitch at our home match against Chester in January 1997, in the presence of Members of Parliament and other distinguished guests. This match was designated the Walter Tull Memorial Match, in honour of the club's first black player. Walter was only the second black professional footballer in history. He joined us from Tottenham Hotspur in 1911, and played over 100 games for us, scoring nine goals from midfield. In 1914 he was among the first to join up at the outbreak of the First World War, and two years later became the first black officer to receive a commission in the British Army. He was killed in action in 1918 on the Somme, only weeks before the Armistice, and has no known grave. In partnership with the Borough Council, we are now establishing a Walter Tull Memorial Garden at Sixfields, where the ashes of those supporters who request it may be interred. This was officially dedicated in May 1999.

We are the first league football club to have adopted an equal opportunities policy. Since then, we have been contacted by a number of other clubs who wish to do the same, and have been told by them that clubs enquiring about this issue to the Football League or the FA are referred to us.

The policy has already had a number of good outcomes in terms of anti-racist education of supporters, who will now habitually report and identify offenders within the crowd. The board has approved a banning policy for those established as guilty of racist words or behaviour.

In October 1997, to mark Black History Month, we held a Day of Action against Racism at our home match against Gillingham, our guest of honour being Angela Billingham, our MEP. Our Working Party continues to meet regularly. Its representatives have included the Supporters Trust, the football club, Northampton Borough Council, ACMS Ltd (the Sixfields Stadium Management Company), the Commission for Racial Equality, Northampton Racial Equality Council, Northamptonshire Police, the Scarman Centre for the Study of Public Order, Leicester University, Middlesex University, the British Asian Association, Northamptonshire County Council, the Kick It Out Campaign, Northampton Town Football in the Community and Nationwide Building Society. It is now akin to a national standing committee on the issue of racism in football.

Northampton Town Football in the Community, of which I am also chair, recently launched a highly successful initiative to establish regular Football Fun Days for the Bangladeshi youth in the town, in collaboration with the local mosque and Muslim community centre. It is believed that this is another 'first' for Northampton Town, reaching out to one of the least accessible groups in the community who for various reasons have little contact with local football, although they love the game.

Improving disabled access

We have been pioneers in addressing the issue of playing opportunities for people with disabilities. Our Football in the Community scheme has taken the lead in organising league football on a national level for players with learning disabilities, so much so that when the England learning disabilities team won the European Cup in Belgium in 1996 (beating Germany 4–2!), eight of the squad and the team manager were from Northampton Town. We have also been in the forefront of establishing the first Duke of Edinburgh's Award Centre with specific emphasis on disabled candidates, at Sixfields in 1997. In 1998 we hosted two of the quarter-finals of the World Cup for players with learning disabilities.

In terms of spectator facilities, Northampton Town FC won the Football League Award and the overall McDonald's Award (England, Scotland and Wales) in 1997 for the best disabled-spectator facilities in British football. Whilst the major credit for this must go to Northampton Borough Council, who built the stadium, the award was not only for physical facilities but for customer services. The

Supporters Trust, too, has played its part. Since its inception in 1992, it has held a large annual event to raise funds for disabled-supporter facilities, raising several thousand pounds, most recently for the purchase of Sennheisser units to relay a match commentary to supporters with sight problems within the stadium.

Supporter involvement in the running of clubs

Since its formation, Northampton Town Supporters Trust has organised regular monthly open forums for all supporters, whether Trust members or not. Speakers have included the chairman and directors of the football club, the manager, the club secretary, members of the playing staff, the local police and the stadium management company.

At all meetings the elected director is present and available to answer any questions about the policy and running of the club. Many policies have been changed or improved as a result of discussions at these meetings, including issues of ticket pricing. The elected director is subject to annual re-election by single transferable vote, and must therefore remain active and sensitive to the views of the membership if he or she is to retain the position. After seven years, the Trust's membership now stands at a record level, as do attendances at its meetings which average over 100.

In the time since the Trust joined the board, average gates have risen from 2,000 to over 6,000. This is, of course, due to playing success and the new stadium, but the increase exceeds comparable situations elsewhere and, in my view, is partly because supporters now know they are stakeholders and not just turnstile fodder. Price increases at the gates have been accepted because they were properly explained and justified and not just imposed. There is a feeling of everyone being on the same side in a common enterprise, rather than 'us and them'.

That is not to say that there are not disagreements and tensions – there are – but there is a forum for resolving them and arriving at acceptable solutions. The club's historic debt has now been paid off in its entirety, the last payment of £50,000 being made in August 1998.

Thus it can be seen that the involvement of supporters at board level has produced commercial as well as social advantages for the football club. But the chief benefits, I believe, have been felt in the areas identified above: anti-racism, equal opportunities and disability, on which the voice of the Trust has been specific and radical. In these areas we are delivering the policies and services of the local authority in a very high-profile context, and are thus truly equal partners with them. In addition, they are not issues which would necessarily rate as high priority with the average board of directors.

Historically, it has usually taken a crisis such as potential insolvency before directors have turned to supporters for help and participation. There is no good reason why this should be so, given the number of successful outcomes we have witnessed from it at Northampton which were unrelated to the club's financial position. Northampton Town is living proof that supporter democracy, and close attention to social issues, do not preclude success on the pitch. Two Wembley play-offs in successive seasons and promotion tell their own story!

Conclusions

Over the last seven years, and particularly recently, I have been contacted by officials and/or supporters of nearly twenty clubs, who either wish to form a Trust similar to our own, or achieve democratic supporter representation on their board of directors, or both. As a result of detailed discussions with all these people, I believe that in order to be effective on any lasting basis, a scheme for supporter representation on the board must have five hallmarks:

- It must be fully executive, that is, not non-voting or purely observer status, as has been tried elsewhere. It must be registered as a directorship at Companies House, and must carry with it the entitlement to full access to all board meetings in their entirety, and to all written and financial information available to the other directors. Symbolic or bogus experiments like the one by Francis Lee at Manchester City expose the limitations of anything less.
- It must be truly democratic, that is, one person one vote, not one pound one vote. A bond scheme such as was launched at Charlton Athletic entitling subscribers to elect a director with one vote for each unit purchased is not democratic, and in fact merely enshrines the concept that money speaks louder than supporters in football.
- It must be affordable for all supporters. If a subscription is the basis of the electorate, it must not be set at a level which is beyond the purse of any supporter, despite the temptation to use subscriptions as a quick fundraiser. Our own subscriptions are £5 per year for adults, £2 per year for 'concessions' (old and young) and £25 for life. These rates have not been increased since our formation. An otherwise splendid scheme at Lincoln City, 'Impetus', is marred only by the subscription level which has been set at £50.
- It must be entrenched, that is, not able to be set aside at the whim of the board if the representative says or does something they do not

like, or fails to come up with a sum of money requested. As previously stated, we at Northampton are fortunate to have our position guaranteed in the stadium lease until 2019 at least. Similar opportunities arise wherever clubs become involved in partnerships with the local authority, whether over the stadium or some other financial contract or arrangement. The sad example of Kettering Town, where the Trust representative was cast aside by the new owners following a short period of administration, illustrates the importance of this point.

- It must be independent, that is, the representative, and the Trust where applicable, must retain the right to criticise the club and the board on behalf of supporters when all other avenues have failed. This, it appears to me, is the snag with the otherwise highly successful example of AFC Bournemouth, where a Trust, initiated by key supporters but comprising a coalition of local interests, acquired the football club two years ago. When the honeymoon period ends, as inevitably one day it will, who will the supporters criticise? Themselves? And who will be in a position to represent them in doing so? Neither am I aware of any democratic structures having been put in place there during the last two years to enable supporters to decide who they want to represent them in future.

Lastly, we at Northampton have been greatly encouraged by the endorsement we have received from the Football Task Force in all three reports which they have published so far, most notably the third, 'Investing in the Community'. This report gives approval to the twin principles of democratic Supporters Trusts and of elected supporter representation on boards of directors. It even proposes a funding mechanism via the Football Trust to enable these principles to be established in clubs generally. (For further discussion of the mechanics of the establishment of trust ownership structures see chapters 8 and 13). I hope this proves to be a prelude to a period when full supporter involvement is the rule rather than the exception.

12. The Struggle for Democracy at Barcelona FC

L'Elefant Blau

In recent years, the Spanish football world has undergone dramatic change, as clubs have been transformed from non-profit associations to private corporations. Today, only four professional football clubs out of the 42 playing in the national Spanish leagues are not corporations. Barcelona Football Club (or 'Barça' to its friends) is one of them. The rapid change in the organisation and governance of Spanish football arose because of a lack of regulation concerning the economic and financial administration of football clubs. There is no equivalent in Spain to the English and Welsh Football Association's Rule 34 which, although now circumvented (see chapter 2 by Conn for a discussion of this) served to delay the flotation of clubs in England. In Spain, the criteria ruling football's economic and financial administration are rather obscure. The lack of specific rules in the face of the growing influence of media and sponsors is now more obvious than ever and threatens the traditional values of the game. Clubs like Barça, with a stadium capacity of almost 100,000 seats and a fan following that adds up to several million, have become a major target of the TV channels.

The 'Elefant Blau' (Blue Elephant) is an association of Barça fans established two years ago with the aim of democratising the club's governance structure and preserving its original status as a non-profit sports organisation. The association is trying to save footballing traditions by putting emphasis on the need for updating Spanish football legislation to take account of the present challenges. The management of a professional club like Barça, with a multi-billion-peseta annual budget, requires greater regulatory control. The days when the club was run by a handful of enthusiastic and altruistic sportsmen are over.

The past

Barcelona Football Club will be 100 years old in November 1999. At the end of last century the city of Barcelona experienced an economic boom. In the wake of the 1888 Universal Exhibition, the town underwent a period of intense development. A rush of foreign capital in search of the high returns granted by fast growing industries and services such as textiles, metals, water, transport and energy supplies, poured in. Barcelona Football Club was founded by a group of foreign sportsmen (mostly British and Swiss residents) working on the technical staff of different ventures set up at the turn of the century by international companies and Catalan investors. The first president of the club was Mr Walter Wild, a British citizen, and the first match, played only a few days after the club's foundation (8 December) was played between the newly founded Barcelona Football Club and a team formed by a group of young British residents. Barcelona Football Club was legally conceived as a non-profit private association financed by the contributions of its members.

Despite the leading role of its foreign founders, the club immediately assumed the main objectives of the Catalan society of which it was a part. 'Sport and Citizenship' was a slogan of the time strictly followed by the first presidents of the club, who always gave their support to initiatives invigorating the cultural identity of Catalonia. Therefore, Barça was not only a sports club but a civic entity that participated in the most significant Catalan movements of the time including the campaigns for autonomy for Catalonia, for Catalan schools, for Catalan language courses for club members, and so on. It thus became the only Spanish football club with a really active cultural programme.

This goes some way to explaining why the two military dictatorships suffered by Spain in the present century both tried to shut down the club. Both regimes considered the 'unity' of Spain as something holy and languages other than Castilian as something evil. General Primo de Rivera closed the club in 1925. General Franco did the same thing 14 years later when his troops occupied Barcelona at the end of the Spanish Civil War. But the outcome of both closures was exactly the same: the reinforcement of the idea that Barça was in fact playing the role of a non-existent Catalan national team; a last refuge for Catalan nationalism. Therefore, to win a championship always meant something more than a mere trophy for Barça. During the military dictatorships our club, like a few other cultural institutions, became one of the last outlets left for the expression of the Catalan identity. Hence, to win against Real Madrid meant for years a victory of democracy against the tyranny of a politically centralised and culturally uniform Spain.

The present

Nowadays, the role of the club as a shelter for traditional Catalan values is somehow outdated. Post-Franco Spain is a democracy, Catalonia has got back in large measure its national political rights and institutions, the use of the Catalan language in everyday life is increasing and there are almost as many Catalan schools as can reasonably be expected. The problem is that in the last 20 years, under the club presidency of Mr Núñez, our rights as members of the club have been dramatically reduced. In short, as Catalonians our situation has improved, but as members of Barcelona Football Club our situation has deteriorated.

Every new statutory reform introduced by Mr Núñez and his board of directors has resulted in an erosion of the members' social rights. Just over 3,000 club members form the assembly of delegates, the highest governing body of the club, but they are not elected; they are selected every two years using a mysterious computer program not noted for its impartiality. Moreover, the board does not make public the names of the appointed delegates. In the Franco period, 30 years ago, the club had to publish the list of names, including the delegates' addresses, so that every member could know who was actually representing them at the assembly. Today, the members get only a long list of numbers: the 3,000 numbers of the 3,000 member cards drawn from the computer lottery. It is hard to imagine how a member can submit a motion to the assembly without knowing who his delegates are or how to meet them. As a result, the 100,000 club members are prevented from effectively exercising their democratic rights to raise issues via their delegates.

The control and supervision of the list of members is another key responsibility of the assembly that has been taken over by the current president and the board. Like the list of delegates, the list is withheld by the board on the excuse of people's privacy in case of unwanted commercial or political marketing. Without a means to canvass the members it is hard to imagine how a member of the club might attempt to challenge the existing president in an election. Unless completely foolhardy, no one is likely to be willing to take the risk of standing for the presidency in such an unfair competition.

As a result of the emergent lack of democracy in the club, the club's management is now able to act practically uncontrolled, not only in the social field but also in respect of the club's economic activity. For instance, there is a lack of transparency on accounting procedures: there are no clear rules that specify exactly how players are accounted for, and the accounting criteria concerning the club's other intangible assets are even cloudier. Until recently, an independent committee appointed by the assembly assumed economic control. This Economic Committee was supposed to monitor the expenses and the execution of the annual budget. But today, the assembly (which includes an ever-increasing number of delegates directly appointed by the president) simply rubber stamps the selection of the Economic Committee proposed by the club's managers. The fact that the Economic Committee is currently chaired by Mr Núñez's son gives some indication of the degree of its independence.

The present anti-democratic trend is strengthened by another factor, namely the diminishing participation of the members' contributions to the club's global income. Twenty years ago, the revenue from season tickets used to cover almost the whole budget. Today, these contributions amount to only about one third. New income sources (primarily television) make up the gap. This tendency is likely to continue in the foreseeable future. The last Barcelona Football Club budget (for the 1997/98 season) was almost 15 billion pesetas. Expenses are rising at an impressive rate and the members' economic contributions cannot keep up with that pace. But this should not and cannot be used as an argument for cutting down the members' social and democratic rights. The club's main assets are its 100,000 members and its millions of fans. Similarly, the members are also the club's only proprietors. No matter how much income the club earns, the whole income of the club depends on its members, not on the television networks or on the sports equipment multinationals. That, at least, is our point of view, despite the fact that in the event of the club folding, nobody knows precisely to whom the assets would go.

To summarise, the club executives are trying to take full control of an institution that runs a multi-billion-peseta budget. The next step is easily predictable: its partial or total transformation into a pure commercial company increasingly engaged in other fields than those of football, and able later on to be quoted on the Stock Exchange. Other people's property, other people's business.

Like many other Spanish clubs, Barcelona Football Club has been intrigued by the American model of the NBA with its enormous advertising returns, its rewarding marketing operations and its 'pay-per-view' incomes. Our feeling is that all those clubs have ignored fundamental differences between American basketball and European football. Basketball fits much better than football into the show business frame. Basketball admits the pure exhibition of a star-team like the Harlem Globetrotters. Moreover, the sport has been packaged in a television format geared towards multiple commercial breaks, cheerleaders and pre-match entertainment designed to attract a large variety of audiences. But a football match is something else; it is a far cry from a circus. It requires the partisan engagement of the audience.

It is the 'shared emotional ownership' (fan equity) evoked by Sean Hamil in his discussion of the social fabric of football (chapter 1). Without this key ingredient, football can be a rather lukewarm and passionless form of entertainment. Football is a game that both depends on and inspires a strong sense of community identity which, in turn, engenders support from the fans.

A realistic approach to the football business has to keep in mind that a club is a social entity, which embraces far more complicated elements than the figures that appear in its balance sheet. A football club's life cannot be bound to the policies of a telecommunication's mogul or to the interests of a multi-national shoemaker. That is the reason why the 'Elefant Blau' was founded. Its first mission was the promotion of a vote of censure against President Núñez and his board, as provided by the 49th article of the club statutes.

In the beginning, there were only six people in the 'Elefant Blau', but very soon the group increased substantially, thanks in large measure to the board's strong resistance and opposition to our project. This resistance was so openly treacherous and mafia-like that it ultimately proved to be beneficial to the 'Blue Elephant's' cause. It could be said that Mr Núñez and his colleagues gave 'The Elephant' wings. To explain the campaign in detail would take up too much space and go beyond the main focus of this chapter. However, an important aspect of our strategy was to establish support for a vote of censure. We gathered more than 6,000 members' signatures (more than the required 5 per cent – or 4,500 – of the electorate) and on Sunday, 8 March 1997, a match day against Real Madrid in the Barça stadium, the vote took place with an astonishing success for the 'Blue Elephant'. Some 40,000 members voted, almost 15,000 of them for the censure. As usual, Mr Núñez got the votes of his untouchable army of 25,000 followers. The explanation of such high fidelity would divert us as well from this chapter's main subject.

Needless to say the 'Elefant Blau' did not win the battle. However, it gave the club's board a serious warning. At least one of its most worrying designs, namely the macro-project called 'Barça-2000', has been apparently postponed. The idea behind 'Barça-2000' was to build a kind of Disneyland park surrounding the stadium with all sorts of bars, cinemas, shops and other facilities tangential to our club's vocation, which is (as declared by the first article of the statutes) the promotion, practise, diffusion and exhibition of football and other sports. If the proposal for 'Barça-2000' had gone ahead it would have paved the way for the conversion of the club into a joint-stock company.

The future

The democratisation of Barcelona Football Club is, of course, our primary goal but it cannot be reached under the present circumstances. The short-term objective must therefore be to put an end to the megalomania of President Núñez, who is seriously jeopardising the club's future. We need to democratise the club statutes, in order to boost membership participation and increase the degree of accountability and transparency. The President's mandate should be limited to no more than two terms of four years each and the delegates should be appointed through democratic elections. At the very least, the updating and publication of the membership roll must occur if the present questionable electoral practices are to be democratised. In short, our club needs efficient and transparent management. Last but not least, it also needs to be modernised, but this process should look at the next century without overlooking the positive developments made this century.

As Europeans we favour freedom of movement for everybody. So, footballers should be able to play wherever they want in the European Union, as the Bosman ruling has instituted. It would not be consistent with the tradition of our club, which was founded by foreigners, to refuse foreign players. Also inconsistent, however, would be to disregard the development of our own young players. This is an economic requirement as well. The massive import of foreign stars has its limits. The cost of the players is presently absorbing about half of the club's annual budget. Clubs are inflating transfer fees and salaries in an irresponsible competition and it would seem that many of them have already gone too far. This is true for Barcelona Football Club, which has already overspent in advance of the expected revenues from its TV contracts.

There is more than the simple economics of football at stake. Many football amateurs have been in the game from their childhood with the dream of one day reaching the Barça professional team. However, the traditionally strong incentive to play football is losing momentum in Catalonia. The dream is fading as the club relies more and more on foreign stars and sells its own home players for cash. As discussed above, supporters and communities need to identify with their players. But it is obviously more difficult to keep this relationship going as commercial pressures threaten to undermine traditional links between football clubs and local communities.

That is why we would like to propose for discussion some ideas we have in mind for a new model for the European championships in general, but more specifically on the relation between football and television. No doubt television can be an extremely efficient medium for spreading football's popularity. But it could become a very dangerous weapon as well. The concentration of television broadcasting rights in a few hands together with the control of one or more clubs is a worrying prospect. (For a discussion of the implications see chapter 5). Securing free and fair competition on the football field must become a key priority. To attain this goal we advocate:

- open European championships, which means the rejection of monopolies of any kind for a few big clubs
- football clubs to be independent of broadcasting companies
- national leagues limited to a maximum of 16/18 clubs
- maximum legal term (4/6 years) for players' contracts
- price of transfers in accordance with players' salary
- abolition of cancellation clauses in players' contracts

To conclude, we find ourselves in agreement with the arguments made by Michie and Walsh (chapter 13) that the revamp of the European Champions League should not be inspired by the TV and commercial interests. Priority must be given to the broader wishes of supporters and players.

Notes

The main authors of this chapter are Elefant Blau members Armand Carabén, Alfons Godall, Joan Laporta and Jordi Moix.

13. What Future for Football?

Jonathan Michie and Andy Walsh

The attempted take-over of Manchester United by BSkyB in 1998 highlighted what had been apparent for some time. Football has become increasingly commercialised. It is now big business. This is discussed and demonstrated in previous chapters – see particularly chapter 1 by Sean Hamil and chapter 2 by David Conn. Indeed, the fact that the game was becoming over-commercialised was one of the reasons for the government establishing the Football Task Force, as detailed by Task Force member Adam Brown in chapter 3. We do not therefore intend going into detail here on these issues. Our chapter takes all this as understood.

Associated with this increasing commercialisation has been a second worrying development. At most Premier League clubs in England there has been a gentrification or yuppification of the fan base, amounting to a form of social exclusion. This is nicely illustrated at Newcastle Football Club which infamously rips off – according to the directors themselves whose conversation was, unknown to them, being recorded – their fans by selling the replica shirts which so many of them can be seen wearing at the club's matches. As with most grounds now, significant sums are also made from the more expensive seats in executive boxes. The replica shirts that the traditional supporters wear in such numbers are banned from these executive boxes.

More serious than the spread of executive boxes, and executive seats more generally, or the activities of clubs' commercial departments with over-priced replica shirts, has been increased ticket prices. Ticket price increases have priced many traditional football fans out of regular attendance. This is particularly the case with young fans.

On the positive side, there has at least been wide recognition not only of the dangers to the game from these twin developments, but also of the need for action to deal with the problem. The problem of social exclusion, and the need to tackle it, has been made a particular priority for action by today's government, although to date the links with football appear not to have been fully made.

However, there has also been the welcome establishment of the Football Task Force that has issued useful reports and recommendations which it is to be hoped will be acted on by government and the football authorities, although at the time of writing the final report has yet to be published.

However, the BSkyB bid was more significant than simply having served to draw attention to these existing problems. It also represented a serious additional threat to the game. Firstly, such a take-over would have exacerbated the problems just referred to. And secondly, it would have created new threats to the game, most particularly the threat that all the top, glamour clubs would then be taken over by media companies. This would result in these clubs being run in the interests of the media companies that own them. Indeed, it would be the legal requirement of the companies' directors to so act, regardless of whether their actions were in the best interests of the football club or not.

According to British company law, if the directors were presented with a course of action that would be in the interests of the parent company but not the football club, they would be legally obliged to adopt the course of action that was in the interests of the parent company of which they were directors. The interests of the football club, and their fans, would have to be sacrificed.

A practical example might have been when, in 1998, the Premier League threatened Manchester United with expulsion (along with the other clubs involved) if they joined the European Super League about which the clubs were in discussion. Had BSkyB owned Manchester United at the time, it might well have been considered to have been in the interests of the broadcasting company to go ahead with the European Super League, and to therefore use Manchester United to help launch it, regardless of the longer-term damage which would have been done to the football club through expulsion from the Premier League.

Another example would be if BSkyB had been allowed to own Manchester United and had then merged with Canal Plus. Such a merger, between BSkyB and the French cable company, was being seriously considered in February 1999. (The talks in February were secret, but widely reported). Canal Plus owns the French club, Paris St Germain. But under UEFA rules, no one owner is allowed to enter more than one club in the same European competition. If both clubs qualified for the Champions League it would then be up to BSkyB/Canal Plus to decide which club to drop.

There would, though, be a far more general, continual potential conflict of interest than these examples, between the football club and the media owners. Most obviously, over matters such as the amount of money to be put into the operation of the football club in lieu of the fact that nothing was being paid for the right to screen live matches, which otherwise would generate large revenues for the club. And there would always be the danger of asset stripping by selling players, or selling the club's football ground as commercial property.

The need to consider alternative forms of ownership and governance for football clubs is therefore urgent. Our chapter aims to contribute to this task. We consider various possible options. Some of these are undeniably ambitious and perhaps utopian, but others are very much on the immediate agenda. Before speculating on where we would like to be, though, it is important first to consider where we are now and how we got here.

Another fine mess

The establishment of plcs in football is based more on the desire to take money out of the game than, as football club directors would have one believe, put money in. The flotation of a football club is often accompanied by a club director or financial advisor talking the language of 'people's capitalism'. Manchester United's 1991 prospectus declared a wish to 'give employees and supporters a greater opportunity to invest in Manchester United' and talked of a desire to 'widen the ownership' of the club. The latter is ironic as it was Louis Edwards, the father of United's current chief executive Martin Edwards, who deliberately set out to concentrate the ownership of Manchester United in his own hands in order that he might exploit the club for his own gain. One story from the time recalls Louis taking the late Sir Matt Busby into his confidence about a potential new share issue; Sir Matt rejected the idea. Instead he suggested that the board go to the fans if money was needed who 'would gladly throw money over the wall'. It is no surprise to learn that one of Louis's advisors at the time was Roland Smith, now *Professor Sir* Roland Smith and chairman of MUFC plc, one of the alleged architects behind the United board's attempt to sell out to BSkyB.

From club to company

Around one hundred years ago football clubs began to form themselves into limited companies – a move intended to protect those running the clubs from personal liability should the newly found professionalism of the era go awry. In an effort to protect the integrity of the game the Football Association imposed Articles of Association that debarred profiteering by club directors. Rule 34 imposed a maximum dividend payout and outlawed payments to club directors. It also laid down the provision that in the event of a club folding, the assets would have to go to other local sporting institutions. As illustrated below – and also in chapter 12 by the Barcelona supporters' group – we can see that this principle was adopted abroad where the idea of football being organised into 'clubs' was enshrined in the constitutions of famous institutions such as FC Barcelona. As can be seen in the case of Barcelona, the concept was developed to give the 'club' a real link with its community and its supporter base.

This move for the good of the game stands in stark contrast to the FA's capitulation to the bigger clubs one hundred years later when the FA allowed itself to be used in the establishment of the Premier League, breaking away from the rest of league football.

Football plc

In 1983 Tottenham Hotspur became the first English club to go to the market. Few regarded it as a good idea; the City was unenthusiastic, and fans and others in football were suspicious. It was not until the Hillsborough Disaster and the financial implications of Lord Justice Taylor's report that the idea of using the financial markets to raise investment capital really took hold. There are around twenty clubs now quoted on the markets with capitalisation ranging from a couple of million at Swansea City to over half a billion at Manchester United. In the meantime, as this development was taking place the vision shown by the FA in devising Rule 34 was being circumvented. The formation of plcs as holding companies was used to allow clubs to appoint paid directors. Gone were the days when local businessmen became involved in football just to boost their prestige and standing in the local community. Now the far more 'modern' pairing appears to be boosting personal wealth and massaging egos.

Football at the crossroads

At the time of writing, the idea of a regulator for football is being widely floated in the media, and is being seriously considered by the Football Task Force. The incoming Labour Government set up the Task Force as a direct response to widespread public concern for the health of 'The People's Game', thus honouring its pre-election pledge. This new approach to football is in contrast to the attitude of previous governments who thought that the problems of football should be resolved from within. There appears to be for the first time proper recognition that sports such as football play an important part in the social and cultural fabric of society. In addition, the government to date appears to have recognised the important role that all the various interest groups in football have to play. For the first time, fans' and players' representatives have a recognised place at the table and though there is still a great deal of cynicism about what the eventual outcome may be, a start has at least been made in tackling some of the most pressing problems.

Greed and power

Ironically the FA already has the power to carry out the role of regulator but appears unwilling to act. Rule 34 still stands but in the 16 years since Spurs first floated, the FA has failed to come up with a plan of how to protect the game from the commercial pressures that now threaten to suffocate it. The European governing body, UEFA, is now the latest target of attack from the big clubs. The insatiable desire of these clubs for more control and more money has forced the revamping of the European club competitions. This has been driven not by the wishes of the fans, players or, it seems, the managers, but by TV and commercial interests.

The European clubs who accepted the ethos that a football club was part of the community, enshrining that tenet in their constitutions, are now also threatening to float on the stock-market. Franz Beckenbauer and other European football directors have cast avaricious glances at what is available to their English counterparts. They may dress up the aims in the language of the 'greater common good' but that is precisely what directors of English football clubs have done before. Often the appointment of a new 'suit' from the City to a football club boardroom is accompanied by the declaration that the esteemed individual is a life-long fan; by implication they are not a threat to the existing order. It is doubtful whether any of the fans following the team around the country, paying ever-increasing prices for the privilege, would recognise these individuals from their travels.

Yet it is a tacit acknowledgement that the approval of the club's supporters for the actions taken in the boardroom is still seen as in some way necessary. The antics and comments of the Newcastle United FC directors Douglas Hall and Freddie Shepherd may have exposed a mindset that extends beyond the river Tyne; at the very least this episode demonstrated that taking the fans for granted can have serious consequences, at least in the short-term.

World Championship?

It took seven years from the formation of the breakaway Premier

League to the threats of a break-away European Super League but there are signs now of a quickening of the process. Within a few months of matters reaching an uneasy settlement at a European level, a world-wide dimension for club football was being broached. FIFA general secretary Sepp Blatter's declared wish for a two-year World Cup was seized upon by Rupert Murdoch: his response was to agree with the proposal except that the competition should be contested by clubs not countries. (While Mr Murdoch can always try to own a football club, a country may be a little trickier).

Football the world over recognises the authority of bodies such as the national FAs, UEFA and the world governing body FIFA but that authority is undermined by the secrecy and exclusivity of these organisations. There is little involvement or input at the administrative level from those at the sharp end: fans, players, managers and staff. This allows media moguls like Berlusconi and Murdoch to exploit divisions and cynicism for their commercial advantage.

Possible ways to combat the commercial threat to our national game are explored later in this chapter. Arguments are made for government intervention not because football is a charity case, far from it. Rather, those charged with protecting the welfare of the sport and the interests of its participants have reneged on their responsibility, allowing the very future of the sport to be placed in real jeopardy.

Back to the future, or a third way?

We are faced with a choice. We can allow the further commercial-isation of the game, with the glamour clubs being bought up by global media corporations, further weakening the social, cultural and sporting role of the local football club and exacerbating the current process of social exclusion; or we can recognise the wider public interest, and strengthen the links between clubs and fans. How can the second choice be implemented? What would it mean in practice?

There are a number of ways in which aspects, at least, of the wider public interest have been recognised. Lessons can therefore be learned from some of these examples from the past, from other countries, and even from the operation of some English clubs today. We are not, however, simply advocating a return to the past. On the contrary, that would be to return to the structure that created the current mess.

Mutualisation

The ultimate form of fan involvement would be to have a mutual structure. Here the fans would own the club itself. This would be through their membership of the club and their involvement through attendance, rather than the ownership of share capital. This is discussed in chapter 10 by Michie and Ramalingam and so we do not analyse it further here, other than to note the following. Firstly, the problem of how to get from here to there would be large, given the existing share capital that would need, in the case of most clubs, to be bought out. Secondly, the case of Barcelona indicates that even given such an option, much depends on the detail regarding the actual operation of such a structure. (On which, see chapter 12 by L'Elefant Blau).

Trust status

Apart from mutualisation, the other way to move from a plc to an alternative structure that would avoid the continual danger of take-over by outside commercial interests wanting to use football clubs for their own (media) ends, would be the use of trust status. (For a discussion of how a Supporters Trust works in practice, at Northampton Town FC, see chapter 11 by the elected director Brian Lomax). This for example is how the ownership and operation of *The Guardian* newspaper is structured. To have a football club operated as a trust has the added advantage over a plc that no dividends have to be paid out to share owners. The club's revenues can be kept within the game. The problem, again, is how to get from here to there. The question can be posed in two ways. Firstly, how to persuade the existing shareholders to accept the change in the status of their shares – into a form in which no dividends are paid? Or secondly, where to find the money to buy out the existing shareholders?

In the case of those clubs that are already plcs, it seems unlikely that the institutional shareholders would agree to the change in the status of their shares. They would, presumably, need to be bought out. The bulk of the other shareholders would in most cases be fans of the club, either directors of the club who may hold large shareholdings, or else the large number of small shareholders. Here it might be thought there would be more chance of the shareholders agreeing to the change in status of their shares, into shares in a Trust. For most of these shareholders the prospect of an annual dividend would not be particularly important. However, what would be important in most cases would be that the individuals could sell their shares at any time, to realise the capital.

There are two issues here. Firstly, could one sell one's shares in the Trust? To whom? And secondly, how much would one get? How would the price be determined, if the shares were not being traded on the Stock Exchange? To be a practical proposal, any move to Trust status would need to provide the desired answer to both these questions. Firstly, it would have to be possible to sell one's Trust shares. And secondly, there would have to be the expectation that one would receive as good a price as if they had remained plc shares.

One way of answering these questions is to refer back to how the problem of the institutional shareholders would be dealt with. Ironically, what appears at first sight to be a problem might turn out, in the context of the British football industry, to represent instead the answer as to how Trust status might be a realistic and practical way forward. The problems just referred to arise in the context of the move from plc to Trust being 'all or nothing'. With all the shares being Trust shares, how will these be valued? And who would buy them, if they pay no dividends, and if the question of whether or not one will be able to sell them again in the future – and for how much – is rather uncertain?

These questions would be answered if the company were actually to remain a plc, with its shares still traded on the Stock Exchange. The problem of the institutional shareholders would be solved if it was ignored, by not attempting to bring them into the Trust, leaving them instead as they are, as holders of dividend-paying shares in a plc traded on the Stock Exchange. So where does the Trust come in? The suggestion here is that a part, but not all, of the shares might be transferred to a Trust. One would then have a plc in which a block of the shares would be owned by a Trust. This Trust would have trustees. The Trust might have one or more of their members as directors of the plc. They would certainly make it their business to ensure that the plc board had suitable directors and that the board acted at all times in the interests of the club. One of the key points would be to have this block of shares held by the Trust sufficiently large to prevent a take-over of the plc by outside commercial interests who might misuse the club for their own commercial ends.

Both sets of problems – those of how to overcome the objections of the institutional shareholders, and those of how to overcome the objections of the non-institutional shareholders – would thus be dealt with simultaneously. All shares would, in effect, continue to be treated in like manner, as they are now. This would require that those who had transferred their shares to the Trust would have to be able to sell them at any time, and to be able to receive the same as if they were non-Trust shares being sold on the Stock Exchange. But if those who held their shares within the Trust sold them on the Stock Exchange, the proportion of shares held by the Trust would diminish. The preferred method of dealing with this would therefore be for the Trust itself to automatically buy the shares from anyone who held shares within the Trust who wanted to sell. Where, though, would they get the money to do this?

The answer to this is also provided by the 'problem' of the institutional shareholders having prevented a wholesale transfer to Trust status. Because the company continues to be a plc – albeit with a large block of the plc shares held collectively in a Trust, administered by trustees – all shares would need to be treated symmetrically in terms of dividend payments. One implication of having only a part-Trust structure is that the advantage referred to above, of not having to pay dividends, would not be fully realised. However, the Trust could be established as follows. When given the choice of whether to transfer your shares into the Trust, we have already said that it would be a risk-free option, in that you could still sell them outside the Trust, as plc shares, at any time on the Stock Exchange. In addition, although dividends would no longer be receivable, they would have to be paid by the plc to the Trust on all the shares just as they are individually on all the plc shares. Thus each of the shares you transfer to the Trust would be paid a dividend, administered by the Trustees, and this annual income would be used to buy additional shares for the Trust, and would be allocated in proportion to all those holding their shares in the Trust. Thus, if one chose to transfer one's shares to the Trust, then instead of being paid a cash dividend of say 5 per cent a year, one would instead receive additional shares each year, to be added to one's existing shareholding within the Trust, equivalent to 5 per cent of one's holdings.

If a shareholder actually wanted the cash that would have come as a dividend then they could of course just sell the additional 5 per cent of shares. And rather than go through this slightly convoluted procedure, the Trust might ask as a matter of course which option each shareholder wanted to elect – to take the dividend in cash, or in additional shares, or in some mixture of the two. The hope would be that the additional shares which the Trust would need to buy to add to the existing shareholdings of those whose shares were held within the Trust would outweigh any sales of shares by those whose shares were held within the Trust. Put another way, it was said above that there might be a problem with the Trust representing a declining proportion of shares if those who held shares within the Trust chose to sell. The point is that such shares would be bought by the Trust using their annual dividend receipts, and these shares would be allocated to the remaining Trust shareholders in lieu of dividends.

In addition to the annual purchase of plc shares by the Trust – for allocation to Trust shareholders in lieu of dividends – it might be that other plc shareholders would transfer to the Trust, so that the proportion of shares held by the Trust would rise by a greater amount than would be accounted for just by their annual purchase of plc shares. Or perhaps more likely than plc shareholdings moving to the

Trust, new shareholders buying plc shares through the Stock Exchange might elect to have these shares held within the Trust. Indeed, the Trust would presumably continually campaign for local people to buy shares and have them held in this way.

One specific target for such a campaign might be the employees of the club, including the players. There are government tax incentives for people to take up shares in their company. And in the case of the Premiership clubs – which are the ones where the scale of the sums involved make it particularly difficult to imagine a complete buy-out from plc status to any other (Trust, mutual or the like) – the players often have large sums to invest to make provision for their post-playing days, and in any such investment it would make sense to receive the annual income in the form of additional shares rather than cash.

International examples

Some reference has already been made to overseas examples and the chapter from Barcelona's 'L'Elefant Blau' goes into greater detail for that particular football club. Elsewhere in Spain there are similar examples of other clubs being owned and democratically run by the fans. Typically a board of directors is elected to run the club and remains directly accountable to the members. There has been widespread adoption of some of the principles established in England prior to the First World War. The English FA's Rule 34, for example, recognises that football clubs have sprung from the local sporting community and provides for the assets to be distributed to the local sports institutions if the football club is ever wound up.

This 'ashes to ashes' view of a professional football club is not just a quaint tradition; it is regarded as sacrosanct to many fans on the continent of Europe used to nothing less. The current constitution and rules of many Spanish clubs have been in place for over sixty years having been adopted under General Franco's regime in 1930s Spain. There has been evidence in recent years of a desire to follow the English example once more, to change the present rules and to allow the establishment of publicly quoted companies. This is a threat of which the fans in general are deeply suspicious – rightly so, in our view.

In Germany similar examples exist of clubs being owned by the members. As recently as December 1994 Schalke 04 adopted a new constitution, for the club to be owned by its members. This was drawn up in conjunction with the German FA, with the aim of providing a model for the whole *Bundesliga*. Each year up to 11 people are elected to an administrative 'board', called the *Aufsichtsrat*. Though football predominates, Schalke field teams in many sports including table

218

tennis, athletics, basketball and handball. The *Aufsichtsrat* includes a representative elected from the *Sportbeirat*, a committee representing all the sporting staff of the club. In addition Schalke has around 400 fan clubs across the world organised into a federation; they too elect a representative to the *Aufsichtsrat*. A further six members are elected at the club AGM and the *Aufsichtsrat* has the power to co-opt up to three further members should they feel specialist advice or expertise in a certain area is needed. (At the present time the *Aufsichtsrat* consists of just nine as only one member has been co-opted). For the day-to-day running of the club, an executive of between three and five members is elected by the *Aufsichtsrat* called the *Vorstand*; all of those on the *Vorstand* are paid and employed full time.

In England the supporters and staff are only ever involved in the running of clubs when there is a crisis. On the European Continent it is an accepted part of the club culture that the game is administered with all members of the club having an interest and taking part. To change attitudes will require a momentous effort. But as FC Barcelona and others have shown over the years, a democratic club structure is no bar to running a successful club. Indeed, in the case of the existing plcs, developing such a structure would protect against the danger of short-term financial interests getting in the way of longer-term development and success.

Whose game is it anyway?

It needs to be remembered that one of the main aims of the various examples and options referred to above is to ensure that the interests of the fans are taken properly into account and that fans are not, over time, excluded from the clubs. The social exclusion that has, undoubtedly, taken place to some extent over the past few years, must be overcome. This means that the various ownership options should not be viewed mechanistically, as technical 'solutions'. Such options will only be as good as their implementation. Conversely, some progress could be made even within existing plc structures. Proper representation of fans' interests could be required of football clubs by Government. This could be through a code of conduct, which clubs would have to comment on in their annual reports, or even by requiring appropriate Articles of Association to be incorporated by all companies whose business included owning a football club.

Again it would be crucial to pay attention to the detail. Most football plc boards would no doubt claim that the directors are all supporters of the club. Such fan representation would therefore have to be seen to be genuinely elected and independent of the club.

The independence of a supporter on the board is vital if the members of the club, the fans, are to have any faith in the system. The fans' representative must be seen to be independent and to carry the same authority as other board members. This cannot be achieved when the level of authority in the boardroom is determined by the number of shares held by the individual as is the case today – unless of course the director elected by fans also represented a block of shares held in Trust, as described in chapter 11 by Brian Lomax for the case of Northampton Town FC.

The board of directors should be a team of individuals put in place to achieve the best possible set of outcomes for the club and its members. In this respect any supporter representation at board level must be meaningful. At Manchester City, Francis Lee used the carrot of a fan on the board to show how different he was going to be when he took over from Peter Swales. The fans' representative on City's board was Dave Wallace, editor of the fanzine *King of the Kippax*. The experience was not a happy one. Wallace was not treated as an equal by other members of the board. He was seen as a means of demonstrating 'a new openness' but the board merely wanted him to act as their PR agent amongst the fans. The board did not allow Wallace to be present at all of their discussions and when Wallace refused to toe the line the post of fans' representative was abolished.

Northampton Town and Bournemouth

It is ironic that with Swales and Lee long gone Manchester City now find themselves in the Nationwide League Second Division where *real* fan power is active in the boardrooms of AFC Bournemouth and Northampton Town FC.

In 1992 Northampton Town were in receivership. The fans and the local community saved the club from extinction. As described by Brian Lomax (chapter 11), although the club is not wholly owned by its members, a supporters' trust now has approaching 10 per cent of the shareholding and elects a director to the board. The local authority now owns the ground, freeing the club from expensive upkeep as well as preventing the threat of a speculative purchaser coming in and selling the land for development as has happened at other clubs.

When Bournemouth found themselves in financial difficulties in 1996 they looked to the trust fund set up at Northampton Town and called on the local community to help establish their own supporters' trust which now runs the club. The involvement of the wider communities in Northampton and Bournemouth in running their football clubs has definite parallels with the continental approach to football as part of the community.

Local government

Local government has played – and continues to play – an important role in football clubs. This is usually most crucially with regard to the ground. This involvement by the local authority has often been used as a lever to try to tackle problems such as racism at grounds, for example at both Millwall and Leeds.

On the other hand, it is important not simply to advocate greater local authority involvement to solve the problem of how to take account of the wider public interest, or in reaction to the success stories we have been discussing. Local authorities are already over-stretched. The reasons that the individuals concerned have become local councillors or local authority officers may be quite unrelated to the sort of issues referred to above and the sort of skills required to tackle them. A vision for the future of football in Britain should certainly include a careful consideration of the role that the local authority could and should play. But this will be both more complex and varied than any simple ownership structure that could be set out in the context of the current chapter. Certainly, though, in cases where local authorities currently lease the football ground to the club, we would suggest that the Department of Culture, Media and Sport could brief local authorities on the sort of arrangements for fan involvement that might be proposed to football clubs as part of the agreement when clubs seek to negotiate, or renegotiate, the lease on the ground. Such considerations might also include introducing the role of 'golden shares'.

Golden shares

During the privatisations of the 1980s, the practice of the government retaining a 'golden share' was used to prevent, for example, foreign interests buying up newly privatised concerns that were considered to be of strategic importance to Britain. There can surely be few companies where the importance of maintaining a degree of local ownership is greater than the case of local football clubs. Thus while it is not our intention in this chapter to be prescriptive about what role local and national government might play in the ownership and management of football clubs, there is clearly a strong case for using this sort of notion of 'golden shares', held perhaps by both local and central government. These would serve more as a blocking mechanism, as with their use in the 1980s' privatisations, than as a real ownership stake. The most obvious purpose would be to prevent take-overs of football clubs, at least without explicit consideration and approval by local and central government.

Next steps: beyond the Task Force

The above discussion has not been intended to be prescriptive. Rather, it has considered various options and has suggested that there are a variety of lessons that can be learned from examples of different football clubs, here and now, as well as from abroad and in the past. One of the reasons for not having been overly prescriptive is that while the danger to football in Britain was made urgent and imminent with the BSkyB threat to take over Manchester United, it is still early days in terms of a consideration of the Football Task Force recommendations and possible legislative and/or regulatory responses to that.

Beyond that, there are certain general themes that come through from the various examples and proposals reported above.

The first and foremost is the importance of staying focused on the goal, and the key danger to it. The goal is to develop football as an important part of Britain's social, cultural and sporting life, and within that, to strengthen and further develop the links between the clubs and the local communities. It may prove no exaggeration to say that whether or not this government succeeds in one of the key goals it has set itself – namely to overcome social exclusion – will depend to a significant degree on whether it can rise to the challenge facing football in Britain. Football has perhaps been, in a small way, part of the problem. It threatens to become part of the problem in a big way. Yet there is no doubt that given the political will, it could become part of the solution to many of the problems of social exclusion, not just by encouraging young people back into football grounds but also through the wider community programmes.

The second general theme is that it is not just what is done that is important, it is how it's done. While a proper elaboration of the legal and institutional mechanisms are important, equally vital are matters such as the representation of fans' views and interests. Any proposal needs to be specific about ensuring that such representation is arrived at democratically, and that the process is not subverted by a board of directors at a club which is unenthusiastic about having any input from the fans.

Thirdly, while some of the general principles need to be applied throughout the game, when it comes to specific ownership structures there may be no 'one best way'. In some cases the ideal of a mutual, with the club owned and run as precisely that – a club – may be achievable. In other cases the existing ownership structure may be acceptable provided the sort of general principles referred to above – relating to the representation of fans' views and the protection from take-over – are acted on. Then there are the existing plcs for which the big question is how to get from here to there when that might involve buying out the existing shareholders. Where would the money come from? As discussed above, there may be ways of overcoming even these problems. But the answers may be different from club to club.

Fourthly, there are practical legislative and regulatory measures the government could take, both to advance the general goals of overcoming social exclusion and also to underpin and assist the various specific actions that might be taken from club to club. Thus, a golden share could be taken in all plcs that own football clubs to at least prevent their take-over and misuse by outside commercial interests. And the proper and independent involvement of fans in the running of clubs could be made a requirement through specified Articles of Association for such companies, or at the very least through guidelines that had to be commented upon in the companies' annual reports.

Conclusion

The aim of this chapter has been to consider the various ownership and governance options for football. This is an important issue given the increased commercialisation that has been generally recognised as having, to some degree at least, taken the game away from the fans and the fans away from the game. But the problem over these past few years has not been fan apathy. On the contrary, this period has witnessed the emergence of an independent culture with the launch and growth of fanzines and the founding and growth of independent supporters' associations. Alongside the growth of the problem has developed activity that could be crucial to the solution.

There is clearly a great deal more work needed to flesh out the ideas raised in this and the other chapters, and to implement the proposals from the Football Task Force. Focusing on this long-term horizon should not be used as an excuse, by government or anyone else, for taking their eye off the immediate and urgent danger to the game from the threatened take-over of football clubs by media companies. If that had been allowed to happen in the BSkyB/Manchester United case it would have done more damage to the longer-term work needed than would just about anything else. British football would have become split between a few glamour clubs to be owned and run by global media interests on the one hand, with the majority of Premiership clubs – not to mention the non-Premiership clubs – carved out.

But these immediate concerns should be seen within the broader and longer-term need to develop the game positively, to overcome the damaging effects of commercialisation and social exclusion. Without this further work to take the game forward, the 'glamour' clubs will be left sitting on the Stock Exchange waiting for the next corporate raiders to come along. The immediate campaigning issues need to be seen as inextricably linked to the longer-term vision. To be successful on both fronts calls for a solid defence combined with some imaginative thinking by all those involved in the game.

Index